Laboratory Manual

PRENTICE HALL

Chemistry

Connections to Our Changing World

Pearson Education

PRENTICE HALL
Upper Saddle River, New Jersey
Needham, Massachusetts

Laboratory Manual

PRENTICE HALL
Chemistry
Connections to Our Changing World

Contributing Writers

Bette Bridges
Chemistry Teacher
Bridgewater-Raynham High School
Bridgewater, Massachusetts

John C. Hugo
Chemistry Teacher
Carman-Ainsworth High School
Flint, Michigan

George E. Hussey
Chemistry Teacher
Falmouth High School
Falmouth, Massachusetts

Cristina Kerekes
Chemistry Teacher
Phillips Academy
Andover, Massachusetts

Kenneth Lyle
Chemistry Teacher
St. John's School
Houston, Texas

Joseph W. MacQuade, Jr.
Former Science Program Administrator
Marblehead High School
Marblehead, Massachusetts

Thomas L. Messer
Former Chemistry Teacher
The American School in Japan
Tokyo, Japan

Karen M. Robblee
Chemistry Teacher
Millbrook High School
Raleigh, North Carolina

Pamala Schupp
Chemistry Teacher
Kelly Walsh High School
Casper, Wyoming

Patricia Soghigian
Chemistry Teacher
Beverly High School
Beverly, Massachusetts

Clarice Wenz
Chemistry Teacher
Goose Creek High School
Goose Creek, South Carolina

Safety Expert
James A. Kaufman
Director
Laboratory Safety Workshop
Natick, Massachusetts

ISBN 0-13-436222-5

2 3 4 5 6 7 8 9 10   02 01 00

CONTENTS

The symbol 🔍 denotes small-scale investigations.

Safety in the Chemistry Laboratory

In the laboratory, you will be working with equipment and materials that can cause injury if they are not handled properly. Accidents happen because of carelessness, haste, and disregard of safety rules and practices. The laboratory can be a safe place to work, however, and accidents can be avoided if you know what risks are present and take steps to reduce them.

Safety rules for the laboratory are listed below. Before beginning any lab work, read these rules and learn them. When working in the lab, follow them carefully. If you have any questions about these rules, ask your teacher before starting lab work.

General Precautions

1. Be prepared to work when you arrive at the laboratory. Familiarize yourself with the lab procedures before beginning the lab.
2. Carefully follow all written and oral instructions. Perform only those activities assigned by your teacher. Never do anything in the laboratory that is not called for in the lab procedure or by your teacher.
3. Notify your teacher if you have any medical problems that might be affected by lab work, such as allergies or asthma.
4. Never work in the laboratory without supervision.
5. Never eat or drink in the laboratory.
6. Never smoke in the laboratory.
7. Keep work areas clean and tidy at all times. Only notebooks and lab manuals or written lab procedures should be brought to the work area. All other items, such as books, purses, and backpacks, should be left at your desk or in a designated storage area.
8. Wear appropriate clothing for working in the laboratory. Remove jackets, ties, and other loose garments. Roll up or secure long sleeves. Remove jewelry, such as dangling necklaces, chains, and bracelets, that might present a hazard in the lab.
9. Tie back or cover long hair, especially in the vicinity of an open flame.
10. Never wear open shoes or sandals in the laboratory.
11. Wear goggles and a lab coat or apron at all times during an investigation.
12. Avoid wearing contact lenses in the lab. Change to glasses, if possible, or notify your teacher.
13. Do not engage in horseplay.
14. Set up apparatus as described in the written laboratory procedures or by your teacher. Never use makeshift arrangements.
15. Always use the prescribed instrument, such as tongs, test-tube holder, or forceps, for handling apparatus.
16. Keep all combustible materials away from open flames.
17. Never put your face near the mouth of a container that holds chemicals. Never smell any chemical directly. When testing for odors, use a wafting motion to direct the odors to your nose.

18. Conduct any experiment involving poisonous vapors in a fume hood.
19. Dispose of waste materials as instructed by your teacher.
20. Clean and wipe dry all work surfaces at the end of class. Wash your hands thoroughly.
21. Know the location of emergency equipment, such as the first-aid kit, eye-wash station, fire extinguisher, fire shower, and fire blanket, and how to use them.
22. In case of chemical spills, notify your teacher immediately.
23. Report all injuries to your teacher immediately.

Handling Chemicals

24. Read and double-check labels on chemical bottles before removing any chemical from a container. Take only as much as you need.
25. To avoid contamination, do not return unused chemicals to stock bottles.
26. When transferring chemicals from one container to another, hold the containers away from your body.
27. Avoid touching chemicals with your hands. If chemicals do come in contact with your hands, wash them immediately.
28. Wear latex gloves when handling concentrated acids and bases.
29. When mixing an acid and water, always add the acid to the water.

Handling Glassware

30. Carry glass tubing, especially long pieces, in a vertical position to minimize the likelihood of breakage and to avoid stabbing anyone.
31. Always wear heavy gloves when inserting a piece of glassware, such as tubing or a thermometer, into a stopper. Before inserting glassware into a stopper, lubricate the glassware with water or glycerin. Use a twisting motion when inserting or removing glassware from a stopper—never apply force. If a piece of glassware becomes stuck in a stopper, take it to your teacher.
32. Do not place hot glassware directly on a table. Always use some type of insulating pad.
33. Allow plenty of time for hot glass to cool before touching it. Remember: Hot glass *looks* cool but can cause painful burns.
34. Never handle broken glass with your bare hands. Use a brush and dustpan to clean up. Dispose of the glass as directed by your teacher.

Heating Substances

35. Use extreme caution with gas burners. Keep your head and clothing away from the flame.
36. Always turn off burners and hot plates when not in use.
37. Do not bring any substance into contact with a flame unless instructed to do so.
38. Never heat anything unless instructed to do so. Never leave unattended anything that is being heated or is visibly reacting.

39. When heating a substance in a test tube, make sure that the mouth of the tube is not pointed at you or anyone else. Never look into a container that is being heated.
40. Never heat a closed container.

In Case of an Injury

41. If an injury should occur, it is important to remain calm.
42. Notify your instructor immediately.
43. Be familiar with the first-aid practices that are to be followed.
44. Know how to use the emergency equipment.
45. Know how to summon assistance.

First Aid

Accidents do not often happen in well-equipped chemistry laboratories if students understand safe laboratory procedures and are careful to follow them. When an occasional accident does occur, it is likely to be a minor one.

In many schools, the nurse is responsible for treating injuries. For some types of injuries, though, you must take action immediately, before the nurse takes over. Find out what your school's emergency procedures are and make sure that they are posted in the laboratory. Always notify your teacher if there is an injury in the classroom, no matter how minor it may seem.

Bleeding from a Cut

Most cuts that occur in the chemistry laboratory are minor. For minor cuts, apply pressure to the wound with a clean, absorbent cloth. If blood begins to soak through, add more layers of cloth. If possible, keep a sheet of plastic over the topmost layer or wear latex or plastic gloves. Take the victim to the nurse.

If the victim is bleeding badly, raise the bleeding part, if possible, and apply pressure to the wound with a clean, absorbent cloth. While first aid is being given, send someone to notify the school nurse.

Acid or Base Spilled on the Skin

Remove all clothing that has the chemical on it and flush the skin with water for at least 15 minutes. Take the victim to the school nurse.

Chemicals in the Eyes

Getting any kind of chemical in the eyes is undesirable, but certain chemicals are especially harmful. They can destroy eyesight in a matter of seconds. Because you will be wearing safety goggles at all times during investigations, the likelihood of this kind of accident is remote. However, if it does happen, go to the nearest eyewash station and begin flushing the eyes with water immediately. It is important to flush with water for at least 15 minutes. While flushing continues, send someone to inform the school nurse. Do NOT attempt to go to the nurse's office before flushing your eyes.

Chemicals in the Mouth

Many chemicals are poisonous to varying degrees. Any chemical taken into the mouth should be spat out and the mouth rinsed thoroughly with water. Tell the victim NOT to swallow the water. Note the name of the chemical and notify the nurse immediately.

If the victim swallows a chemical, note the name of the chemical and notify the nurse immediately. Do NOT give the victim anything to drink.

If necessary, the nurse will contact the Poison Control Center, a hospital emergency room, or a physician for instructions.

Clothing or Hair on Fire

A person whose clothing or hair catches on fire will often run around frantically in an unsuccessful effort to get away from the fire. This action only provides the fire with more oxygen and makes it burn faster. If your clothing catches fire, drop to the floor and roll around to extinguish the flames. If you are helping another person whose clothing is on fire, smother the flames by rolling the person on the floor, in a fire blanket, or in a heavy coat. For hair fires, use a fire blanket to smother the flames. Send someone to notify the nurse immediately.

Breathing Smoke or Chemical Fumes

Inhalation of smoke or chemical fumes is unlikely if all experiments that give off smoke or noxious gases are conducted in a well-ventilated fume hood.

If smoke or chemical fumes are present in the laboratory, all persons—even those who do not feel ill—should leave the laboratory immediately. Since smoke rises, crawl along the floor while evacuating a smoke-filled room. Close all doors to the laboratory after the last person has left. Notify the nurse immediately. Make sure the room is thoroughly ventilated before anyone returns.

Shock

People who are suffering from any severe injury (for example, a bad burn or major loss of blood) may be in a state of shock. A person in shock is usually pale and faint. The person may be sweating, and have cold, moist skin and a weak, rapid pulse.

Shock is a serious medical condition. Do NOT allow a person in shock to walk anywhere—even to the nurse's office. Call for emergency help immediately. While emergency help is being summoned, loosen any tightly fitting clothing and keep the person comfortable.

Safety Symbols

 SAFETY CLOTHING
This symbol is to remind you to wear a laboratory apron over your street clothes to protect your skin and clothing from spills.

 SAFETY GOGGLES
This symbol is to remind you that safety goggles are to be worn *at all times* when working in the laboratory. For some activities, your teacher may also instruct you to wear protective gloves.

 GLOVES
This symbol is to remind you to wear gloves to protect your hands from contact with corrosive substances, broken glass, or hot objects.

 HEATING
This symbol indicates that you should be careful not to touch hot objects with your bare hands. Use either tongs or heat-proof gloves to pick up hot objects.

 FIRE
This symbol indicates the presence of an open flame. Loose hair should be tied back or covered, and bulky or loose clothing should be secured in some manner. This symbol also alerts you to the hazard of working with a flammable liquid.

 CORROSIVE SUBSTANCE
This symbol indicates a caustic or corrosive substance—most frequently an acid. Avoid contact with skin, eyes, and clothing. Do not inhale vapors.

 BREAKAGE
This symbol indicates an activity in which the likelihood of breakage is greater than usual, such as working with glass tubing, funnels, and so forth.

 DANGEROUS VAPORS
This symbol indicates the presence of or production of poisonous or noxious vapors. *Use the fume hood* when directed to do so. Care should be taken not to inhale vapors directly. When testing an odor, use a wafting motion to direct the vapor toward your nose.

 EXPLOSION
This symbol indicates that the potential for an explosive situation is present. When you see this symbol, read the instructions carefully and *follow them exactly*.

 POISON
This symbol indicates the presence of a poisonous substance. Do not let such a substance come in contact with your skin and do not inhale its vapors.

 ELECTRICAL SHOCK
This symbol indicates that the potential for an electrical shock exists. Read all instructions carefully. Disconnect all apparatus when not in use.

 RADIATION
This symbol indicates a radioactive substance. Follow your teacher's instructions as to proper handling of such substances.

 DISPOSAL
This symbol indicates that a chemical should be disposed of in a special way. Dispose of these chemicals only as directed by your teacher.

 HYGIENE
This symbol is to remind you always to wash your hands thoroughly after completing a laboratory investigation. Never touch your face or eyes during a laboratory investigation.

Safety Contract

After you have read all the safety information on pages *vii–xi* in this laboratory manual and are sure you understand all the rules, fill out the Safety Contract that follows. Signing this contract tells your teacher that you are aware of the rules of the laboratory. The signature of your parent or guardian indicates an awareness of the need for adult supervision if you work on laboratory assignments at home. Return your signed contract to your teacher.

Safety Contract

I, _____ , have read the section *Safety in the Chemistry Laboratory* on pages *vii–xi* of this laboratory manual. I understand its contents completely and agree to comply with all the safety rules and guidelines that have been established in each of the following categories:

(please check)

_____ General Precautions

_____ Handling Chemicals

_____ Handling Glassware

_____ Heating Substances

_____ First Aid

_____ Safety Symbols

Certain laboratory investigations, such as those involving the preparation of food, may need to be performed at home. If so, I agree to follow all established safety rules and to work only under the supervision of an adult.

Signature _____ Date _____
(student)

Signature _____ Date _____
(parent or guardian)

Using This Laboratory Manual

The laboratory investigations in this manual provide an opportunity for you to observe chemical principles in action and to become familiar with the techniques used by chemists. Each investigation follows a standard outline that will help you tackle the stated problem in a systematic manner. The sections of each investigation are described below.

Introduction The Introduction provides background information and ties the investigation to specific concepts discussed in your textbook.

Pre-Lab Discussion The Pre-Lab Discussion asks questions that will prepare you to carry out the investigation. These questions help ensure that you understand the purpose and plan of the investigation.

Problem This section presents a problem in the form of a question. Your job during the investigation is to solve the problem based on your observations.

Materials A list of all the materials you will need to conduct the investigation appears at the beginning of each investigation.

Safety This section warns you of potential hazards and tells you about precautions you should take to decrease the risk of accident. The safety symbols that are relevant to the investigation appear next to the title of the Safety section. They also appear next to certain steps of the Procedure. A chart explaining these symbols is found on page *xi*.

Procedure This section tells how to conduct the investigation. Make sure you read the entire Procedure carefully before you begin the investigation. Diagrams are included where necessary to explain a technique or to show an experimental setup. If safety symbols appear next to a certain step, follow the corresponding safety precaution for that step and all subsequent steps. CAUTION statements within the Procedure warn of possible hazards.

Observations As you carry out the investigation, you need to record your observations. You may be asked to describe your observations in words (qualitatively) or you may be required to record quantitative data such as measurements of mass, temperature, and volume. Be sure to record your observations as they occur—do not rely on your memory.

Calculations Once you have recorded your observations, further calculations may be required in order to reach a conclusion. If no further processing of data is necessary, the Calculations section is omitted.

Critical Thinking: Analysis and Conclusions Two steps of the traditional scientific method—analyzing data and forming a conclusion—are represented in this section. Using data gathered during the investigation and knowledge gained from your textbook and the Introduction, you are asked to analyze and interpret your experimental results. You will need to support your analysis and conclusions with the data you collected during the investigation.

Critical Thinking: Applications This section challenges you to apply the concepts learned in the investigation to other scientific and real-world situations.

Going Further This section suggests additional activities for you to pursue on your own. Some of these are brief extensions of the investigation. Others involve library or other types of research. Still others suggest experiments you might perform with your teacher's permission.

Common Laboratory Equipment

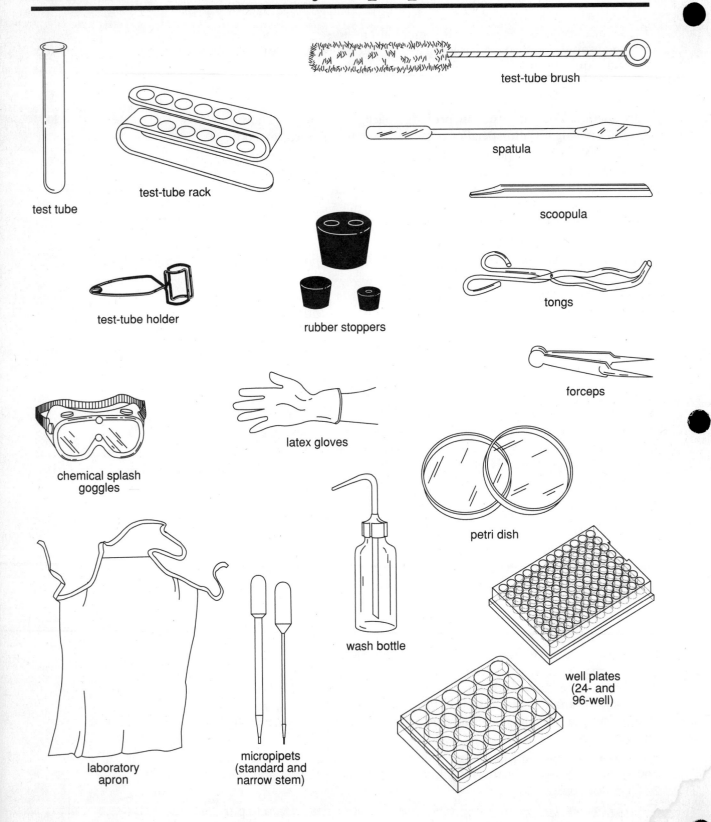

test-tube brush

spatula

scoopula

test tube

test-tube rack

test-tube holder

rubber stoppers

tongs

forceps

chemical splash
goggles

latex gloves

petri dish

wash bottle

well plates
(24- and
96-well)

laboratory
apron

micropipets
(standard and
narrow stem)

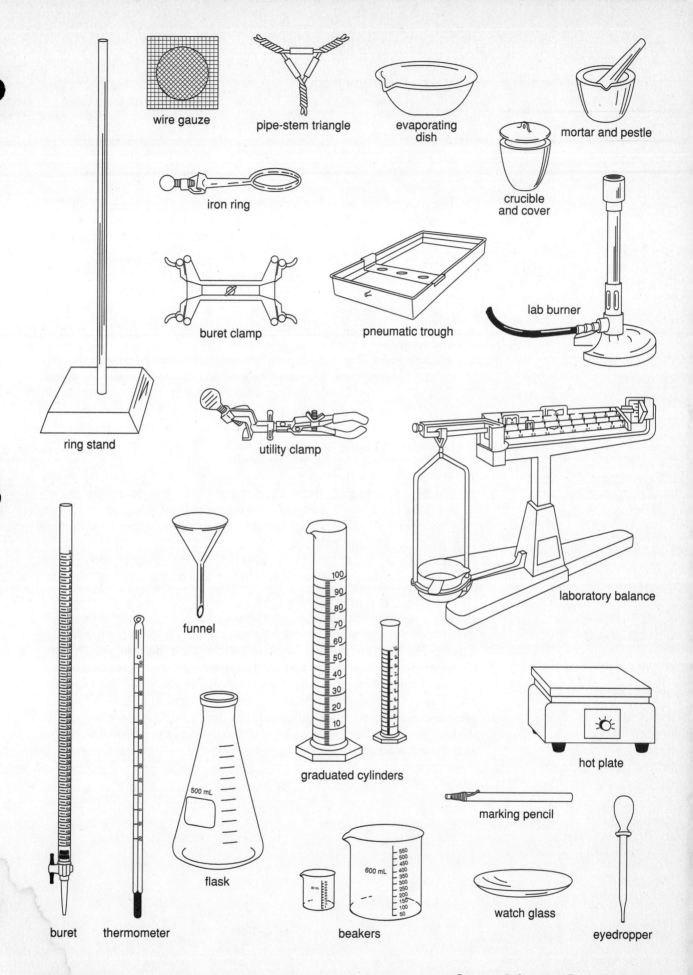

wire gauze

pipe-stem triangle

evaporating dish

mortar and pestle

iron ring

crucible and cover

buret clamp

pneumatic trough

lab burner

ring stand

utility clamp

laboratory balance

funnel

graduated cylinders

hot plate

500 mL

flask

600 mL

marking pencil

watch glass

buret   thermometer

beakers

eyedropper

Using a Laboratory Balance

In chemistry investigations, you will frequently use a laboratory balance to measure mass. Although balances vary somewhat in style, and you may use more than one type of balance in your class, they all work on the same principle. One common balance is shown in Figure 1 on the next page. Note that it consists of a suspended pan for holding material and a set of calibrated beams with riders. An object to be measured is placed on the pan, and the riders are moved until the pointer is centered. Then the mass is read.

The balance is a sensitive instrument and must be handled properly. Read the following steps for using a balance, and practice a few times with familiar objects until you become comfortable with the procedure.

1. Carry the balance with two hands. Place it on a level surface.
2. Set all the riders to zero and remove any material from the balance pan.
3. Calibrate the balance by turning the adjustment screw until the pointer on the end of the beam swings equally on either side of the midpoint. See Figure 1.
4. A single solid object, such as a nail or a coin, can be placed directly on the balance pan. Liquids or loose solids, such as salt or sugar, should be placed in a premeasured container or on a weighing paper.
5. Move the largest rider along the beam one notch at a time until the pointer drops. Then move the rider back one notch. Repeat this procedure with the next smaller rider. Continue in the same manner until you are using the smallest rider.
6. The beam on which the smallest rider moves does not have any notches. Slowly slide the rider along until the pointer on the end of the beam is swinging equally on either side of the midpoint. You may prefer to use a pencil to move the rider in order to minimize disturbance to the balance.
7. The mass of the object on the pan is the sum of the masses shown on the beams. Be sure to subtract the mass of the container, if any.

A balance is a graduated measuring device. As such, the precision of any measurement depends on the smallest division of the scale. In the case of the quadruple-beam balance, the smallest division is 0.01 g. A value can be estimated to one place smaller than the smallest division. For example, the mass indicated by the balance in the figure is 123.456 g.

Electronic balances are more accurate and easier to use than conventional balances. Simply place a container or weighing paper on the pan, press the zero (sometimes called tare) button, and add the material you wish to measure. The balance will give the mass of the material indicated as a digital readout.

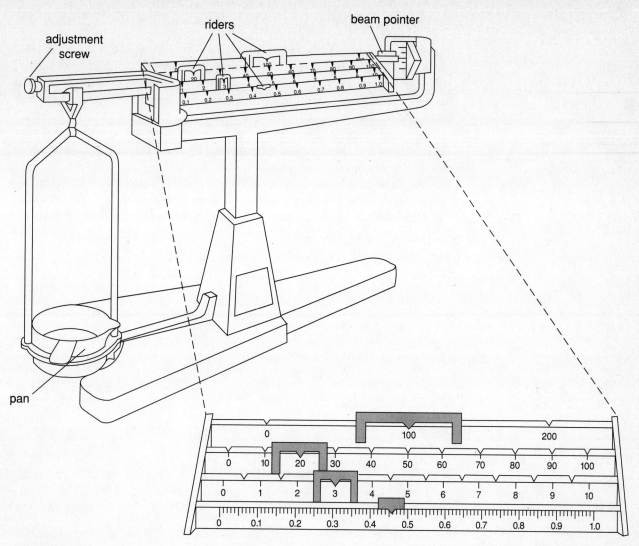

Figure 1

Using a Burner

When heating materials in the laboratory, you most often will use a hot plate. There are times, however, when a burner is specified. A burner is fueled by gas and supplies an open flame. As such, it is important for you to know how to operate a burner safely in order to minimize risk of injury or fire.

Learn the following directions for operating a burner. Make sure you understand them before attempting to use a burner, and work only under the supervision of your teacher.

1. Tie back any loose hair or clothing. Put on your safety goggles.
2. Examine the burner to familiarize yourself with its construction. Operate the air intake control and, if present, the fine adjustment valve. See Figure 2.

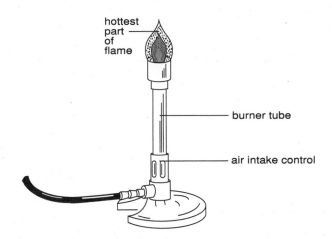

hottest part of flame

burner tube

air intake control

Figure 2

3. Make sure that the opening of the burner tube is clean and free from debris.
4. Push one end of the rubber tubing onto the burner inlet pipe. Push the other end onto the gas valve. The tubing should be securely in place before you go on to the next step.
5. Make sure the burner is level and on a flat surface. There should be no flammable material near the burner.
6. Light a match and hold it against the side of the burner tube about 2 cm below the top. Turn on the gas slowly and move the match up until the gas ignites.
7. Adjust the flame by manipulating the air intake control. A good burner flame gives off little light and has two distinct cones, as shown in Figure 2. Adjust the flame as follows:

   - If the flame is too large, slowly turn down the gas.
   - If the flame is yellow and/or smoky, adjust the air intake control.
   - If there is a gap between the top of the tube and the base of the flame, slowly turn down the gas.
   - If the flame disappears down the tube, turn off the gas, decrease the air intake, and relight the burner.

8. Turn off the burner as soon as you no longer need it.
9. NEVER leave a lighted burner unattended.

Working with Chemicals

Success in laboratory chemistry depends on many factors, one of which is your confidence in handling the materials that you must work with during investigations. Knowing how to safely dispense and transfer chemicals, to use equipment, and to protect yourself helps to create a productive working environment for you and your classmates. In other sections of this book you will find general safety guidelines and specific instructions for using a laboratory balance and burner. The information that follows will help you become acquainted with some of the other standard procedures you will use throughout this course.

Measuring Liquids

When you need an approximate volume of liquid, you can measure it simply by pouring the liquid into a beaker or flask that is imprinted with volume calibrations. If you need a more exact volume, use a graduated cylinder or micropipet. Choose the size of the graduated cylinder that best matches the volume you need to measure. A micropipet may be used to measure volumes of 1 to 6 milliliters or to add drops of liquid to a precise mark in a 10-milliliter graduated cylinder.

In graduated cylinders made of glass, liquids will form a meniscus, or curved surface, with the sides of the cylinder. For most liquids, you should read the volume indicated by the bottom of the meniscus, as shown in Figure 1–1 on page 4 of Investigation 1.

Transferring Liquids

Most high school students are unfamiliar with the techniques for safely transferring liquids. The first thing you need to know is how to get the liquid out of the reagent bottle and into another container without contaminating the class supply. With your palm facing upward, grasp the stopper between your first two fingers, as shown in Figure 3A, and remove it. Hold the stopper while you pick up the reagent bottle with the same hand. Pour out the amount of liquid you need and replace the stopper. In this way, the stopper never touches another surface, preventing contamination of the stopper and the work area.

To minimize splashing when you pour a liquid into a wide-mouth container, such as a beaker, place a stirring rod in the container and

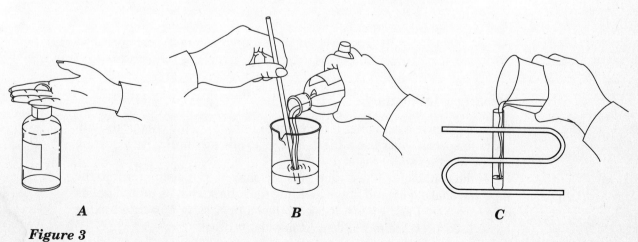

A   **B**   **C**

Figure 3

pour the liquid down the rod, as shown in Figure 3B. When pouring liquid into a small-mouth container, such as a test tube, place the liquid into a beaker first. You then will have more control over the liquid when pouring it from the beaker's spout. By placing the test tube in a test-tube rack, as shown in Figure 3C, you protect your fingers from spills.

Transferring Solids

If you want to transfer a solid chemical to a wide-mouth container, tilt the supply bottle toward the container and slowly rotate your wrist back and forth as you tap the side of the bottle so that the solid falls gently from the mouth. (See Figure 4.) If you are transferring a solid into a small-mouth container, such as a test tube, first pour the solid onto a piece of paper into which you have folded a crease. Then pour the solid out of the crease.

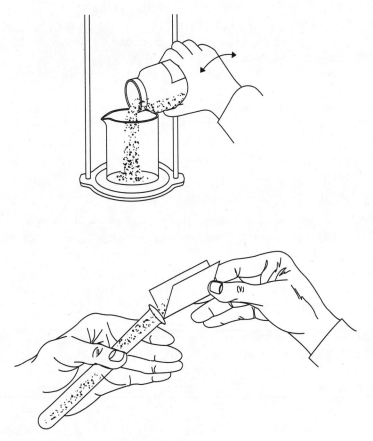

Figure 4

Mixing Materials

Be sure you use a container large enough to hold all the chemicals with room to spare. Never use a thermometer to stir mixtures. Use a stirring rod or wooden splint instead.

If the contents of a test tube must be shaken, put a stopper into the tube and shake it up and down, holding the tube so that its mouth points away from you and others. Remove the stopper slowly in case mixing has caused pressure to build up inside the tube.

Heating Materials

Whenever possible, use a hot plate instead of a laboratory burner to heat chemicals. The absence of a flame reduces the risk of fire. If you are boiling a liquid, place two or three boiling stones or a stirring rod in the container to reduce the amount of bumping and allow the boiling to proceed smoothly. Never add boiling stones to a hot liquid because large amounts of vapor may form and cause splashes. Never heat a closed container, and be sure that open test tubes point away from you and others while being heated.

If you must use a lab burner, follow the safety instructions described elsewhere in this book. Never heat flammable material or leave the flame unattended. Be sure to adjust the burner as described on page *xviii* to use the minimum flame necessary.

Materials that are heated become too hot to touch with bare hands. Be sure to use a test-tube holder to handle glass test tubes. Hold porcelain crucibles and evaporating dishes with tongs as shown in Figure 5. Allow containers to cool before touching them directly.

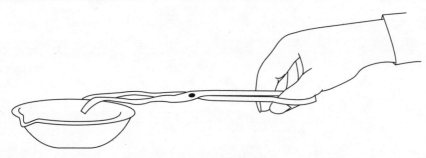

Carrying an evaporating dish

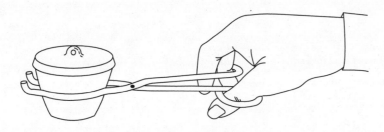

Carrying a crucible

Figure 5

Filtering Mixtures

A mixture of an insoluble solid and a liquid can be separated by pouring the mixture through a filter. To prepare a filter, fold a round piece of filter paper in half and then in quarters as shown in Figure 6. Tear off a small corner from the fold and open the paper to form a cone as shown. Note the position of the torn corner, which allows the paper to lie flat against the funnel.

Place the filter paper into a funnel and set the funnel in an iron ring attached to a ring stand. Place a container under the funnel to catch the

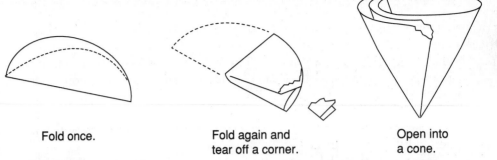

Fold once.

Fold again and
tear off a corner.

Open into
a cone.

Figure 6

filtered liquid, or filtrate. You will have to wet the filter paper to make it stick to the funnel. Press out air bubbles that might slow the filtration, and pour the mixture into the funnel, taking care not to let the mixture overflow. Use a stirring rod, as mentioned earlier, to guide the liquid into the funnel and reduce spillage.

Uncertainty and Measurement

Lab 1

Introduction

Suppose you have a summer job monitoring the pollution in a local lake. You are instructed to collect three 100-mL water samples at certain locations at set times each day. To each sample, you add 5 mL of a coloring agent that reacts and changes color intensity in proportion to the amount of pollutant in the water. You then check each sample with an instrument that detects color intensity and gives a quantitative, or numerical, measure of the amount of pollutant in each sample. Unfortunately, your measurements of similar samples vary by 10 to 20 percent. How could you increase the accuracy and precision of your measurements?

Every measurement has an uncertainty, or a built-in error. This error is due to limitations in the measurement scale, the manufacturing process, and the ability of the human eye to detect small differences. For example, when measuring volume with a graduated cylinder, the width of the scale lines, variations in glass thickness, and slight changes in the angle of sight when reading the scale are some of the factors that cause uncertainty. Because of this uncertainty, no measurement should be thought of as an exact value, but rather as a value within a range that varies with the uncertainty. For example, the uncertainty of a volume measurement made with a 100-mL graduated cylinder may be ±0.5 mL. Thus, if you measured 100.0 mL of water, the actual volume would be 100.0 ±0.5 mL, or within a range of 99.5 mL to 100.5 mL. Although ±0.5 mL represents only a ±0.5% error for a 100.0 mL measurement, it becomes a much larger error of ±10% when you measure a smaller quantity, such as 5.0 mL.

There are two important lessons you should learn about making measurements. First, you should familiarize yourself with the scale of each piece of lab equipment and learn to read each scale as accurately as possible. Second, you should know the uncertainty of your measurements, because your results cannot be more accurate than the built-in error allows.

In this laboratory investigation, you will become familiar with the measurement scale of a balance, graduated cylinders, and a thermometer. Then you will determine the uncertainty of measurements made with this equipment. If you really do get a job monitoring water pollution, you will know how to increase the accuracy and precision of your measurements so that they are scientifically useful.

Pre-Lab Discussion

Read the entire laboratory investigation and the relevant pages of your textbook. Then answer the questions that follow.

Name _____

1. Why is it important to wear eye protection at all times in the chemistry laboratory, even when you are not using an open flame or dangerous chemicals? _____

_____

_____

2. In the diagram of the graduated cylinder shown in Figure 1–1, what fraction of a mL does each division, or increment, between the 1-mL markings represent? _____

3. What is the volume of the liquid shown in Figure 1–1? (Hint: Read the volume measurement at the bottom of the curved meniscus.)

_____

4. Which do you think will have a more predictable impact on the measurements you make in the laboratory, human error or uncertainty in the measurement scales of the lab equipment? Explain.

_____

_____

Problem

How large are the uncertainties in measurements made with common lab equipment?

Materials

safety goggles   distilled water (at 20°C)
laboratory apron   dropper
laboratory balance   Celsius thermometer
standard masses   heat-proof gloves
2 objects of unknown mass   beaker containing boiling water
graduated cylinder, 10-mL   plastic tub
graduated cylinder, 100-mL   ice

Safety

Wear your goggles and lab apron at all times during the investigation. Your eyes are fragile, and you should always protect them from potential laboratory hazards such as shattering glass or splashing boiling water. Note the caution alert symbols here and with certain steps of the Procedure. Refer to page *xi* for the specific precautions associated with each symbol.

Procedure

Part A: Estimating the Uncertainty of a Balance

1. Put on your goggles and lab apron. Obtain a laboratory balance and use the zeroing adjustment so the scale reads zero with no mass on the pan. Gently disturb the pan by touching it, and check to make sure that the balance returns to zero with no visible deviation.

2. Study the balance scale that has the smallest counterweight. Determine the mass increment size (in grams) represented by any one of the smallest scale divisions (between two adjacent marks), and record this value. Once you know this value, determine the mass represented by one half and one fifth of this scale increment. Record these values. (Note: If you are using an electronic balance, skip this step.)

3. Obtain a standard mass and place it on the balance pan. Adjust the counterweights to find its mass. The mass should be equal or very close to the standard's given value. Once the exact balance point is found, record the mass as accurately as the smallest scale increment allows (e.g., 10.00 g).

4. Shift the smallest counterweight just slightly until you observe the slightest deviation from the zero point. The shift may be less than one scale division. Do the same for a shift in the opposite direction. These slightly higher and lower mass readings represent the apparent uncertainty range. Record the masses for the upper and lower ends, or limits, of the range. (Note: If you are using an electronic balance, the apparent uncertainty is represented by the range between the higher and lower masses that may flicker on the display.)

5. As exactly as possible, measure and record the mass of each of the two objects of unknown mass. Contribute your measurements to the class data bank for later use. While waiting for your turn with the two unknowns, you can proceed with Part B of this investigation.

Part B: Estimating the Uncertainty of Graduated Cylinders

6. Using the laboratory balance, measure and record the mass of a dry 10-mL graduated cylinder and a dry 100-mL graduated cylinder. **CAUTION:** *If glass cylinders are being used, take care not to knock them over and break them. If a cylinder does shatter, do not pick up the broken pieces with your bare hands.*

7. Record the volume represented by the smallest volume increment on each of the cylinders. Also determine and record the volume represented by one half and one fifth of the smallest volume increment.

8. Use a dropper to add 10.0 mL of distilled water to each cylinder. Add the last few drops to each cylinder carefully so that the bottom curve of the meniscus (observed in glass cylinders only) is on the 10.0-mL mark. Figure 1–1 shows you where to position your sight line so that you obtain an accurate reading.

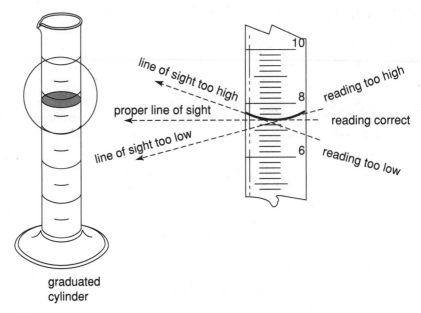

graduated
cylinder

Figure 1–1

9. With the laboratory balance, measure and record the mass of each cylinder containing 10.0 mL of water. **CAUTION:** *If glass cylinders are being used, take care not to knock them over and break them.* Subtract the mass of the empty cylinder to find the mass of water in the 10-mL and 100-mL cylinders. Record and contribute your measurements to the class data bank for later use. Pour the water into the sink and return all your lab equipment to the supply area. Then proceed with Part C.

Part C: Estimating the Uncertainty of a Thermometer

10. Obtain a Celsius thermometer. Determine and record the temperature represented by the smallest scale increment. Also determine and record the temperature represented by one half and one fifth of the smallest scale increment. **CAUTION:** *Thermometers are fragile. Handle with care.*

11. Put on a pair of heat-proof gloves and place the thermometer in the beaker of boiling water provided by your teacher. For 1 to 2 minutes, hold the thermometer in the boiling water so that the tip is not touching the beaker bottom. Remove the thermometer from the boiling water and quickly read it. Record the temperature, estimating to tenths of a degree. Contribute your measurement to the class data bank. **CAUTION:** *Do not touch the beaker or hot plate with your bare hands.*

12. Turn off the hot plate. Allow the thermometer to cool to room temperature. Then place it in a tub of ice water provided by your teacher. Leave the thermometer in the ice bath for 1 to 2 minutes. Record the temperature and contribute your measurement of the freezing point of water to the class data bank.

13. Return all equipment to the supply area. Clean up your work area and wash your hands before leaving the laboratory.

Name _____

Observations

Part A: Laboratory Balance

Smallest mass scale increment   _____

One half of smallest mass scale increment   _____

One fifth of smallest mass scale increment   _____

Mass of standard weight   _____

        Highest limit _____   Lowest limit _____

Mass of unknown #1   _____

Mass of unknown #2   _____

Part B: Graduated Cylinders

	10-mL	100-mL
Smallest volume scale increment	_____	_____
One half of smallest volume scale increment	_____	_____
One fifth of smallest volume scale increment	_____	_____
Mass of empty cylinder	_____	_____
Mass of cylinder with 10.0 mL of water	_____	_____
Mass of 10.0 mL of water	_____	_____

Part C: Thermometer

Smallest temperature scale increment   _____

One half of smallest temperature scale increment   _____

One fifth of smallest temperature scale increment   _____

Temperature of boiling water   _____

Temperature of freezing water   _____

Calculations

Part A: Uncertainty for Laboratory Balance

1. Use your data for the mass of the standard weight to find the apparent uncertainty of your balance. Subtract the lower limit mass of the standard weight from the higher limit and divide this difference by 2. Round to one significant digit to get the apparent uncertainty (e.g., 0.0125 g rounds off to 0.01 g). Write the mass of the standard weight followed by the uncertainty (e.g., 10.00 g ± 0.01 g).

                                                      mass _____

2. With classmates, evaluate the class measurements of the masses of the unknowns. Discard any values that are much greater or much

smaller than the majority of values. List and average the remaining masses for each unknown to find an average mass for each.

Class Data Bank: Masses of Unknowns (g)
Unknown #1   Unknown #2

Average mass _____   Average mass _____

3. Determine the practical uncertainty for the lab balance by doing the following steps:
   a. To find the deviation in mass measurements for each unknown, compute the difference (absolute value) between the average mass value (see answer to Question 2) and each of the mass measurements in the data list for Question 2.

Deviations from Average Mass (g)
Unknown #1   Unknown #2

   b. Average the list of mass deviations for each unknown and round to one significant figure (e.g., 0.0125 g rounds off to 0.01 g). This is the practical uncertainty.

   Average deviation (uncertainty)   Unknown #1 _____
                                      Unknown #2 _____

   c. Report the average mass of each unknown followed by its uncertainty (e.g., 5.25 ± 0.01 g).

   Average mass with uncertainty   Unknown #1 _____
                                      Unknown #2 _____

Part B: Uncertainty for Graduated Cylinders

1. With classmates, evaluate the class measurements of the masses of 10 mL of water. Discard any values that are much greater or much smaller than the majority of measurements. List the remaining measurements and compute an average mass for the water in each cylinder.

Class Data Bank: Mass of 10 mL of Water (g)
10-mL cylinder   100-mL cylinder

Average mass _____   Average mass _____

2. Determine the practical uncertainty of the mass measurements made in the 10-mL and the 100-mL graduated cylinders by doing the following steps:

a. Take the difference (absolute value) between the average mass of water and each individual mass of water in the data list for the 10-mL graduated cylinder. This gives a list of data deviations. Do the same for the 100-mL cylinder.

Deviations from Average Mass (g)
10-mL cylinder   100-mL cylinder

b. Average the deviations for each cylinder and round to one significant digit (e.g., 0.133 g rounds off to 0.1 g). This practical uncertainty of the mass measurement is equivalent to the practical uncertainty of the cylinder volume because 1.00 g of water at 20°C has a volume of 1.00 mL.

Average deviation (uncertainty) 10-mL cylinder _____

100-mL cylinder _____

c. Report the volume of water (10.0 mL) in each cylinder, followed by the calculated uncertainty for each cylinder from Part B.

Average volume with uncertainty 10-mL cylinder _____

100-mL cylinder _____

Part C: Uncertainty of a Celsius Thermometer

1. With classmates, evaluate the class measurements of the boiling points and freezing points of water. Discard any values that are much higher or lower than the majority of temperatures in each list. List the remaining temperatures and compute an average boiling point temperature and an average freezing point temperature.

Name _____

Class Data Bank: Water Temperature (°C)
Boiling point   Freezing point

Average boiling point _____ Average freezing point _____

2. Determine the practical uncertainty of the thermometers by doing the following steps:

   a. Take the difference (absolute value) between the average boiling point and each boiling point in the data list. This gives a list of data deviations. Do the same with the average freezing point data.

   Deviations from Average Temperature (°C)
   Boiling point   Freezing point

   b. Average the deviations for the boiling points and the freezing points and round to one significant figure (e.g., 0.455°C rounds off to 0.5°C). These are the practical uncertainties for the thermometers.

   Average deviation (uncertainty)   Boiling point   _____

   Freezing point _____

   c. Report the average boiling point and freezing point of water followed by the calculated uncertainty of each.

   Average boiling point with uncertainty   _____

   Average freezing point with uncertainty   _____

Critical Thinking: Analysis and Conclusions

1. Why do students measuring the mass of the same object on similar balances report slightly different masses? *(Drawing conclusions)* ____

   _____

   _____

2. Which did you find to have a smaller uncertainty, the 10-mL or 100-mL graduated cylinder? Give a reason why one has a smaller uncertainty. *(Interpreting data)* _____

   _____

3. Based on your uncertainty determinations, tell whether balances or graduated cylinders appear to be more accurate measuring devices. Explain your answer. (*Making comparisons*) _____

_____

4. Assuming that the equipment was functioning properly, explain the probable source of error in data values that were discarded because of their large deviations. (*Making inferences*) _____

_____

5. Do the uncertainties you calculated for each type of lab equipment more closely match the size of the smallest scale division, one-half division, or one-fifth division? (*Interpreting data*) _____

_____

6. Based on your answer to Question 5, what uncertainty would you assign to each type of equipment used? (*Evaluating*)

Balance _____   10-mL graduated cylinder _____

Thermometer _____   100-mL graduated cylinder _____

Critical Thinking: Applications

1. If the uncertainty of a balance is ±0.005 g, how many significant figures would you use to report a scale reading when the counter-weights lie exactly on the 8-gram mark? Explain your answer. (*Applying concepts*) _____

_____

2. Suppose a student asks your advice about how to measure 9 mL of a liquid as accurately as possible using a graduated cylinder. Would you recommend a 10-mL or a 100-mL graduated cylinder? Support your answer using the results of this investigation. (*Making judgments*)

_____

_____

3. What procedural change would you recommend to increase the accuracy and precision of the measurements discussed in the Introduction to this lab? (*Evaluating*) _____

_____

Going Further

1. Determine the uncertainty of a carpenter's tape measure, a tape measure used for sewing, or a measuring cup used for cooking. To make this determination, use methods similar to those used in this investigation. Present your findings to your class.

Cleaning Up an Oil Spill

Text reference: **Chapter 1**

Introduction

Have you ever considered the difficulty of cleaning up an oil spill? You may have read about the *Exxon Valdez* oil spill in Prince William Sound off the coast of Alaska. It was one of the largest oil spills in North American history. Many scientists in chemistry, marine biology, wildlife physiology, and shoreline ecology worked together to clean up the spill and to save as much wildlife as they could. The cleanup was a very time-consuming and difficult operation. Scientists continue to monitor the long-term effects of the spill on the environment.

As you probably know, oil is less dense than water. It not only floats on top of the water, but also spreads rapidly on the water's surface. The first step that scientists take in cleaning up an oil spill is to contain the oil if possible. Because cleanup crews need time to reach a spill site, however, some oil is carried away before containment procedures can be employed. Also, waves and currents in the ocean make containment difficult over an extended time period. Thus, other methods must be employed to clean up the spill.

Natural processes, such as evaporation, wave action, and the biological breakdown of oil by bacteria, begin the process of cleaning up an oil spill immediately, but they often occur too slowly to save the organisms whose habitats have been polluted or destroyed. A big factor in the cleanup of the Prince William Sound oil spill was bioremediation—introducing large numbers of oil-eating bacteria to remove oil. Unfortunately, this process is long and slow. Scientists are searching for faster methods to clean up spills in order to save more wildlife.

In this investigation, you will evaluate some physical and chemical techniques that can be used to clean up an oil spill. As you do the investigation, keep in mind that your goal is to remove as much of the oil as fast as possible and with the minimum amount of damage to your model environment.

Pre-Lab Discussion

Read the entire laboratory activity and the relevant pages of your textbook. Then answer the questions that follow.

1. Why is containment alone not a satisfactory answer to the oil spill problem? _____

_____

_____

Name _____

2. Of the methods you will be using in this investigation, which do you predict will be the best for cleaning up an oil spill and minimizing further damage to the environment? Explain your reasoning. _____

_____

_____

_____

3. In Step 5 of the Procedure, why are you told to tie back long hair and loose clothing? _____

_____

4. What effect do you think the sand will have on the oil? _____

_____

Problem

What are some effective, environmentally safe methods for cleaning up an oil spill?

Materials

chemical splash goggles   string, 25-cm piece
laboratory apron   2 beakers, 150-mL
newspapers   graduated cylinder, 10-mL
masking tape   2 wooden splints
aluminum pie pan   matches
tap water   sand
motor oil   natural straw
container   liquid detergent
2 droppers   paper towels

Safety

Wear your goggles and lab apron at all times during the investigation. Tie back long hair and secure loose clothing to avoid any fire hazard while working with the matches and burning splints. Clean up any spilled oil immediately to avoid the potential hazard of slipping on the floor or ruining clothing from oily work areas. If a spill occurs, tell your teacher immediately.

Dispose of excess oil, waste oil-and-water mixtures, and oil-soaked sand and straw in the containers provided by your teacher. Do not pour any oil down the drain.

Note the caution alert symbols here and with certain steps of the Procedure. Refer to page *xi* for the specific precautions associated with each symbol.

Procedure

1. Put on your goggles and lab apron. Cover your work area with sheets of newspaper, secured with masking tape.

2. Fill the pie pan with water to a depth of about 2 cm. Add two drops of oil to the center of the water. Tie the ends of the string together and gently place the circle of string around the oil on the water's surface.

3. Carefully add another 2 mL of oil inside the string. Try using the string to pull the oil to one side of the pan. Record your observations in the Data Table.

4. Using one of the droppers, try to suction the oil from the containment area. Place the oil from your dropper in one of the beakers and dispose of it in the container provided by your teacher. **CAUTION:** *Do not pour any oil down the drain.* Record your observations.

5. Remove the string from the pan and dispose of it in the container provided by your teacher. Using a graduated cylinder, measure 5 mL of oil and add it to the water. Fill a clean 150-mL beaker with tap water. Ignite a wooden splint with a match. Using the burning splint, ignite the oil on the water in the pie pan. Extinguish the splint by placing it in the beaker of tap water. **CAUTION:** *Avoid contact with the flame from the match and the burning splint. Tie back hair and loose clothing.* Record your observations of the ignited oil.

6. If you were able to remove all the oil in Step 5, add another 5 mL of oil to the pan. If the oil was not cleaned up in Step 5, proceed using the oil already in your pan. Spread a handful of sand lightly over the surface of the oil. Wait one or two minutes. Record your observations.

7. If all the oily sand from Step 6 is below water level, add another 5 mL of oil to the pan. If the sand is above water level, dispose of the contents of the pan in the container provided by your teacher. Then add a fresh supply of water to a depth of about 2 cm and add 5 mL of oil to the water. Sprinkle a handful of straw on the surface of the oil. Record your observations until no further changes occur.

8. Dispose of the contents of the pan in the container provided by your teacher, and rinse and wipe your pan. Again, fill the pan with water to a depth of 2 cm and add one drop of oil. Now add one drop of liquid detergent to the oil and stir the two together using a clean wooden splint. Record your observations.

9. Dispose of the contents of the pan in the container provided by your teacher. Clean up your work area and wash your hands before leaving the laboratory.

Name _____

Observations

DATA TABLE

Cleanup Procedure	Observations
containment with string	
suction with dropper	
burning the oil	
sand	
straw	
detergent	

Critical Thinking: Analysis and Conclusions

1. The string used in Steps 1–3 of the procedure shows how a boom works to contain oil spills. Were you able to contain your oil with the string provided? Why or why not? *(Drawing conclusions)* _____

_____

_____

_____

_____

2. Do you think it would be possible to use a suction device—like the dropper used in this investigation—to remove a large oil spill? Explain. *(Drawing conclusions)* _____

_____

_____

3. Why did the sand cause the oil to sink? *(Making inferences)* _____

_____

_____

4. Does sinking the oil with sand appear to be an effective method of cleaning up an oil spill? Explain your answer. *(Drawing conclusions)*

_____

_____

_____

5. Why did the straw not cause the oil to sink? *(Making inferences)* _____
_____

6. What effect did the detergent have on the oil? Would this effect aid in cleaning up an oil spill? *(Interpreting data)* _____
_____
_____
_____

Critical Thinking: Applications

1. If the oil could be ignited, would you consider this an effective and safe way to clean up an oil spill? Explain. *(Making judgments)* _____
_____
_____

2. Based on your results, which method of cleanup tested in this investigation do you think is the most effective? Defend your answer. *(Evaluating)* _____
_____

3. If scientists are able to reclaim oil by removing it from the water's surface, what problems would they encounter in trying to make the oil suitable for reuse? *(Applying concepts)* _____
_____
_____

4. If you had to develop a plan to be used in cleaning up an oil spill, taking into consideration factors such as speed of removal, damage to the environment, and cost, what strategies would you include? *(Developing models)* _____
_____
_____
_____

Going Further

1. Research the most recent major oil spills around the world. Prepare a report describing the cleanup methods used and their effectiveness.
2. Research the use of bioremediation in cleaning up oil spills. Discuss the advantages and disadvantages of using this technology.
3. Research the way that oil is transported. Find out if other, more environmentally safe methods exist for transporting oil. If they do, discuss why you think some of these methods have not been put to use.

Simulating a Cold Pack

Lab **4**

APPLICATION

Text reference: **Chapter 2**

Introduction

Suppose you are on a hike and you sprain your ankle. The immediate application of a cold pack would be a wise first-aid practice. Injuries such as a sprained ankle are accompanied by an increase in blood flow to the affected area, which brings excess heat and contributes to swelling. A cold pack is much colder than your injured ankle, so it removes some of the heat, causes blood vessels to constrict, and reduces swelling, inflammation, and pain.

How exactly does a cold pack work? An instant cold pack, shown in Figure 4–1, usually consists of a tough plastic bag with two compounds inside: water and a salt such as ammonium nitrate (NH_4NO_3), a common lawn fertilizer. The water is sealed inside a fragile inner bag to keep it separated from the ammonium nitrate.

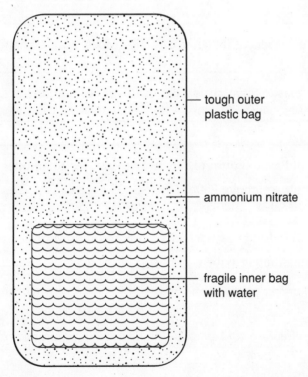

— tough outer plastic bag

— ammonium nitrate

— fragile inner bag with water

Figure 4–1

When the cold pack is needed, the ammonium nitrate is brought into contact with the water by squeezing the pack until the fragile inner container pops open. As the ammonium nitrate dissolves in the water, a subtle chemical change occurs. The water breaks the solid ammonium nitrate into positively and negatively charged particles (ions).

Name_____

Chemical changes always involve changes in energy. Often, heat is released, which may be detected as an increase in temperature. Other times, heat energy is absorbed, which results in a decrease in temperature.

In this investigation, you will experiment with the materials that make up an instant cold pack. You will combine water and ammonium nitrate in an insulated cup. The cup will prevent any heat exchange with the environment while the dissolving process removes heat from the water. In order to have a useful cold pack, there must be more than enough solid ammonium nitrate present to reduce the temperature of the liquid in the bag to near zero and keep it cold for an additional 10 to 15 minutes. You will determine the amount of ammonium nitrate solid necessary to lower the temperature to that of melting ice or below and to maintain that temperature for at least 10 minutes.

Pre-Lab Discussion

Read the entire laboratory investigation and the relevant pages of your textbook. Then answer the questions that follow.

1. Define *heat*. _____

_____

2. Define *temperature*. _____

_____

3. In your experience, in what direction does heat exchange occur?

_____

4. Why are plastic foam cups used in this investigation? _____

_____

_____

5. Why should ammonium nitrate not be exposed to an open flame or

to temperatures above 250°C? _____

_____

6. Why should clothing splashed with ammonium nitrate solution be

rinsed immediately with water? _____

_____

Problem

How can an effective cold pack be made from ammonium nitrate and water?

Materials

chemical splash goggles	laboratory balance
laboratory apron	spatula
graduated cylinder, 100-mL	ammonium nitrate (NH_4NO_3)
tap water	thermometer
plastic foam cup	stirring rod
4 large pieces weighing paper	clock

Safety

Wear your goggles and lab apron at all times during the investigation. Ammonium nitrate is poisonous and can burn or explode when dry or if it is exposed to temperatures above 250°C. Do not expose ammonium nitrate to fire or store in a hot environment. Clothing splashed with ammonium nitrate solution becomes flammable when dried. If ammonium nitrate accidentally comes in contact with your skin or clothing, rinse it off with large quantities of water and inform your teacher immediately. Dispose of the ammonium nitrate solution as instructed by your teacher.

Note the caution alert symbols here and with certain steps of the Procedure. Refer to page *xi* for the specific precautions associated with each symbol.

Procedure

 1. Put on your goggles and lab apron. Fill the graduated cylinder with 50 mL of tap water that is at room temperature, and pour the water into the plastic foam cup.

 2. Place a weighing paper on the laboratory balance and determine the mass of the paper. Then use a spatula to measure out a mass of 15.0 g of ammonium nitrate, allowing for the mass of the paper. Repeat this step three more times, so that you have four 15.0-g portions of ammonium nitrate. **CAUTION:** *Ammonium nitrate is poisonous and may explode or burn when dry. Avoid contact with skin and clothing. If contact occurs, rinse with large quantities of water.*

3. Using the thermometer, measure the temperature of the water and record this value in the data table.

4. Add one of the 15.0-g portions of ammonium nitrate to the cup and stir it slowly with the stirring rod until it is dissolved. Measure and record the temperature of the water. Also record your observations, such as how much time it takes for the ammonium nitrate to dissolve and how quickly the temperature of the solution changes.

5. Repeat Step 4 with each of the remaining 15.0-g portions of ammonium nitrate until enough of the compound is present to maintain the temperature of the water at 0°C or below for at least 10 minutes.

 6. Dispose of the ammonium nitrate solution according to your teacher's instructions. Clean up your work area and wash your hands before leaving the laboratory.

Observations

Data Table

Mass of NH₄NO₃ in Solution (g)	Temp. (°C)	Change in Temp. (°C)	Observations
0.0			
15.0			
30.0			
45.0			
60.0			

Calculations

1. Calculate the change in temperature that occurs after each 15.0-g portion of ammonium nitrate is added to the water, and write these values in the Data Table.

Critical Thinking: Analysis and Conclusions

1. At what point did the largest change in temperature occur? How can this observation be explained? *(Interpreting data)* _____

   _____

   _____

   _____

2. Identify any patterns that you observed as the portions of ammonium nitrate were added to the water. *(Making comparisons)* _____

   _____

   _____

3. What do you think would happen if you tried to dissolve another 15.0 g of ammonium nitrate in the water? Explain your reasoning. *(Drawing conclusions)* _____

   _____

   _____

Critical Thinking: Applications

1. In this investigation, the insulated cup prevents the cold solution from being warmed by the outside environment. Would you expect a commercial cold pack to remain as cold for the same length of time if it was applied to an injured ankle? Explain. *(Applying concepts)*

   _____

   _____

2. Predict what happens to any undissolved ammonium nitrate in the cold pack as heat is absorbed. *(Making predictions)* _____

_____

_____

_____

3. One of the dangers of using a cold pack made of ice—especially one taken from a freezer—is frostbite. In light of the temperatures reached by the addition of the final portions of ammonium nitrate, would you expect the danger of frostbite to exist with a cold pack made from ammonium nitrate? Explain. *(Making judgments)* _____

_____

_____

_____

_____

Going Further

1. Describe how you would design an instant cold pack from common household items, ammonium nitrate, and water. Include a list of the materials needed, directions for using the cold pack, and the appropriate safety warnings. Make a sketch of your design. (Note: You can calculate the ratio of the mass of ammonium nitrate per gram of water used in the investigation, and use the ratio to specify the amount of each compound needed in your design.)

2. Ammonium nitrate is commonly used as a fertilizer. You might think that it could be disposed of simply by adding it to soil or water. Consult an environmentalist or do library research to determine what problems might be created by dumping large amounts of ammonium nitrate into the environment.

Candy Coatings: Compounds or Mixtures?

Text reference: Chapter 2

Introduction

Perhaps you are familiar with the small, round, candy-coated chocolates whose manufacturer once claimed: "Melts in your mouth, not in your hand." The manufacturer could make such a claim because each candy is covered with a hard coating. Although the candy doesn't necessarily melt right away, the dyes in the coatings eventually do dissolve, making one's hands turn different colors.

In this investigation, you will use two separation techniques to determine whether the dyes in candy coatings are compounds or mixtures. In the first part of the investigation, you will use wool yarn in a series of chemical reactions to separate the dyes from the sugar, chocolate, and other nondye substances in the candies.

In the second part of the investigation, you will explore the makeup of the dye by using a separation technique called paper chromatography. In this technique, a liquid medium, or solvent, is used to dissolve the dyes and carry them along a piece of paper. Different chemicals will have different rates of travel. The results will show whether the dye is a compound or a mixture of compounds.

Pre-Lab Discussion

Read the entire laboratory investigation and the relevant pages of your textbook. Then answer the questions that follow.

1. What is the chemical definition of a compound? A mixture? _____

    _____

    _____

    _____

2. Why should you wear chemical splash goggles and a safety apron

    throughout this investigation? _____

3. Why would it be inappropriate to eat the candy? _____

    _____

    _____

4. What does it mean "to decant" the liquid with the dissolved dye

    in it? _____

    _____

Name_____

5. What is the purpose of the paper wick? _____

_____

Problem

Are the dyes found in candy coatings one compound or many?

Materials

Part A
chemical splash goggles
laboratory apron
hot plate
20 cm wool yarn
beaker, 150-mL
tap water
4 small candies, same color
large test tube, 18 × 150 mm
test tube rack

graduated cylinder, 10-mL
distilled water
acetic acid, 3 M
2 small test tubes, 13 × 100 mm
tongs
stirring rod
paper towel
ammonia water (NH_3), 1%
watch glass

Part B
micropipet
filter paper, 11-cm diameter
scissors
well plate
toothpick

graduated cylinder, 10-mL
developing solution
petri dish
ruler

Safety

Wear your goggles and lab apron at all times during the investigation. Never eat any foodstuffs in the laboratory. Acetic acid and ammonia can irritate or burn your skin. Do not rub your eyes or touch your skin without first washing your hands. If these solutions contact your skin or clothing, wash the area with large amounts of water and notify your teacher.

The solutions used in Part B are extremely flammable. Be sure there are no burner flames in the laboratory. Turn off the hot plate during Part B. Note the caution alert symbols here and with certain steps of the Procedure. Refer to page *xi* for the specific precautions associated with each symbol.

Procedure

Part A

1. Put on your goggles and lab apron. Fill a 150-mL beaker one-third full of water, and place it on the hot plate. Turn on the hot plate and start the water to boil. Meanwhile, place four small candies of the same color in a large test tube and set the test tube in the test-tube rack. **CAUTION:** *Foodstuffs should never*

be eaten in the lab. Do not eat any of the candies. Measure 7 mL of distilled water using a 10-mL graduated cylinder and pour it into the test tube with the candies.

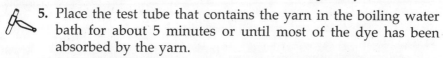

2. Add 3 drops of concentrated acetic acid to the water-candy mixture. **CAUTION:** *Concentrated acetic acid can irritate or burn your skin. If you spill any, rinse the affected area immediately with large amounts of cold water and report the spill to your teacher.*

3. As soon as the colored coating is dissolved, slowly pour, or decant, the liquid dye into a small test tube, making sure the candy or any other solid residue is left behind. Discard the candy and other solid residue.

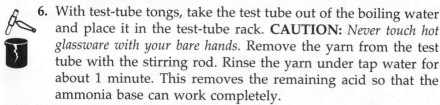

4. Using a stirring rod, add a 20-cm piece of woolen yarn and 3 drops of concentrated acetic acid to the liquid-dye mixture.

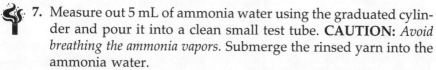

5. Place the test tube that contains the yarn in the boiling water bath for about 5 minutes or until most of the dye has been absorbed by the yarn.

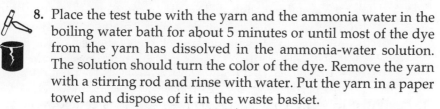

6. With test-tube tongs, take the test tube out of the boiling water and place it in the test-tube rack. **CAUTION:** *Never touch hot glassware with your bare hands.* Remove the yarn from the test tube with the stirring rod. Rinse the yarn under tap water for about 1 minute. This removes the remaining acid so that the ammonia base can work completely.

7. Measure out 5 mL of ammonia water using the graduated cylinder and pour it into a clean small test tube. **CAUTION:** *Avoid breathing the ammonia vapors.* Submerge the rinsed yarn into the ammonia water.

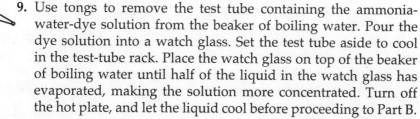

8. Place the test tube with the yarn and the ammonia water in the boiling water bath for about 5 minutes or until most of the dye from the yarn has dissolved in the ammonia-water solution. The solution should turn the color of the dye. Remove the yarn with a stirring rod and rinse with water. Put the yarn in a paper towel and dispose of it in the waste basket.

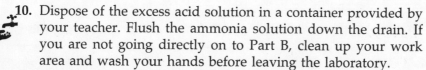

9. Use tongs to remove the test tube containing the ammonia-water-dye solution from the beaker of boiling water. Pour the dye solution into a watch glass. Set the test tube aside to cool in the test-tube rack. Place the watch glass on top of the beaker of boiling water until half of the liquid in the watch glass has evaporated, making the solution more concentrated. Turn off the hot plate, and let the liquid cool before proceeding to Part B.

10. Dispose of the excess acid solution in a container provided by your teacher. Flush the ammonia solution down the drain. If you are not going directly on to Part B, clean up your work area and wash your hands before leaving the laboratory.

Part B

11. Put on your goggles and lab apron. Transfer the concentrated dye to a micropipet.

Name _____

 12. Obtain a piece of filter paper and fold it in half. Unfold the paper and cut a 2-cm-wide wick in the paper by making two cuts from the edge to the crease in the middle. Your filter paper with wick should look like Figure 6–1. **CAUTION:** *Make sure all hot plates have been turned off and there are no flames in the laboratory before going on with this investigation. The solvent is highly flammable.*

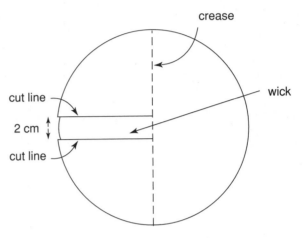

Figure 6–1

13. Transfer a few drops of the concentrated dye solution from the micropipet to a well in the well plate. Take a toothpick and crush one end by placing it on the lab bench and pushing down until the end flares slightly. Dip the crushed end of the toothpick into the dye solution and make a very small spot of dye on the creased filter paper where the wick meets the rest of the paper. Allow the spot to dry. Repeat at least ten times on the same spot to concentrate the dye on the filter paper. Make the spot as small as possible. Record the initial color of the spot.

14. Using a graduated cylinder, pour 8 mL of developing solution into the bottom half of a petri dish.

15. Cut the wick in half crosswise and bend it down to make a stand. Place it into the developing solution, as shown in Figure 6–2. Carefully place the other half of the petri dish over the filter paper, not allowing the wick to be crushed or flattened. Allow to develop undisturbed for about 35 minutes.

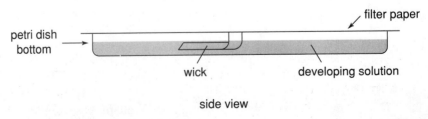

Figure 6–2

16. Observe how far your dye traveled from the original spot and mark the outer limit of the solvent.

 17. Dispose of all your solvents as directed by your teacher. Clean up your work area and wash your hands before leaving the laboratory.

Observations

1. Initial color of spot _____

2. Final color of spot _____

3. Color(s) present after developing _____

4. Distance traveled by solvent _____

5. Distance traveled by dye _____

6. Sketch what you saw on the filter paper after the chromatography was done.

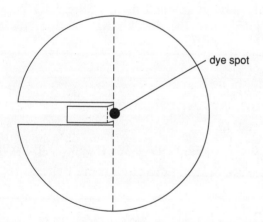

Figure 6–3

Critical Thinking: Analysis and Conclusions

1. Was the dye you tested a single compound or a mixture? Explain your answer. *(Interpreting data)* _____

2. Complete the table on the next page by pooling your data with those of other students in the class. Are the colors of the candy all one color (dye) or are they made from a several different colors (dyes)? Are these results consistent with what you know about colors? Explain your reasoning. *(Drawing conclusions)*

DATA TABLE 1

Color	Component Colors	Compound or Mixture
green		
red		
yellow		
purple		
brown		
orange		

_____

_____

_____

3. Why was it important to keep the spot applied to your filter paper as small as possible? *(Designing experiments)* _____

_____

_____

4. What would have happened if the entire filter paper, and not just the wick, had sat in the developing solution? *(Making predictions)*

_____

_____

Critical Thinking: Applications

1. What do you think would have happened if you had used an ink pen to mark the initial spot on the paper? Why? *(Applying concepts)*

_____

_____

2. Do you think the coating of the candies you tested is made with the same type of food coloring sold in grocery stores? How could you test your hypothesis? *(Developing hypotheses)* _____

_____

_____

_____

_____

Going Further

1. Test the dyes in some other brands of candies and compare their intensity of color.
2. Design an experiment to see if the same chemicals are used in commercial and household food colorings.

Rutherford's Experiment

Lab 7

Introduction

Have you ever seen a large package and immediately thought you knew what was inside? Just as you cannot see inside a sealed package, no one can see inside an atom. How then can we describe the structure of an atom? We use indirect evidence. Indirect evidence has enabled scientists to visualize many unseeable phenomena: ancient climates, the center of the earth, as well as the structure of atoms.

In the early 1900s, the New Zealand scientist Ernest Rutherford (1871–1937) discovered that radioactive alpha particles were helium atoms with the electrons removed. Rutherford and his colleagues were curious to see what would happen if they aimed a beam of positively charged alpha particles at thin sheets of gold—one of the densest elements known. When they did the experiment, they found that most of the alpha particles passed straight through the gold foil—as if nothing were there. A very tiny fraction of the particles was reflected back from the foil, however, and Rutherford realized that something quite small, but quite massive, was scattering the alpha particles. This experiment was the first evidence for the existence of a nucleus within the atom.

In the lab investigation in Chapter 3 of your textbook, you had an opportunity to probe the contents of various sealed boxes and then open them. In this investigation, you will probe a box that cannot be opened. You will gather indirect information about the contents of a sealed box and then draw a model based on this information. You will eventually be able to compare your results with others in your class, but you will not know the real answer for certain, just as scientists do not know the real answer for certain when they publish their data.

Pre-Lab Discussion

Read the entire laboratory investigation and the relevant pages of your textbook. Then answer the questions that follow.

1. In what ways is the sealed box similar to Rutherford's gold atoms?

    _____

    _____

2. What did Rutherford use to probe gold atoms, and what will you

    use to probe the inside of a sealed box? _____

    _____

Name _____

3. Why would it be too difficult for you to duplicate Rutherford's alpha-scattering experiment in your chemistry laboratory? _____

_____

4. List some of the procedures you expect will help in your investigation of the sealed box. _____

_____

_____

Problem

How can you use indirect evidence to study the nature of something you cannot see?

Materials

safety goggles   ceramic magnet
sealed box   metric ruler

Safety

Wear your goggles at all times during the investigation.

Procedure

 1. Put on your goggles. Obtain a sealed box whose contents are to be investigated, a ceramic magnet, and a metric ruler. You should be able to hear a steel ball rolling inside the box.

2. You can investigate the contents of the box by shaking or tipping it, but you cannot open the box or make holes in it. Use the steel ball as a probe to determine the box's contents. Use the magnet on the outside of the box to guide the steel ball.

3. Probe the contents of the box. Determine as many characteristics—such the texture, size, and shape—of the contents as you can. Record each procedure you use (for example, rolling the ball in a particular direction) and what it reveals (for example, the position and size of any obstacle that is encountered). Vary your procedures to obtain as complete and exact an image of the contents of the box as possible. Use the clues you gather about the contents to draw the features and shapes of the structures inside the box.

4. Do not open the box at any time, pry up the lid, or make openings of any kind. Draw the best image you can of the box's contents using only information you gather by investigating the sealed box. Be prepared to present your methods and findings before the class. Remember that you are simulating a scientific investigation in which only student investigations can provide an answer to the problem. Your answer may or may not agree with the results of others.

5. Clean up your work area and wash your hands before leaving the laboratory.

Observations

DATA TABLE

Procedure	Results
1.	
2.	
3.	
4.	
5.	

Critical Thinking: Analysis and Conclusions

1. Based on your observations, draw a picture of the contents of your box in the space below. *(Drawing conclusions)*

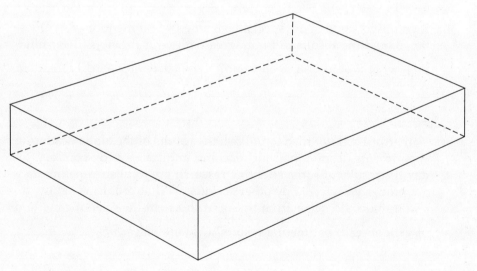

Figure 7–1

2. Compare your drawing of the contents of the box with the drawings of others in the class. How do scientists know when their experimental results are correct? *(Making comparisons)* _____

_____

_____

3. If two or three groups present images of the box contents that are very similar, what does this suggest to you about the validity of these results compared with the singular results of others? *(Making judgments)* _____

_____

Critical Thinking: Applications

1. In Rutherford's experiment, most of the positively charged alpha particles passed directly through the gold foil. However, a very small percentage of the alpha particles rebounded or changed course. What do these results suggest to you about the structure of gold atoms as compared to the contents of your box? *(Making comparisons)* _____

   _____

   _____

2. In what ways could you test your model of the contents of the box? *(Developing models)* _____

   _____

   _____

3. What other tests would you like to do if you had more equipment? *(Designing experiments)* _____

   _____

4. If you used some of the special instruments you mentioned in Question 3, and the results did not agree with your previous determination, what would you need to do? *(Developing hypotheses)* _____

   _____

   _____

5. Rutherford did not rush to publish the results of the alpha-scattering experiments despite their far-reaching implications. By contrast, today the results of some scientific research are published before they are properly reviewed by other scientists. What problems, if any, do you think could occur from trying to short-cut the scientific method of validating experimental results? *(Making judgments)* _____

   _____

   _____

Going Further

1. Investigate one of the people connected with uncovering the structure of the atom. How did the person's personality or philosophy affect the scientific results? What role did history play?
2. No one has ever seen a black hole in space. Why then should people believe that black holes exist? Find out what a black hole is and what evidence there is for the existence of black holes. Share your findings with your class in a brief oral report.

Finding the Charge of an Electron

Lab 8

Introduction

An electron is too small to see or to have its mass measured in a school laboratory, but a flow of electrons (an electric current) can produce large-scale changes in matter. An electric current in the form of a lightning bolt, for example, can incinerate a tree. On a smaller scale, you probably know from experience that the electric current in a toaster can easily make your breakfast waffle too hot to touch.

In this investigation, you will monitor a chemical change, called an electroplating reaction, produced by an electric current. In an electroplating reaction, a source of electric current is connected to two metal electrodes immersed in a solution that can conduct electricity. The solution is composed of water and a compound that dissolves into charged particles, called ions. The current causes metal atoms to leave one electrode and dissolve into the solution. At the same time, metal atoms plate out, or attach, onto the other electrode.

You will use zinc metal (Zn) for the electrodes in this investigation. At the positive electrode, zinc atoms lose two electrons each and dissolve as Zn^{2+} ions. These ions travel freely in the solution. At the negative electrode, Zn^{2+} ions from the solution gain two electrons and plate out as neutral zinc atoms. You will be able to measure the change in mass at each electrode and from these data derive the number of zinc atoms gained or lost. Since changes in each zinc atom involve two electrons, the number of electrons involved is double the number of atoms.

The electroplating reaction is driven by an external battery, which causes electrons to move through a wire toward the negative electrode and away from the positive electrode through another wire. You will measure the flow of electrons through the external wire using an ammeter. With the data you have, you can use a series of calculations to find the charge on one electron.

Pre-Lab Discussion

Read the entire laboratory investigation and the relevant pages of your textbook. Then answer the questions that follow.

1. What quantities do you need to know in order to determine the charge of the electron? _____

   _____

   _____

Name_____

2. How is each quantity in Question 1 obtained? _____

_____

_____

3. What quantity is measured by the ammeter? _____

4. How is the total charge calculated? _____

_____

5. Why must the number of zinc atoms be doubled to find the number of electrons that flowed through the circuit? _____

_____

_____

6. What hazards are present in this investigation, and what safety precautions should you follow? _____

_____

_____

Problem

How can the charge of an electron be determined?

Materials

chemical splash goggles	3 wire leads with alligator clips
laboratory apron	ammeter
2 zinc (Zn) electrodes	stopwatch or clock with a second hand
steel wool	
marking pen or pencil	beaker containing tap water
beaker, 250-mL	beaker containing denatured alcohol
zinc sulfate solution, (ZnSO₄) 1.0 M	laboratory balance
4 D batteries	

Safety

Wear your goggles and lab apron at all times during the investigation. The denatured alcohol bath contains methyl alcohol, which is poisonous and highly flammable. Wash any spills and splashes immediately with plenty of water and make sure there are no open flames in the laboratory. Use the alcohol bath only under your teacher's supervision.

Note the caution alert symbols here and with certain steps of the Procedure. Refer to page *xi* for the specific precautions associated with each symbol.

Procedure

  1. Put on your goggles and lab apron.

2. Rub both sides of the two zinc electrodes with steel wool to remove any dirt or grease. Use the marking pen to draw a + (positive sign) on one electrode and a − (negative sign) on the other electrode. Measure the masses of the electrodes, and record these values in Data Table 1.

3. Assemble the apparatus shown in Figure 8–1 as follows. Bend one end of each electrode so that it can rest on the rim of the 250-mL beaker. Then place the electrodes on opposite sides of the beaker and add 200 mL of the zinc sulfate solution to the beaker. **CAUTION:** *Be sure that the electrodes do not touch each other.* Connect one of the wire leads to the positive zinc electrode and the other end of that lead to the negative terminal of your ammeter. Connect a second lead to the negative zinc electrode and the other end of that lead to the negative terminal of the batteries. Do not connect the third wire yet.

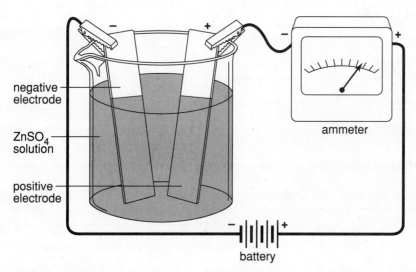

Figure 8–1

4. After your teacher has checked your apparatus, connect the third lead between the positive terminal of the ammeter and the positive terminal of the batteries. Watch the ammeter for a few moments until the current remains unchanging, and then adjust the current to between 0.70 and 0.80 amperes by moving the electrodes closer together or further apart. Do not allow the electrodes to touch.

5. In Data Table 2, record the current indicated by the ammeter. Take a reading at the beginning of each minute for 20–25 minutes. If the current varies beyond the 0.70–0.80 ampere range, readjust the positions of the electrodes. Be sure to wait until the end of a 1-minute interval to make any adjustments.

6. Disconnect the wire leads from the electrodes when you have finished taking readings. Carry your beaker containing the electrodes to the washing area set up by your teacher. Holding each electrode by its dry end, rinse it very carefully by dipping it first in a large beaker of water and then in a beaker of denatured alcohol. Do not shake or swirl the electrodes in the rinse liquids, or you may dislodge pieces of zinc. **CAUTION:** *The alcohol is toxic, and its vapors are flammable. Use only under your teacher's supervision. Be sure there are no flames in the laboratory. Avoid touching the alcohol. Wash spills or splashes on your skin with plenty of water.*

7. Set the electrodes gently on a paper towel, and place them in a protected area to dry. Return the zinc sulfate solution to a container provided by your teacher.

8. Measure the mass of each electrode when it is completely dry, and record these values in Data Table 1.

9. Clean up your work area and wash your hands before leaving the laboratory.

Observations

DATA TABLE 1

	Negative Electrode	**Positive Electrode**
initial mass (g)		
final mass (g)		
change in mass (g)		

DATA TABLE 2

Time (min)	Current (amp)	Time (min)	Current (amp)
1		11	
2		12	
3		13	
4		14	
5		15	
6		16	
7		17	
8		18	
9		19	
10		20	

Calculations

1. Find the change in mass for each electrode and write this value in Data Table 1.

2. The mass of a zinc atom is 1.09×10^{-22} g. Find the total number of zinc atoms involved at each electrode by dividing the change in mass by the mass of one atom.

3. Calculate the average current flowing through the ammeter. Then find the total charge in ampere-seconds by multiplying the average current by the time elapsed in seconds. (Remember to convert minutes to seconds.)

4. In SI units, charge is measured in coulombs. One coulomb is equal to one ampere-second. Convert your value for total charge to coulombs and calculate the charge per zinc atom involved at each electrode.

5. Find the charge per electron. (Note: Remember that for every zinc atom in the reaction, two electrons are involved.)

Critical Thinking: Analysis and Conclusions

1. How closely do your two values for the charge of an electron match the accepted value given in your textbook? *(Making comparisons)*

_____

_____

_____

2. Are the charge values you calculated for the two electrodes the same? If not, how might the discrepancy be explained? *(Making inferences)*

_____

_____

_____

3. What source of energy caused the change in masses of the electrodes? *(Making inferences)* _____

4. Are the changes in mass measured at each electrode consistent with the reactions taking place? Explain. *(Interpreting data)* _____

_____

_____

_____

_____

Critical Thinking: Applications

1. If you were to try this experiment using a different metal for the electrodes (and an appropriate conducting solution), predict whether or not you would find similar values for the charge on the electron. Explain. *(Making predictions)* _____

_____

_____

2. How do you think the number of zinc ions in solution at the start of the reaction compares to the number at the end? Explain your reasoning. *(Developing hypotheses)* _____

_____

_____

_____

Going Further

1. Under your teacher's supervision, redo this experiment using a different metal (lead or copper are recommended). See if you arrive at the same value for the charge on an electron.

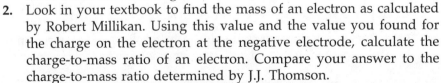

2. Look in your textbook to find the mass of an electron as calculated by Robert Millikan. Using this value and the value you found for the charge on the electron at the negative electrode, calculate the charge-to-mass ratio of an electron. Compare your answer to the charge-to-mass ratio determined by J.J. Thomson.

Isotopes of "Pennium"

Small Scale
Lab 9
A P P L I C A T I O N

*Text reference: **Chapter 3***

Introduction

Unless you're a coin collector, you probably think all United States pennies are pretty much the same. To the casual observer, all the pennies in circulation do seem to be identical in size, thickness, and composition. But just as elements have one or more isotopes with different masses, the pennies in circulation have different masses. In this investigation, you are going to use pennies with different masses to represent different "isotopes" of an imaginary element called pennium, or Pe. Remember that chemical isotopes are atoms that have the same number of protons, but different numbers of neutrons. Thus, chemical isotopes have nearly identical chemical properties, but some different physical properties.

In this investigation, you will determine the relative abundance of the isotopes of pennium and the masses of each isotope. You will then use this information to determine the atomic mass of pennium. Recall that the atomic mass of an element is the weighted average of the masses of the isotopes of the element. This average is based on both the mass and the relative abundance of each isotope as it occurs in nature.

Pre-Lab Discussion

Read the entire laboratory investigation and the relevant pages of your textbook. Then answer the questions that follow.

1. What do the 20 pennies in this investigation represent? _____

    _____

2. What do the different masses of the pennies represent? _____

    _____

3. What information do you need to calculate the average atomic mass

    for an element? _____

    _____

Problem

What are the masses and relative abundances of isotopes of pennium and what is the atomic mass of the element?

Materials

safety goggles   20 pennies in a resealable bag
laboratory balance

Isotopes of "Pennium"   **51**

Name _____

Safety

Wear your goggles at all times during the investigation.

Procedure

 1. Put on your goggles. Remove the pennies from the resealable bag and count them to make sure that there are 20. Determine and record the combined mass of your 20 pennies.

2. Find the mass of each penny separately. In the Data Table, record the year the penny was minted and its mass to the nearest 0.02 g.

3. Place the 20 pennies in the resealable bag and return the pennies and the laboratory balance to the area designated by your teacher. Clean up your work area and wash your hands before leaving the laboratory.

Observations

Combined mass (to nearest 0.02 g) of 20 pennies _____

DATA TABLE

Penny	Year	Mass (g)
1		
2		
3		
4		
5		
6		
7		
8		
9		
10		
11		
12		
13		
14		
15		
16		
17		
18		
19		
20		

Calculations

1. Inspect your data carefully. Determine the number of isotopes of Pe that are present. _____
_____

2. Calculate the fractional abundance of each isotope in your sample.

3. Calculate the average atomic mass of each isotope.

4. Using the fractional abundance and the average atomic mass of each isotope, calculate the atomic mass of Pe.

Critical Thinking: Analysis and Conclusions

1. Was the mass of 20 pennies equal to 20 times the mass of one penny? Explain. (*Making comparisons*) _____
_____
_____

2. In what year(s) did the mass of Pe change? How could you tell? (*Interpreting data*) _____
_____

3. How can you explain the fact that there are different "isotopes" of pennium? (*Making inferences*) _____
_____
_____

Critical Thinking: Applications

1. Why are the atomic masses for most elements not whole numbers?
   (Applying concepts) _____
   _____
   _____

2. How are the three isotopes of hydrogen (hydrogen-1, hydrogen-2, and hydrogen-3) alike? How are they different? *(Making comparisons)*
   _____
   _____
   _____

3. Copper has two isotopes, copper-63 and copper-65. The relative abundance of copper-63 is 69.1% and copper-65, 30.9%. Calculate the average atomic mass of copper. *(Applying concepts)*

Going Further

1. Repeat this investigation using dimes (Di). Are there different "isotopes" of dimes? Calculate the atomic mass of dimes.
2. Find out the chemical composition of pennies and dimes. How have these changed over the years?

Flame Tests

Introduction

According to the Bohr theory of the atom, electrons may occupy only specific energy levels. When an atom absorbs sufficient energy, an electron can "jump" to a higher energy level. Higher energy levels tend to be less stable, however, and if a lower energy level is available, the electron will "fall" back, giving off energy in the process. The difference in energies between the two levels is emitted in the form of a photon of electromagnetic radiation. The energy of each photon is described by the equation $E = h\nu$, where h is Planck's constant and ν is the frequency of the radiation. If the wavelength of the released photon is between 400 and 700 nm, the energy is emitted as visible light. The color of the light depends on the specific energy change that is taking place.

White light is a continuous spectrum in which all wavelengths of visible light are present. An excited atom, however, produces one or more specific lines in its spectrum, corresponding to the specific changes in energy levels of its electrons. Because each element has a distinct electron configuration, each has a unique line spectrum.

Flame tests are a quick method of producing the characteristic colors of metallic ions. The loosely-held electrons of a metal are easily excited in the flame of a lab burner. The emission of energy in the visible portion of the spectrum as those electrons return to lower energy levels produces a colored flame. The color is a combination of the wavelengths of each transition, and may be used to determine the identity of the ion.

In this investigation you will perform flame tests on seven metallic ions, then use your results to determine the identity of several unknowns.

Pre-Lab Discussion

Read the entire laboratory investigation and the relevant pages of your textbook. Then answer the questions that follow.

1. Write out the electron configurations for each of the metallic ions to be tested in this investigation.

    Ba^{2+} _____

    Cu^{2+} _____

    Li^{+} _____

    K^{+} _____

    Sr^{2+} _____

    Ca^{2+} _____

    Na^{+} _____

Name _____

2. What does a flame test indicate about the energy changes taking place among the electrons in a metallic ion? _____

_____

_____

3. Explain why a metallic ion produces a characteristic color in a flame test, regardless of the compound used as the source of the ion. ___

_____

_____

4. What wavelengths correspond to the visible spectrum? Which color has the shortest wavelength? The longest? _____

_____

5. What precautions should be taken when using 6.0 M HCl? _____

_____

_____

6. Why is it important to use a clean nichrome wire for each test? ___

_____

Problem

What colors are characteristic of particular metallic ions in a flame test?

Materials

chemical splash goggles
laboratory apron
latex gloves
well plate
marker pen
solutions of the following salts:
   barium nitrate ($Ba(NO_3)_2$)
   copper nitrate ($Cu(NO_3)_2$)
   strontium nitrate ($Sr(NO_3)_2$)
   lithium nitrate ($LiNO_3$)

potassium nitrate (KNO_3)
sodium chloride ($NaCl$)
calcium nitrate ($Ca(NO_3)_2$)
nichrome wire loop
beaker, 50-mL
hydrochloric acid
   (HCl), 6.0 M
lab burner
wash bottle with distilled water
3 unknown solutions

Safety

Wear your goggles and lab apron at all times during the investigation. The 6.0 M HCl is corrosive and irritating to skin, nasal passages, eyes, and clothing. The salt solutions, with the exception of NaCl, are toxic. Handle all of the solutions with care, and do not inhale their vapors. If a solution should splash on your skin, wash the affected area with large amounts of water and notify your teacher. When you work near the burner flame, tie back or cover loose hair, and secure loose or bulky clothing.

Note the caution alert symbols here and with certain steps of the Procedure. Refer to page *xi* for the specific precautions associated with each symbol.

Procedure

 1. Put on your goggles and lab apron. Obtain a well plate and use a marker to label seven wells with the names of the known solutions. Put a dropperful of each known solution into its labeled well.

 2. Put on your latex gloves. Obtain a beaker with about 10 mL of 6.0 *M* HCl and a nichrome wire loop. Light the burner, and adjust the flame to low. **CAUTION:** *Hydrochloric acid is corrosive to skin and clothing and its vapors are irritating to lungs and eyes. Avoid contact with the solution and inhalation of its vapors. Loose hair should be tied back or covered, and bulky or loose clothing should be secured in some manner.*

3. For each test, be sure that the nichrome wire is clean, so as not to contaminate the solutions. To clean the wire, first rinse it with distilled water, using the wash bottle. Then dip it in the 6.0 *M* HCl solution. Place it in the burner flame for a few moments, as shown in Figure 10–1. Determine the color of the clean nichrome wire in the flame. This is the color you should see after every trial.

 4. Sodium has a very strong color, which may affect your other tests, so test the sodium solution last. Dip the clean nichrome wire in one solution. Place the wire in the burner flame and observe. Record your observations on Data Table 1. Clean the wire and repeat this step with the next known solution until you have tested all seven solutions. **CAUTION:** *Do not let these*

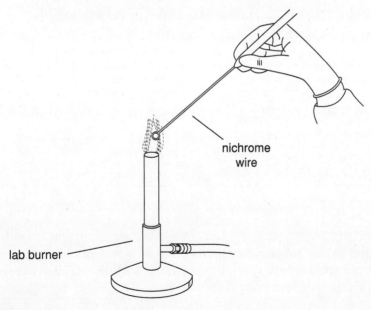

nichrome wire

lab burner

Figure 10–1

Name_____

substances come in contact with your skin. If a solution should splash on your skin, wash the affected area with large amounts of water and notify your teacher.

5. Obtain three unknowns from your teacher. Repeat Step 4 for each unknown. Record your observations on Data Table 2.

6. Turn off the burner. Clean up your work area and wash your hands before leaving the laboratory.

Observations

DATA TABLE 1   Flame Tests of Known Solutions

Salt Solution	Color
$Ba(NO_3)_2$	
$Cu(NO_3)_2$	
$LiNO_3$	
KNO_3	
$NaCl$	
$Ca(NO_3)_2$	
$Sr(NO_3)_2$	

DATA TABLE 2   Tests of Unknown Solutions

Unknown	Color

Critical Thinking: Analysis and Conclusions

1. What metallic ions are present in the unknown solutions? *(Drawing conclusions)* _____

_____

2. Summarize the process that produces the colors seen in the flame tests. *(Applying concepts)* _____

_____

_____

_____

3. What is the relationship of the colors you saw and the lines of the electromagnetic spectrum produced by the metals? *(Making inferences)* _____

_____

Critical Thinking: Applications

1. When a glass rod is heated, a yellow flame is observed around the point of heating. What does this yellow flame indicate? Why is it observed when glass is heated? *(Developing hypotheses)* _____

   _____

   _____

   _____

2. The line spectrum of lithium has a red line at 670.8 nm. Calculate the energy of a photon with this wavelength. *(Making predictions)*

3. What other equipment could you use in this investigation if burners were not available? *(Designing experiments)* _____

   _____

   _____

4. How do you think metallic salts are used in fireworks? *(Applying concepts)* _____

   _____

   _____

Going Further

1. Get some copper metal filings from your teacher. Work under your teacher's supervision. Pick up a small piece of copper filing with the wire loop, and put it in the burner flame. Is the color of copper in the flame the same as the color of copper nitrate solution?
2. Neon is a gas that has a reddish-orange emission spectrum. Find out why neon lights can display a multitude of colors.
3. The invention of the spectroscope by Robert Bunsen and Gustav Kirchoff opened up a new era of chemical investigation and research. Bunsen and Kirchoff discovered two elements through the use of their invention. Find out which elements they discovered, and how the spectroscope is now used.

Electron Distribution Using Peas

Lab 12

Text reference: **Chapter 4**

Introduction

Could you determine the exact position and momentum of a baseball as it soared through the air? Of course, you could—by taking a timed series of snapshots of the baseball as it moved. Why then can't scientists follow a similar procedure to determine the position and momentum of an electron?

You can see a moving baseball or its image because of the light bouncing off the baseball. The effect of light on either the position or the momentum of the baseball is negligible. By contrast, an electron has such an extremely small mass that light disturbs it in an unpredictable way. How then can the position and momentum of an electron be determined?

Knowledge of the behavior of electrons in the atom comes from theoretical work done in the 1920s by the German physicist Werner Heisenberg (1901–1976) and the Austrian physicist Erwin Schrodinger (1887–1961). Heisenberg postulated that it was impossible to determine exactly both the position and momentum of an electron at the same instant. Heisenberg deduced that the more precisely you know the position of an electron, the less certain you are about its momentum, and vice versa. Because its exact position and momentum can never be established at any given time, the exact path of an electron around the nucleus cannot be determined. Instead the quantum-mechanical model of the atom gives the probabilities of finding an electron in a particular region around the nucleus.

In this investigation, you will model the probable locations of electrons around the nucleus of an atom. You will use peas to represent electrons to help you visualize regions of high and low electron density.

Pre-Lab Discussion

Read the entire laboratory investigation and the relevant pages of your textbook. Then answer the questions that follow.

1. Why isn't it possible to determine the exact path of an electron in an atom? _____

   _____

   _____

2. What does the quantum-mechanical model of the atom tell you about the location of an electron in an atom? _____

   _____

   _____

3. What do the peas represent in this investigation? What setup do you use to distribute the peas around the nucleus? _____

_____

_____

_____

_____

_____

4. How will you process your data to illustrate the probabilities of finding electrons in particular regions around the nucleus? _____

_____

_____

_____

Problem
How can a model be used to represent the probable locations of electrons in an atom?

Materials

safety goggles
filter paper, circular
metric ruler
marker pen
scissors
tripod ring stand

compass
sheet of newsprint or butcher
 paper
dried peas
beaker, 150-mL
plastic container

Safety
Wear your safety goggles during this investigation.

Procedure

1. Put on your goggles. Fold the filter paper in half and then fold it again into quarters. Using the ruler, measure up 1.5 cm from the closed point of the paper and make a mark. Make a small hole in the bottom of the folded filter paper by cutting at the 1.5-cm mark with the scissors. Insert the cut filter paper into the ring of the tripod ring stand to create a funnel with the small hole at the bottom.

2. Use the compass to draw a circle with a radius of 3 cm in the center of a large sheet of paper. Then draw four more concentric circles 3 cm apart, around the first circle. Number the rings 1–5, starting from the center.

3. Mark the center of the innermost circle with a large dot. Let this dot represent the nucleus of the atom. Place the ring stand so that the hole in the filter paper is exactly above the large dot, or nucleus, as shown in Figure 12–1.

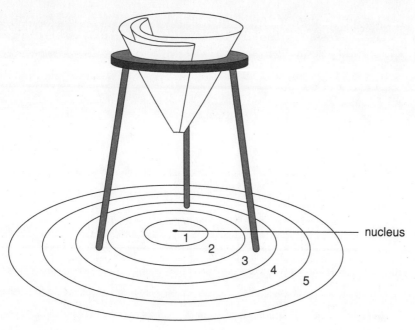

Figure 12–1

4. Count out 100 dried peas and place them in a plastic container. Pinch closed the hole at the base of the filter paper and add the 100 dried peas, or "electrons," to the filter. Let go of the filter, allowing the peas to fall through the small hole onto the target beneath the ring stand. If the peas jam up in the filter, push them gently to keep them moving.

5. Count the number of peas in each ring around the nucleus, as well as any that fall outside the rings. Record the data in the table, beginning with the innermost ring number 1.

 6. Gather up the peas and place them in the plastic container. Return all equipment to the supply area. Clean up your work area and wash your hands before leaving the laboratory.

Observations

DATA TABLE Distribution of Peas

Ring	Distance from Nucleus	Number of Peas in Ring
1	3 cm	
2	6 cm	
3	9 cm	
4	12 cm	
5	15 cm	
outside the rings	beyond 15 cm	

Name

Using the data in the table, graph the number of peas (vertical axis) vs. the distance from the nucleus (horizontal axis). This can be either a point average graph or a bar graph.

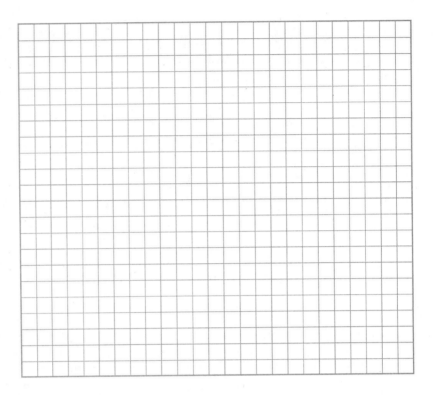

Critical Thinking: Analysis and Conclusions

1. Judging from your graph, in which region would you be most likely to find electrons? In which region would you be least likely to find electrons? *(Interpreting diagrams)* _____

_____

_____

2. Were you able to determine the exact path by which each pea (electron) arrived at its position on the target? How does this finding relate to the quantum theory? *(Developing models)* _____

_____

_____

_____

_____

3. Which orbital do the results of this experiment best approximate? *(Making inferences)* _____

_____

Critical Thinking: Applications

1. What would your graph look like if you had used 200 peas instead of 100? *(Making predictions)* _____
_____

2. Write a brief paragraph explaining how the quantum-mechanical model of electron distribution in an atom differs from the Bohr model. *(Using the writing process)* _____
_____
_____
_____
_____
_____

3. Why do you think that many people persist in visualizing the atom according to the out-dated Bohr model as opposed to accepting the quantum-mechanical model? *(Making judgments)* _____
_____
_____
_____

Going Further

1. Playing darts is a popular recreational activity. Design an experiment using a dart game to model the probabilities for electron distribution within the atom. Graph the probabilities.

Mendeleev for a Day

Introduction

As more and more elements were discovered during the 1800s, chemists began to categorize them according to similarities in chemical and physical properties. A Russian chemist, Dmitri Mendeleev (1834–1907), was more successful than most. He arranged the elements in vertical columns in order of increasing atomic mass. The columns were then arranged so that elements with similar chemical properties were placed side by side.

Mendeleev left numerous spaces in his table because there were no known elements with the appropriate properties to fill the spaces. (See Figure 13–1.) He then predicted the properties of these unknown elements based on the properties of the elements next to them on the periodic table. When these "missing elements" were discovered, they were found to have properties very similar to those predicted by Mendeleev.

Like Mendeleev, in this investigation you will group unknown compounds according to their chemical behaviors. You will see if a precipitate (solid substance) forms when two solutions are mixed together. You then will observe which precipitates are dissolved by another solution. Finally you will record any color changes that occur when two solutions are mixed together. After analyzing your data, you will place each unknown solution into a group with other solutions of similar characteristics.

```
                        Ti = 50    Zr = 90     ? = 180.
                        V = 51     Nb = 94    Ta = 182.
                        Cr = 52    Mo = 96     W = 186.
                        Mn = 55    Rh = 104,4 Pt = 197,4
                        Fe = 56    Ru = 104,4 Ir = 198.
                Ni = Co = 59       Pd = 106,6 Os = 199.
  H = 1                 Cu = 63,4  Ag = 108   Hg = 200.
        Be = 9,4 Mg = 24   Zn = 65,2 Cd = 112
         B = 11  Al = 27,4    ? = 68  Ur = 116  Au = 197?
         C = 12  Si = 28      ? = 70  Sn = 118
         N = 14  P = 31    As = 75    Sb = 122  Bi = 210?
         O = 16  S = 32    Se = 79,4  Te = 128?
         F = 19  Cl = 35,5  Br = 80    I = 127
Li = 1 Na = 23   K = 39    Rb = 85,4  Cs = 133  Tl = 204
               Ca = 40     Sr = 87,6  Ba = 137  Pb = 207.
                 ? = 45    Ce = 92
               ?Er = 56    La = 94
               ?Yt = 60    Di = 95
               ?In = 75,6  Th = 118?
```

Figure 13–1 *Mendeleev's Periodic Table (1869)*

Pre-Lab Discussion

Read the entire laboratory investigation and the relevant pages of your textbook. Then answer the questions that follow.

1. How does Mendeleev's periodic table differ from the modern periodic table? _____

   _____

   _____

   _____

2. Why did Mendeleev leave blank spaces on his periodic table? Did later discoveries justify his predictions? _____

   _____

   _____

   _____

3. Why is it necessary to mix any solution that does not show an immediate change? _____

   _____

4. Why is it necessary to rinse each test tube thoroughly between trials? _____

5. Which solutions need to be disposed of in a special container? _____

   _____

Problem

How can you group compounds according to their chemical behavior?

Materials

chemical splash goggles
laboratory apron
3 test tubes
marking pen
test-tube rack

graduated cylinder, 10-mL
unknown solutions 1–9
4 micropipets containing test
    solutions A, B, C, and D
stirring rod

Safety

Wear your goggles and lab apron at all times during the investigation. Since you are dealing with unknown solutions, consider them all to be corrosive and toxic, and avoid direct contact. If you spill a solution on yourself, report the spill immediately to your teacher and wash the affected area with large amounts of cold running water. Note the caution alert symbols here and with certain steps of the Procedure. Refer to page *xi* for the specific precautions associated with each symbol.

Name _____

Procedure

1. Put on your goggles and lab apron.

2. Label three test tubes *A, B,* and *C* with the marking pen. Using the graduated cylinder, obtain 3 mL of solution 1. Place 1 mL into each of the three test tubes. **CAUTION:** *Some of the solutions that you will use in this investigation are corrosive. Avoid direct contact with all of them.*

3. To test tube A, add 12 drops of test solution A.

4. To test tube B, add 12 drops of test solution B.

5. To test tube C, add 12 drops of test solution C.

6. Any test tube that does not show an immediate change should be stirred for at least 10 seconds. Rinse the stirring rod after each use. Record all results in the Data Table.

7. To any test tube that contains a precipitate, add 20 drops of test solution D and stir for at least 15 seconds. Rinse the stirring rod after each use. Record all results.

8. Pour the waste materials in test tube A into a labeled container provided by your teacher. Rinse out the test tubes and graduated cylinder thoroughly for use in the next set of tests.

9. Repeat Steps 2 through 8 for each of the other solutions. When you are done testing solutions 4 and 9, pour the waste material into the labeled containers provided by your teacher.

10. Clean up your work area and wash your hands before leaving the laboratory.

Observations

DATA TABLE   Reactions of Unknown Solutions

Unknown	A-ppt?	B-ppt?	C-Color	D-Dissolved?
1				
2				
3				
4				
5				
6				
7				
8				
9				

Name _____

Critical Thinking: Analysis and Conclusions

1. Why do you think that this investigation is titled "Mendeleev for a Day"? *(Drawing conclusions)* _____

   _____

2. Based on your observations, group the unknown solutions into families according to similarities in chemical behavior. Justify your answer with data from this investigation. *(Interpreting data)* _____

   _____

   _____

   _____

   _____

   _____

3. Why didn't all members of the same family show identical reactions? Give an example of a reaction that was similar but not identical.

   (Developing hypotheses) _____

   _____

   _____

Critical Thinking: Applications

1. Suppose you could do experiments with your unknowns in which you reacted each of them with oxygen to form an oxide, as Mendeleev did. How would this information help you determine the location of the compounds in the periodic table? *(Making predictions)*

   _____

   _____

   _____

2. No members of Group 8A (18) of the modern periodic table can be found on the version of Mendeleev's table shown in Figure 13–1. Suggest an explanation for their absence. *(Making inferences)* _____

   _____

   _____

Going Further

1. Research the contributions that scientists other than Mendeleev have made to the development of the modern periodic table. Prepare a short oral report to present to the class.

Chemical Activity of Metals

Small Scale
Lab **14**

Introduction

Have you ever noticed that some people are more active than others? Some people play a variety of physical sports while other people like to sit and read. You can think of elements in much the same way. In the case of an element, its activity level is a measure of its ability to react chemically with other elements.

Many metals will react with ions of another metal in solution. You can tell that a reaction has occurred because the metallic ions that come out of solution form a solid precipitate of that metal. At the same time, atoms of the more active metal go into solution. Chemists use the degree of activity to predict what changes will occur in certain reactions. For example, a more active metal will always replace a less active metal in a compound. This is called a single replacement reaction, which you will study in more detail in Chapter 9.

In this experiment, you will use three metals and four solutions of compounds that contain different kinds of metallic ions. You will put each metal into a separate sample of each solution and observe what happens. If a reaction occurs, you will notice a solid precipitate forming on the metal. If a particular metal reacts with the ions of many other metals, then that metal is a chemically active metal. If a metal reacts with few or none of the other metals, then it is chemically inactive. From your observations in this experiment, you will be able to arrange the four metals in the order of their chemical activity.

Pre-Lab Discussion

1. What does the term *chemical activity* mean? _____
   _____
   _____

2. What evidence of chemical activity will you be looking for in this investigation? _____

3. What are the hazards in handling silver nitrate and what precautions should you follow? _____
   _____

Problem

How does the chemical activity of each of four metals compare?

Name _____

Materials

chemical splash goggles
laboratory apron
well plate
marking pen
latex gloves
4 micropipets, filled with solutions of:
    copper(II) nitrate, (Cu(NO₃)₂)
    magnesium nitrate,
      (Mg(NO₃)₂)

zinc nitrate, (Zn(NO₃)₂)
silver nitrate, (AgNO₃)
4 pieces each of the following
   metals:
   copper
   magnesium
   zinc
eyedropper

Safety

Wear your goggles and lab apron at all times during the investigation. Handle all chemicals with care; avoid spills and contact with your skin. Wear gloves when handling silver nitrate solution. Note the caution alert symbols here and with certain steps of the Procedure. Refer to page *xi* for the specific precautions associated with each symbol.

Procedure

1. Put on your goggles and lab apron. Using the marking pen, label the wells in the well plate from left to right along the top row *1, 2, 3,* and *4.* Label the rows down the left side *A, B, C,* and *D.*

2. Use the micropipet labeled *Cu(NO₃)₂* to place 8 drops of copper(II) nitrate, Cu(NO₃)₂, into wells A1, B1, C1, and D1. See Figure 14–1.

3. Using the micropipet labeled *Mg(NO₃)₂*, place 8 drops of magnesium nitrate, Mg(NO₃)₂, into wells A2, B2, C2, and D2.

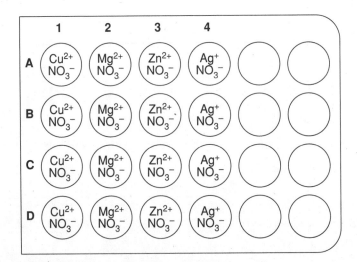

Figure 14–1

4. Using the micropipet labeled $Zn(NO_3)_2$, place 8 drops of zinc nitrate, $Zn(NO_3)_2$, into wells A3, B3, C3, and D3.

5. Put on latex gloves. Using the micropipet labeled $AgNO_3$, place 8 drops of silver nitrate, $AgNO_3$, into wells A4, B4, C4, and D4. **CAUTION:** *Silver nitrate is poisonous if ingested. Be careful not to get it on your skin or clothing, as it will produce a stain that is hard to remove. If any spills occur, ask your teacher how to clean up safely.*

6. Place one piece of copper metal into each of the wells in row A (wells A1, A2, A3, and A4).

7. Place one piece of magnesium metal into wells B1, B2, B3, and B4.

8. Place one piece of zinc metal into wells C1, C2, C3, and C4. (Note: Strips of silver are not used because of the expense. Had silver been used, you would have been directed to put strips of it into wells D1, D2, D3, and D4. The results you would have obtained have been put into the Data Table for you.)

9. Chemical reactions will take place in some of the wells in rows A, B, and C. Placing the well plate on white paper will make it easier to observe any changes that occur. Observe what happens for five minutes. In the Data Table, record what happens to each metal. If a metal does not change, write NR for No Reaction.

10. Look at the metal samples you used. Describe the appearance of the metals on the lines provided.

11. Use an eyedropper to transfer all the silver nitrate solution from the well plate to a container provided by your teacher. Dispose of all other chemicals according to your teacher's instructions. Clean up your work area and wash your hands before leaving the laboratory.

Observations

DATA TABLE

		1 Cu^{2+} NO_3^-	2 Mg^{2+} NO_3^-	3 Zn^{2+} NO_3^-	4 Ag^+ NO_3^-
A	Cu				
B	Mg				
C	Zn				
D	Ag	NR	NR	NR	NR

Appearance of metals _____

_____

_____

Name_____

Critical Thinking: Analysis and Conclusions

1. What similarities and differences in physical properties (e.g., hardness, color, shine) did you see when you looked at the metals? *(Making comparisons)* _____

   _____

   _____

2. Which of the four metals reacted with the greatest number of solutions? *(Interpreting data)* _____

   _____

3. Which of the four metals reacted with the least number of solutions? *(Interpreting data)* _____

4. List the metals from the most active to the least active. *(Making comparisons)* _____

Critical Thinking: Applications

1. The Statue of Liberty is made of copper. Use your investigation results to explain why copper is a better material for a statue than magnesium or zinc. *(Applying concepts)* _____

   _____

   _____

2. Gold does not react with any of the solutions used in this investigation. What does this tell you about gold's chemical activity? *(Making inferences)* _____

3. How does the chemical activity of gold account for its use in jewelry? *(Applying concepts)* _____

   _____

4. Lead is less active than zinc but more active than copper. Predict the results if lead metal is put into separate solutions of zinc nitrate and copper(II) nitrate. *(Making predictions)* _____

   _____

   _____

Going Further

1. Research the metals that are used to make coins. Explain the choice of these coinage metals in terms of their chemical activity.
2. Visit a cookware store or department and find out what metals are used to make pots and pans. What kinds of foods react with these metals? Explain your findings in terms of the activity of metals.

Relative Mass with Beans

Lab 15
APPLICATION

Text reference: ***Chapter 5***

Introduction

A traveler from Honolulu, Hawaii, going to St. Paul, Minnesota, arrives at the airport in Minnesota and sees a sign displaying the local temperature as 20 degrees. At first the traveler wishes she had brought a warm coat and gloves, but she quickly realizes her mistake. A longer look at the sign tells her the temperature is 20 degrees Celsius, which is 68 degrees Fahrenheit. The moment of confusion occurred because the traveler had forgotten that temperature can be measured on more than one scale, or against different standards. A standard is a defined value or measure to which other measurements are compared. For example, the boiling point and freezing point of water are defined as 0 degrees and 100 degrees respectively on the Celsius scale. Other temperatures are measured in Celsius degrees relative to those points.

Another example of the use of a standard is the atomic mass assigned to each element in the periodic table of the elements. The standard for atomic masses is the carbon-12 atom, which is assigned a mass of exactly 12 atomic mass units (amu). The other elements are assigned masses measured by this standard, starting with 1.01 amu for hydrogen, and going above 200 amu for the heaviest elements.

It may be difficult to visualize the concept of the relative mass of atoms. The protons and neutrons in their nuclei are far too small to be counted, and atoms cannot be placed individually on a balance. One way to work with this concept on a visible scale is to use a model. In the present investigation, beans of different varieties represent atoms of different elements. Like isotopes of one element, beans of one variety have individual masses that are very similar, but not identical. Like atoms of different elements, beans of different varieties have average masses that are measurably different.

In this investigation you will measure equal numbers of different bean varieties in order to derive a standard unit for bean mass. You will then be able to assign relative masses to each bean variety based on this standard. While you will certainly be able to distinguish them, you will make no measurements with individual beans.

Pre-Lab Discussion

Read the entire laboratory investigation and the relevant pages of your textbook. Then answer the questions that follow.

1. What is the standard for comparison for the relative masses of the elements listed in the periodic table? What is the relative mass assigned to this standard? _____

_____

Name _____

2. What will you use as the standard for comparison in determining the relative masses of the beans in this investigation? _____

_____

_____

3. What characteristics of beans enable you to use them as models for atoms of different elements? _____

_____

_____

_____

4. In this investigation you will establish an average mass for each kind of bean. How could you use this average to measure out a given number of beans without actually counting them? _____

_____

_____

Problem

How can the principle of relative atomic mass be modeled using beans?

Materials

safety goggles
laboratory apron
graduated cylinder, 50- or
    100-mL
4 beakers, 150-mL
wax marking pencil
funnel

navy beans
kidney beans
pinto beans
lima beans
4 paper cups
laboratory balance

Safety

Wear your goggles and lab apron at all times during the investigation. If any beans spill on the floor, pick them up immediately so that no one slips on them. Note the caution alert symbols here and with certain steps of the Procedure. Refer to page *xi* for the specific precautions associated with each symbol.

Procedure

 1. Put on your goggles and lab apron.

 2. With the marking pencil, label each of the four beakers: *navy, kidney, pinto,* and *lima.* Using the graduated cylinder and a funnel, pour 17–20 mL of navy beans, 55–60 mL of kidney beans, 35–40 mL of pinto beans, and 110–115 mL of lima beans into the respective beakers.

3. Label each of the four paper cups with the name of one variety of bean.

4. Measure the mass of each cup and record the value in your Data Table.

5. Count out 60 beans of each variety and place them in their respective cups.

6. Measure the masses of the cups with their contents and record these values in your Data Table.

7. Return each kind of bean to its original container.

8. Clean up your work area and wash your hands before leaving the laboratory.

Observations

DATA TABLE   Relative Mass of Beans

Bean Variety				
Mass of Cup (g)				
Mass of Cup and Beans (g)				
Mass of Beans (g)				
Average Mass per Bean (g)				
Relative Mass of Beans (u)				

Calculations

1. Calculate the total mass of the 60 beans in each cup and record this value in your Data Table.

2. Calculate the average mass per bean for each variety of bean and record each value in your Data Table.

3. Use the smallest average bean mass among the varieties measured as the standard to calculate the relative mass of each variety of bean. Assign the smallest average bean mass the relative mass of 1.0 u, where *u* stands for relative mass unit. Calculate the relative mass of each of the other varieties to the nearest tenth by using the following equation, and record the values in the data table:

$$\frac{1.0\ u}{\text{smallest average mass (g)}} = \frac{u\ \text{of bean variety}}{\text{average mass for bean variety (g)}}$$

Critical Thinking: Analysis and Conclusions

1. Which bean variety qualified as the standard for comparison? *(Interpreting data)* _____

2. How much greater is the average mass per bean of the largest variety of bean than the average mass per bean of the smallest variety of bean? *(Making comparisons)* _____

   _____

3. If you assigned a relative mass of 1.0 u to the variety with the greatest average mass per bean, which variety would it be, and what would then be the relative masses of the other bean varieties? *(Interpreting data)* _____

   _____

   _____

4. What might be the drawbacks to assigning a relative mass of 1.0 u to the bean variety with the greatest average bean mass? *(Drawing conclusions)* _____

   _____

   _____

5. Once you have set the standard for relative mass of beans, how can you use a chemical balance to measure out equal numbers of two varieties of beans? (Hint: Look back at your answer to Pre-Lab Question 4.) *(Applying concepts)* _____

   _____

   _____

Critical Thinking: Applications

1. Write a description of how your work in this investigation models the work of chemists in assigning relative atomic masses to the elements. *(Using the writing process)* _____

    _____

    _____

    _____

2. When you assign a relative mass to each variety of beans, what property of the beans do you ignore? *(Developing models)* _____

    _____

3. The formula for the compound methane is CH_4. One molecule of methane has one carbon atom and four hydrogen atoms bonded together. Using the relative masses of these elements given in the periodic table, calculate the relative mass of methane in amu.

    (Applying concepts) _____

    _____

    _____

4. As stated in the periodic table, the relative mass for hydrogen is 1.01 amu. In 1.01 g of hydrogen atoms, there are 6.02×10^{23} hydrogen atoms (Avogadro's number). How many carbon atoms will be present in 12.01 g of carbon atoms? (Hint: Refer to the relative masses of carbon and hydrogen in the periodic table.) *(Applying concepts)*

    _____

5. How many atoms of each of the following elements would be present in samples having the following masses? *(Making predictions)*

    a. 14.01 g of nitrogen atoms   _____

    b. 40.08 g of calcium atoms   _____

    c. 32.06 g of sulfur atoms   _____

    d. 4.00 g of helium atoms   _____

6. Based on your answers to Questions 4 and 5, develop a hypothesis that describes the relationship between relative mass, mass in grams, and numbers of atoms. *(Developing hypotheses)* _____

    _____

    _____

7. To find how many atoms are in a sample of an element, would it be more reliable to measure the volume or the mass of the atoms? Explain your reasoning. *(Evaluating)* _____

    _____

    _____

Name _____

Going Further

1. Research the work of John Dalton, who assigned relative masses of the elements using hydrogen as the standard. Describe the mistake he made in his assumptions and the difficulties that resulted. Find out how the mistake was discovered and what led to the use of carbon as the standard of mass.

2. The number 6.02×10^{23}, Avogadro's number, has tremendous significance and usefulness in chemistry. Find out what this number represents, how it was determined, and how it is used in chemistry.

Exploring the Halides

Small Scale
Lab 17

Text reference: **Chapter 6**

Introduction

The elements in Group 7A (17) of the periodic table are nonmetals called the halogens. The word *halogen* comes from two ancient Greek words that mean "salt" and "former." There are five members of the halogen family. They are fluorine, chlorine, bromine, iodine, and astatine. Each halogen can react with a number of different metals to form compounds called halides. For example, when sodium metal reacts with chlorine, the halide sodium chloride is formed. The first four halogens form classes of halides with easily recognizable names, as follows:

fluorides—formed from a metal and fluorine

chlorides—formed from a metal and chlorine

bromides—formed from a metal and bromine

iodides—formed from a metal and iodine

In this investigation, you will observe chemical reactions of small quantities of four halides with specific solutions, or test reagents. You will use your observations of these reactions to determine which halide is present in a solution containing one or more unknowns.

Pre-Lab Discussion

Read the entire laboratory investigation and the relevant pages of your textbook. Then answer the questions that follow.

1. What are the five halogens and what is the chemical symbol for each? _____
    _____

2. What structural characteristic is shared by the atoms of all the halogens? _____

3. What are fluorides, chlorides, bromides, and iodides? _____
    _____
    _____

4. What method will you use to study halide reactions? _____
    _____
    _____

5. What safety precautions should you observe when working with bleach or ammonium hydroxide? _____

_____

_____

6. What are the hazards in handling the silver nitrate solutions, and what precautions should you follow? _____

_____

_____

Problem

How can you determine whether a fluoride, chloride, bromide, or iodide is present in a solution?

Materials

chemical splash goggles
laboratory apron
well plate, 24-well
11 micropipets, each filled with one
    of the following solutions:
        sodium fluoride (NaF)
        sodium chloride (NaCl)
        sodium bromide (NaBr)
        sodium iodide (NaI)
        calcium nitrate ($Ca(NO_3)_2$)

silver nitrate ($AgNO_3$)
sodium thiosulfate ($Na_2S_2O_3$)
ammonium hydroxide
    (NH_4OH)
starch solution
household bleach (NaClO)
unknown solution
20 toothpicks
latex gloves
eyedropper

Safety

Wear your goggles and lab apron at all times during the investigation. Handle all chemicals with care; avoid spills and contact with your skin. Wear gloves when handling the silver nitrate solution. Take particular care not to inhale fumes from the bleach or the ammonium hydroxide. Never mix bleach and ammonium hydroxide together. Note the caution alert symbols here and with certain steps of the Procedure. Refer to page *xi* for the specific precautions associated with each symbol.

Procedure

1. Put on your goggles and lab apron. Add five drops of sodium fluoride solution, NaF, to each of the first four wells in row A of your well plate. Then add five drops of the remaining three halides (sodium chloride, sodium bromide, and sodium iodide) to the wells in rows B, C, and D respectively, as shown in Figure 17–1.

2. Place two drops of calcium nitrate solution, $Ca(NO_3)_2$, into each of the first four wells in column 1 (wells A1, B1, C1, D1). Mix the solutions thoroughly with a clean toothpick. Record your

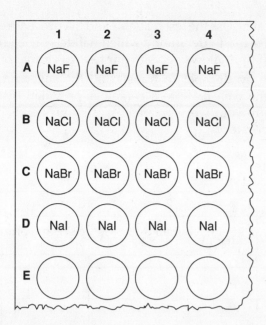

Figure 17–1

observations in the Data Table. Pay particular attention to the color of any precipitate (abbreviated *ppt*) that forms. It may help to observe the well plate first on top of a piece of white paper. If no observable change takes place, write *NR* for *no reaction*.

 3. Put on latex gloves. Into each of the column 2 wells (wells A2, B2, C2, D2), add two drops of silver nitrate, $AgNO_3$. Mix thoroughly with a clean toothpick. Observe as described in Step 2 and record your observations in the Data Table. **CAUTION:** *Silver nitrate is poisonous if ingested. Be careful not to get it on your skin or clothing, as it will produce a stain that is hard to remove. If any spills occur, tell your teacher.*

 4. Into the same column 2 wells tested in Step 3, add two drops of ammonium hydroxide solution, NH_4OH. **CAUTION:** *Avoid inhaling the ammonium hydroxide fumes.* Mix thoroughly with a clean toothpick. Observe as before and record your observations in the Data Table.

5. Following the same procedure as in Steps 3 and 4, add two drops of $AgNO_3$ solution into each of the column 3 wells (wells A3, B3, C3, and D3). Then add five drops of sodium thiosulfate solution, $Na_2S_2O_3$, and record all results.

 6. Into each of the column 4 wells (wells A4, B4, C4, and D4), place two drops of starch solution and then two drops of bleach solution. Make sure to mix the solutions thoroughly with a clean toothpick, and record your observations. **CAUTION:** *Avoid inhaling fumes from the bleach. Do not mix bleach and ammonium hydroxide solutions. The resulting vapors are toxic and explosive. Avoid spilling or splashing bleach on your skin or clothing. Wash any splashes with plenty of water.*

 7. Obtain from your teacher a solution containing one or more unknown halides. Record the solution's identification number in the

Data Table. Use the test reagents and the procedure you followed in Steps 1–6 to determine which halide(s) your unknown contains. If time allows, repeat your tests to verify your results.

8. Use an eyedropper to transfer all the silver nitrate solutions from the well plate to a container provided by your teacher. Clean up your work area and wash your hands before leaving the laboratory.

Observations
DATA TABLE

	Solution	1 $Ca(NO_3)_2$	2 $AgNO_3$ and NH_4OH	3 $AgNO_3$ and $Na_2S_2O_3$	4 Starch and Bleach
A	NaF				
B	NaCl				
C	NaBr				
D	NaI				
E	Unknown ID#				

Critical Thinking: Analysis and Conclusions

1. Describe the reactions that occurred with sodium fluoride. Did they follow the pattern you saw with the other halides? (*Making comparisons*) _____

_____

_____

_____

2. Based on your observations, describe the precipitates formed by the reactions of the halides with silver nitrate. (*Interpreting data*) _____

_____

_____

_____

3. Which of the precipitates dissolved when ammonium hydroxide was added? When sodium thiosulfate was added? (*Interpreting data*) _____

_____

_____

_____

4. How did the halides react to the starch solution? (*Drawing conclusions*) _____

_____

5. How did the halides react to the bleach solution? (*Drawing conclusions*) _____

_____

_____

6. Explain your reasoning in identifying the halide(s) present in your unknown. (*Interpreting data*) _____

_____

Critical Thinking: Applications

1. Chlorine is often added to drinking water to kill disease-causing organisms. Design an experiment to determine if chlorine is present in your tap water. (*Designing experiments*) _____

_____

2. How might you determine the difference between iodized salt and noniodized salt? Can you think of a reason why the results of this experiment might be inconclusive? (*Evaluating*) _____

_____

_____

_____

Going Further

1. Look at the ingredients of several commercial products in a grocery store. Identify products in which you found halides. Make a bulletin board display based on your findings.
2. Chlorine is used to kill infectious agents, such as bacteria, in swimming pools. Find out what chlorine compounds are used and how they work. Report your findings to your class.

Making Micro-*Hindenburgs*

Small Scale Lab **18** APPLICATION

Text reference: Chapter 6

Introduction

The *Hindenburg* was the largest airship ever built. It had a record of 54 successful flights. However, what people remember most about the *Hindenburg* is its tragic end at Lakehurst, New Jersey. On May 6, 1937, the hydrogen-filled *Hindenburg* burst into flames as the pilot was attempting to land it. Thirty-six people were killed while horrified onlookers watched. The exact cause of the explosion has never been determined, but the *Hindenburg* disaster essentially ended wide-scale development and use of airships.

Why was the *Hindenburg* filled with hydrogen? Would another gas have been better? In this lab, you will make hydrogen gas and investigate its properties so that you can answer these questions.

Pre-Lab Discussion

Read the entire laboratory investigation and the relevant pages of your textbook. Then answer the questions that follow.

1. Find hydrogen in the periodic table. Why do you think it is separated from the Group 1A (1) elements? _____

   _____

   _____

   _____

2. What chemicals are used to produce hydrogen gas in this investigation? _____

3. Why should you handle hydrochloric acid with extreme care? _____

   _____

4. What should you do if you accidentally spill some HCl? _____

   _____

5. What is the purpose of the bubble solution in this investigation? _____

   _____

6. What do you predict will happen when you hold the flame near the bubbles of gas produced in this investigation? On what information is your prediction based? _____

   _____

Problem

What properties of hydrogen prevent its use in modern-day airships?

Materials

chemical splash goggles
laboratory apron
latex gloves
scissors
micropipet
one-hole rubber stopper
granulated zinc

test tube
test-tube rack
hydrochloric acid (HCl), 3.0 *M*
micropipet containing bubble
    solution
matches
wooden splint

Safety

Wear your goggles, gloves, and lab apron at all times during the investigation. Hydrochloric acid is corrosive. If you spill any acid, immediately wash the area with plenty of cold water and notify your teacher. Tie back loose hair and clothing when working with a flame. Note the caution alert symbols here and with certain steps of the Procedure. Refer to page *xi* for the specific precautions associated with each symbol.

Procedure

 1. Put on your goggles, gloves, and lab apron.

2. Make a microfunnel, using the scissors to cut off the top of the plastic micropipet bulb. Insert the microfunnel into the one-hole rubber stopper as shown and set aside.

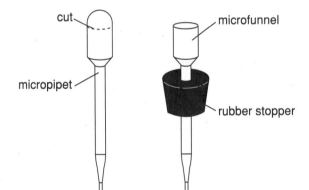

Figure 18–1

 3. Place about 2 g of granulated zinc in the test tube. Place the test tube in the test-tube rack. Then carefully pour 10 mL of 3.0 *M* hydrochloric acid (HCl) into the test tube. **CAUTION:** *Hydrochloric acid is corrosive. Avoid spills and splashes. If you do spill acid, immediately rinse the area with plenty of cold water and report the spill to your teacher.* Record your observations.

4. Insert the rubber stopper with the microfunnel into the test tube so that no gas can escape except by way of the microfunnel. With a micropipet provided by your teacher, place 5–10 drops of bubble solution into the microfunnel, as shown in Figure 18–2. Record your observations.

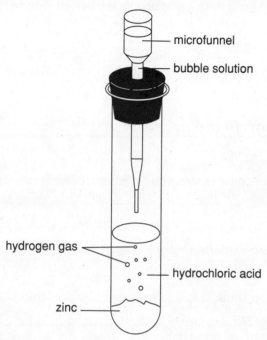

microfunnel

bubble solution

hydrogen gas

hydrochloric acid

zinc

Figure 18–2

 5. Light the wooden splint. **CAUTION:** *Tie back loose hair or clothing when working with the flame.* Carefully bring the flame close to the bubbles rising from the microfunnel. Record your observations. (If generation of gas slows or ceases, extinguish the flame. Remove the stopper and add more zinc and HCl. Then reinsert the microfunnel and stopper, relight the splint, and test the bubbles.)

 6. Disassemble the apparatus and dispose of the reaction products in a container provided by your teacher. **CAUTION:** *The product in the test tube, zinc chloride (ZnCl$_2$), is a severe skin irritant. Avoid direct contact. If spills or splashes occur, wash the area with plenty of water.* Clean up your work area and wash your hands before leaving the laboratory.

Observations

zinc with hydrochloric acid   _____

_____

bubble solution in microfunnel   _____

_____

flame held near bubbles   _____

Critical Thinking: Analysis and Conclusions

1. What evidence in this investigation suggests that a chemical reaction has taken place? *(Interpreting data)* _____

   _____

2. Based upon your data, what properties of hydrogen are demonstrated in this investigation? (Hint: Why did the bubbles float in the air?) *(Making inferences)* _____

3. What purpose did the bubble solution serve? *(Making inferences)* ____

   _____

Critical Thinking: Applications

1. Why do you think that hydrogen gas was used to fill the *Hindenburg?* *(Evaluating)* _____

   _____

2. What other gas would have been a better choice for inflating the *Hindenburg?* Explain. *(Making judgments)* _____

   _____

3. Why do you think that this investigation is entitled "Making Micro-Hindenburgs"? *(Developing models)* _____

   _____

4. Why would it be dangerous to do this investigation on a larger scale where a large quantity of hydrogen is generated in a short time? *(Making predictions)* _____

   _____

Going Further

1. Hydrogen is just one of several gases that can be produced in the laboratory with relative ease. Oxygen gas can be produced by mixing baker's yeast or MnO_2 with a 3% solution of hydrogen peroxide. Carbon dioxide can be produced by mixing baking soda and vinegar (acetic acid).

   Design an experiment in which you compare properties, such as the density and flammability, of hydrogen gas (H_2), oxygen gas (O_2), and carbon dioxide gas (CO_2). Under your teacher's supervision, conduct your experiment and report your results. Would either oxygen or carbon dioxide be an acceptable gas to use in an airship or blimp? Explain.

2. Research and prepare a report detailing the history of lighter-than-air craft. Find out how these craft are used today.

3. Hydrogen gas is a fuel that burns efficiently and cleanly. Research the advantages and disadvantages of using hydrogen gas as a fuel for motor vehicles. How close are scientists to overcoming the disadvantages?

Formula of Lead Iodide

Small Scale
Lab **19**

Text reference: **Chapter 7**

Introduction

In 1808, John Dalton published *A New System of Chemical Philosophy* in which he presented his atomic theory of matter. According to Dalton's theory, chemical compounds form when atoms combine with each other. Another postulate of Dalton's atomic theory is that a given compound always has the same relative numbers and kinds of atoms.

The chemical formula of an ionic compound shows the relative number and kinds of atoms as a whole number ratio. The ratio of elements in a compound can be determined experimentally. Once the ratio is known, the formula for the compound is easily written. In this experiment, you will be reacting sodium iodide and lead nitrate together in various ratios to produce the precipitate, lead iodide. By plotting the data, you will be able to find the ratio that produces the most precipitate. This will be the correct ratio of atoms in lead iodide. From this ratio, you can determine the chemical formula of lead iodide.

Pre-Lab Discussion

Read the entire laboratory investigation and the relevant pages of your textbook. Then answer the questions that follow.

1. How does Dalton's atomic theory of matter apply to this investigation? _____

   _____

   _____

   _____

2. Why should you let the reaction stand for 5 minutes before measuring the height of the precipitate in each test tube? _____

   _____

3. How will the graph help you interpret your data? _____

   _____

4. What is a subscript and what does it mean in the formula of an ionic compound? _____

   _____

   _____

5. Why do lead compounds require caution in handling and disposal?

_____

_____

_____

_____

Problem

Can you determine the chemical formula for lead iodide?

Materials

chemical splash goggles
laboratory apron
9 small test tubes
marking pen
well plate
micropipet

sodium iodide (NaI), 0.1 M
distilled water
latex gloves
lead nitrate ($Pb(NO_3)_2$), 0.1 M
metric ruler

Safety

Wear your goggles and lab apron at all times during the investigation. Lead compounds are toxic. Wear latex gloves when working with them. Do not dispose of any lead nitrate or lead iodide wastes down the drain, but place them in labeled waste containers provided by your teacher. Note the caution alert symbols here and with certain steps of the Procedure. Refer to page xi for the specific precautions associated with each symbol.

Procedure

 1. Put on your goggles and lab apron. Label nine test tubes 1–9 with the marking pen, and place them in a well plate that will serve as a test-tube holder.

2. Fill the micropipet with 0.1 M sodium iodide (NaI) solution. Following Table 19–1 as a guide, add the indicated number of drops to each test tube. For example, place 18 drops in tube 1, 16 drops into tube 2, etc., until all nine tubes are done.

 3. Put on your gloves. Rinse the micropipet four times with distilled water. Then fill it once with 0.1 M lead nitrate ($Pb(NO_3)_2$) solution and immediately discard this solution in the lead waste beaker. **CAUTION:** *Lead nitrate is toxic. Wear gloves. Do not let this substance come in contact with your skin.*

4. Fill the micropipet again with 0.1 M lead nitrate ($Pb(NO_3)_2$) solution. Following Table 19–1 as a guide, add the indicated number of drops to each test tube. For example, place 2 drops in tube 1, 4 drops into tube 2, etc., until all nine tubes are done.

TABLE 19–1

Test Tube	Drops of NaI Solution	Drops of $Pb(NO_3)_2$ Solution
1	18	2
2	16	4
3	14	6
4	12	8
5	10	10
6	8	12
7	6	14
8	4	16
9	2	18

5. Allow the nine test tubes to stand for 5 minutes. If necessary, tap the test tubes gently to help the precipitates settle to the bottom.

6. With a metric ruler, measure the height of the precipitate in each test tube. Record the heights in your Data Table.

7. Dispose of all chemicals according to your teacher's instructions. Clean up your work area and wash your hands before leaving the laboratory.

Observations

DATA TABLE

Test Tube	Height of Precipitate (mm)	Ratio of Drops $Pb(NO_3)_2$:NaI
1		
2		
3		
4		
5		
6		
7		
8		
9		

Name _____

Calculations

1. Compute the ratio of drops of lead nitrate solution to drops of sodium iodide solution in each test tube and record these ratios in the data table. (Hint: Set up each ratio to give the number of drops of sodium iodide solution that would correspond to one drop of lead iodide solution.)

2. Graph your data. Plot the test tube numbers on the horizontal axis and the height of the lead iodide precipitate on the vertical axis. Beside each data point, record the drop ratios for $Pb(NO_3)_2$:NaI.

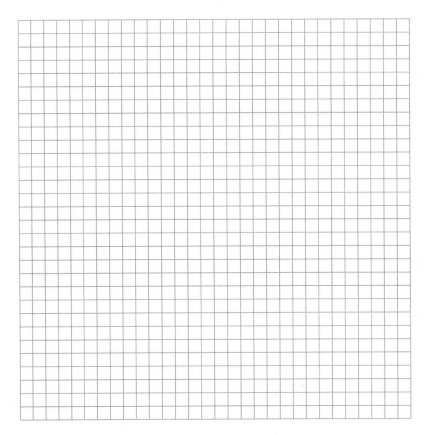

Figure 19–1

Critical Thinking: Analysis and Conclusions

1. Which reactant ratio(s) yielded the greatest amount of precipitate? *(Interpreting data)* _____

2. What can you conclude from your graph of precipitate heights and reactant ratios? *(Interpreting diagrams)* _____

_____

_____

_____

_____

3. Based on the ratio that you determined in response to Question 1, what is the correct formula for lead iodide? *(Making inferences)* _____

_____

4. Which reagent ran out first in tube 2? In tube 7? *(Interpreting data)*

_____

Critical Thinking: Applications

1. Why is it important that the proper ratio be used when writing the formula of a substance? *(Evaluating)* _____

_____

2. Would the procedure you used in this investigation work for any compound? Give an example of a type of compound for which this procedure would not work. Explain. *(Designing experiments)* _____

_____

_____

3. Making an apple pie calls for a reaction among certain ratios of ingredients. How is making an apple pie different from making lead iodide? *(Making comparisons)* _____

_____

_____

Going Further

1. Recipes indicate the ratios of ingredients that are to be used. Analyze some of your favorite recipes to see what ratios are involved. Classify the products according to whether they are compounds or mixtures. Explain why the ratios are not so critical when only mixtures are involved.

Solubility and Bond Type Lab 20

Text reference: **Chapter 7**

Introduction

Compounds may contain ionic bonds, polar covalent bonds, nonpolar covalent bonds, or a combination of these bond types. Several of the investigations in this book provide clues that allow you to predict which type of bond a compound contains. Investigation 21, for example, explores the electrical conductivity of solutions of various compounds. In Investigation 23, the tendency of a liquid to rise in a narrow space is examined. Both of these behaviors depend on bond type. Another way to predict whether a substance has ionic, polar covalent, or nonpolar covalent bonds is to measure its solubility—its ability to dissolve—in different liquids. Substances with polar covalent or ionic bonds tend to dissolve in liquids that contain polar covalent bonds, while substances with nonpolar covalent bonds tend to dissolve in liquids with nonpolar covalent bonds.

In this investigation, you will compare the solubilities of sodium chloride, potassium chloride, sodium iodide, iodine, and camphor in water, ethanol, vegetable oil, and glycerol. You will also determine the solubility of the liquids in each other. Based on your data, you will then classify these substances by bond type.

Pre-Lab Discussion

Read the entire laboratory investigation and the relevant pages of your textbook. Then answer the questions that follow.

1. What are three types of chemical bonds? Do all compounds contain a single type of bond? _____

   _____

2. What special precautions should be taken when working with iodine crystals? _____

   _____

   _____

3. Compound X dissolves in water but not in vegetable oil. Compound Y dissolves in ethanol but not in water. Which of the two more likely contains polar covalent bonds? Explain. _____

   _____

   _____

Name _____

Problem

How can a compound's solubility be used to predict the type of bonds it contains?

Materials

chemical splash goggles
laboratory apron
marking pen
4 test tubes
test-tube rack
graduated cylinder, 10-mL
tap water
ethanol (C_2H_5OH)
glycerol ($C_3H_8O_3$)
vegetable oil

laboratory balance
microspatula
sodium chloride (NaCl)
potassium chloride (KCl)
sodium iodide (NaI)
iodine (I_2)
camphor ($C_{10}H_{16}O$)
forceps
4 stoppers to fit test tubes

Safety

Wear your goggles and lab apron at all times during the investigation. Ethanol and iodine are toxic. Avoid breathing their vapors. All work with iodine should be done in a fume hood. Avoid skin contact with iodine; use forceps to handle it. If iodine does come in contact with skin, rinse the affected area with plenty of water. Ethanol is flammable; be sure there are no open flames in the laboratory. Note the caution alert symbols here and with certain steps of the Procedure. Refer to page *xi* for the specific precautions associated with each symbol.

Procedure

Part A

1. Put on your goggles and lab apron. Label four test tubes from 1–4. Place them in a test-tube rack.

  2. Put 5.0 mL of the listed liquids into separate test tubes as follows. **CAUTION:** *Ethanol is toxic as a liquid and a vapor. Avoid direct contact with it. It is also flammable. Be sure there are no open flames in the laboratory.*

      test tube 1: water   test tube 3: glycerol
      test tube 2: ethanol   test tube 4: vegetable oil

3. Measure four 0.5-g samples of sodium chloride. Using a microspatula, add a few grains of sodium chloride to test tube 1. Stopper and shake the tube. If the solid dissolves, add a few more grains. Keep adding grains until no more will dissolve or until you have used all of the sample.

4. If all the solid dissolves, write *soluble* in Data Table 1. If none of the solid dissolves, write the word *insoluble* in Data Table 1. If some of the solid dissolves, write the words *partially soluble* in Data Table 1.

5. Repeat Steps 3 and 4 for each of the other three test tubes.

6. Pour the contents of the test tubes into the container provided by your teacher. Rinse and dry the test tubes and repeat the procedure, using potassium chloride instead of sodium chloride.

7. Dispose of the materials and clean the test tubes as before. Repeat the procedure for sodium iodide, iodine, and camphor. **CAUTION:** *Iodine crystals and vapors are toxic. Do this part of the procedure in the fume hood. Avoid skin contact with the iodine. Use forceps when handling it.*

8. Dispose of the materials and clean the test tubes. Iodine compounds should be collected in a specially marked container. If you are not going on directly to Part B, clean up your work area and wash your hands before leaving the laboratory.

Part B

9. Put on your goggles and lab apron. Put 3.0 mL of water into each of three test tubes. Add 3.0 mL of ethanol to the water in one of the tubes. Stopper and shake the tube for about 30 seconds. Let it sit for another 30 seconds. Note the appearance of the liquid. If you can see layers, write the word *insoluble* in Data Table 2. If no layers are present, write the word *soluble.*

10. Repeat Step 9 using vegetable oil, and then glycerol, instead of ethanol. Dispose of the materials as before, and rinse out and dry all the test tubes.

11. Following the same procedure as in Step 9, test mixtures of ethanol with vegetable oil, ethanol with glycerol, and vegetable oil with glycerol. Write your observations in Data Table 2.

12. Dispose of the liquids and solids as directed by your teacher. Clean up your work area and wash your hands before leaving the laboratory.

Observations

DATA TABLE 1 Solubility of Solids

	Water	Ethanol	Vegetable oil	Glycerol
NaCl				
KCl				
NaI				
I_2				
camphor				

DATA TABLE 2   Solubility of Two Liquids

	Ethanol	Vegetable oil	Glycerol
water			
ethanol			
vegetable oil			

Critical Thinking: Analysis and Conclusions

1. Predict the type of bonds each of the solids you tested contains. Explain your reasoning. *(Classifying)* _____

_____

_____

_____

2. Which of the liquids can be considered polar? Which are nonpolar? *(Drawing conclusions)* _____

_____

_____

3. Why did NaCl not dissolve in vegetable oil? *(Drawing conclusions)*

_____

4. Why did iodine dissolve in vegetable oil but not in water? *(Drawing conclusions)* _____

_____

Critical Thinking: Applications

1. Salad dressing is a mixture of vegetable oil and vinegar (acetic acid). Why does the dressing have to be shaken before it is used? *(Developing hypotheses)* _____

_____

_____

2. What kind of liquid cleaning agents would be most effective at dissolving oily stains? *(Making judgments)* _____

_____

Going Further

1. You are given a mixture of iodine and NaCl powders. Suggest a method for separating the two. Design an experiment employing your method. Perform the experiment only under a teacher's supervision. Report on your results.

Conductivity of Molecular and Ionic Compounds

Lab 21
APPLICATION

Text reference: **Chapter 7**

Introduction

The salt and sugar on your kitchen table both dissolve easily in water, but the solutions they form have an important difference. One of those kinds of white crystals is an ionic compound, and when it dissolves, it dissociates into ions. The ions are free to move in the solution, and that solution, therefore, conducts electricity. The other kind of crystal, however, is a molecular compound, and its molecules remain whole when they dissolve. With no ions, that solution conducts no electricity.

This investigation involves testing several different liquids that are distributed among the work areas in the laboratory. When you measure the conductivity of each liquid, you will find that some are good conductors, some are fair or poor conductors, and some are nonconductors. Using the conductivities you have measured, you will decide which solutions contain ionic compounds, and which contain molecular compounds.

After you have classified your solutions, you will examine sugar and salt from another point of view. Bonding theory generally predicts that ionic compounds should form from combinations of elements that are far apart on the periodic table, while molecular compounds should form from elements that are close together. You will see whether your findings on conductivity agree with this prediction.

Pre-Lab Discussion

Read the entire laboratory investigation and the relevant pages of your textbook. Then answer the questions that follow.

1. What are ions, and how do they form? _____

   _____

2. What is an ionic bond? _____

   _____

3. What is a covalent bond? _____

   _____

4. How do aqueous solutions of ionic and molecular compounds differ?

   _____

   _____

5. When some ionic compounds dissolve, not all of their bonds dissociate. What kind of conductivity would you expect such a solution

   to have? _____

   _____

Name _____

Problem

How can the conductivity of a solution help you to classify the bonds in the solute?

Materials

chemical splash goggles
laboratory apron
equipment at each work area:

conductivity tester
wash bottle with distilled water
test solution in 250-mL beaker
beaker, 250-mL

Safety

Wear your goggles and lab apron at all times during the investigation. Beware of electrical shocks. Use and dispose of chemicals as specified by your teacher, and wash your hands thoroughly before leaving the laboratory. Note the caution alert symbols here and with certain steps of the Procedure. Refer to page *xi* for the specific precautions associated with each symbol.

Procedure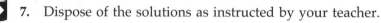

1. Put on your goggles and lab apron.

2. Using the conductivity tester as described by your teacher, test the solution at your lab station. **CAUTION:** *Some of the test solutions may be corrosive, or may stain or discolor clothing. Avoid spills and splashes. If spills occur, wash with plenty of water and notify your teacher immediately. Avoid inhaling fumes from the bleach or ammonia solutions. Do not mix bleach and ammonia solutions. The resulting vapors are toxic and explosive.*

3. Note whether the test light is lit, and if so, how brightly. Record your observations in the Data Table.

4. Rinse the conductivity probes with distilled water over an empty beaker.

5. Move to the next lab station and check the conductivity of the solution at that station in the same manner. Record your observations.

6. Repeat Steps 2–5 until you have tested and recorded data for all the solutions.

7. Dispose of the solutions as instructed by your teacher.

8. Clean up your work area and wash your hands before leaving the laboratory.

Observations

DATA TABLE

Test Solution	Conductivity			
	Good	Fair	Poor	None

Critical Thinking: Analysis and Conclusions

1. What types of bonds do you think the good conductors of electricity have? Explain your reasoning. (*Making inferences*) _____

   _____

   _____

2. What type of bonds do you think the nonconductors of electricity have? Explain your reasoning. (*Making inferences*) _____

   _____

   _____

Name _____

3. How can you account for the fair and poor conductors of electricity? *(Developing hypotheses)* _____

_____

_____

Critical Thinking: Applications

1. What kind of ions does sodium chloride (table salt) produce when it dissolves? *(Applying concepts)* _____

_____

2. Where are sodium and chlorine found on the periodic table? (Consult the periodic table in the back of this laboratory manual, or in your textbook.) Do the relative positions of these elements in the periodic table agree with the prediction made in the Introduction about their structure? Explain. *(Evaluating)* _____

_____

3. Look up the chemical formula for sucrose. Where are the elements that form sucrose found on the periodic table? Do the relative locations of these elements in the periodic table agree with the theoretical prediction about the kind of compound these elements should form? Explain. *(Evaluating)* _____

_____

_____

_____

4. What conclusions can you draw from this investigation? *(Drawing conclusions)* _____

_____

_____

_____

Going Further

1. Using the electronegativity values listed for the elements in the periodic table, compute the electronegativity differences for the bonds in table salt and sugar (sucrose). Use these differences to predict what type of bonding will occur between the various atoms in these compounds. Do the predictions agree with your observations on table salt and sugar?

2. Investigate how Linus Pauling used bond energies to derive electronegativity values.

Models of Molecular Compounds

Lab 22

Introduction

Why should people care about the shapes of molecules? Consider that the properties of molecules, including their role in nature, depend not only on their molecular composition and structure, but their shape as well. Molecular shape determines a compound's boiling point, freezing point, viscosity, and the nature of its reactions.

The geometry of a small molecule can be predicted by examining the central atom and identifying the number of atoms bonded to it and the number of unshared electron pairs surrounding it. The shapes of molecules may be predicted using the VSEPR rule, which states that electron pairs around a central atom will position themselves to allow for the maximum amount of space between them.

Covalent bonds can be classified by comparing the difference in electronegativities of the two bonded atoms. If the difference in electronegativities is less than or equal to 0.4, the bond is called a nonpolar covalent bond. If the difference in electronegativities is between 0.5 and 1.9, a polar covalent bond exists. (If the difference in electronegativities is greater than 2.0, an ionic bond results.) In a polar covalent bond, the electrons are more attracted to the atom with the greater electronegativity, resulting in a partial negative charge on that atom. The atom with the smaller electronegativity value acquires a partial positive charge.

Molecules made up of covalently bonded atoms can be either polar or nonpolar. The geometry of the molecule determines whether it is polar or not. For example, if polar bonds are symmetrically arranged around a central atom, their charges may cancel each other out and the molecule would be nonpolar. If, on the other hand, the arrangement of the polar bonds is asymmetrical, the electrons will be attracted more to one end of the molecule and a polar molecule or dipole will result.

Ball-and-stick models can be used to demonstrate the shapes of molecules. In this experiment, you will construct models of covalent molecules and predict the geometry and polarity of each molecule.

Pre-Lab Discussion

Read the entire laboratory investigation and the relevant pages of your textbook. Then answer the questions that follow.

1. What is a covalent bond? _____

   _____

2. What is a dipole? _____

   _____

3. What two factors determine whether a molecule is polar or not?

_____

_____

4. List the five different molecular geometries that you will be studying in this investigation. _____

_____

5. Calculate the electronegativity difference and predict the type of bond for the following examples: (Refer to Figure 7–19 in your text for a list of electronegativities.)

    a. Na—Cl _____

    b. C—H _____

    c. S—O _____

    d. N—N _____

Problem

How can the polarity of molecules be predicted from their geometry and the types of bonds they contain?

Materials

safety goggles
ball-and-stick model set

Safety

Wear your goggles at all times during the investigation. Note the caution alert symbols here and with certain steps of the Procedure. Refer to page *xi* for the specific precautions associated with each symbol.

Procedure

 1. Put on your goggles. Construct ball-and-stick models of the following compounds:

H_2	HBr	H_2O
PH_3	CH_4	HClO
N_2	CH_3NH_2	CH_3Cl
H_2CO	C_2H_2	H_2O_2
HCOOH	HCN	

2. For each of the preceding compounds, complete the Data Table in the Observations section. As an example, the first line of the Data Table has been filled in for you.

 3. When you have completed this investigation, take apart your models and return the model set to your teacher. Clean up your work area and wash your hands before leaving the laboratory.

Observations

DATA TABLE   Structure and Polarity of Molecules

Formula	Electron Dot Structure (Lewis)	Structural Formula	Shape of Molecule	Molecular Polarity
H_2	H:H	H — H	Linear	Nonpolar
HBr				
H_2O				
PH_3				
CH_4				
HClO				
N_2				
CH_3NH_2				
H_2CO				
C_2H_2				
CH_3Cl				
HCOOH				
HCN				
H_2O_2				

Name_____

Critical Thinking: Analysis and Conclusions

1. Explain how you used the molecular shapes to predict molecular polarity. Support your answer with examples from the results of this investigation. (*Classifying*) _____

_____

_____

_____

_____

2. List the advantages and disadvantages of using ball-and-stick models to construct molecules. (*Developing models*) _____

_____

_____

Critical Thinking: Applications

1. Based on your results, predict the type of bonding, molecular geometry, and molecular polarity of the following molecules. (*Making predictions*)

   a. HI _____

   b. SH_2 _____

   c. NH_3 _____

   d. CO_2 _____

2. The polarity of a substance can have a great effect on its reactivity and solubility. A rough rule of thumb for solubility is "like dissolves like." Knowing this general rule, what can you predict about the polarity of alcohol if you know that alcohol dissolves in water? Why do you think that water is not used to dissolve greasy stains and

   dirt at dry cleaners? (*Applying concepts*) _____

_____

_____

Going Further

1. Use balloons to create three-dimensional models of the five different molecular geometries discussed in this investigation.
2. Research what is meant by the term *isomer*. Give examples of molecular isomers.

Capillary Action and Polarity of Molecules

Small Scale Lab **23**

*Text reference: **Chapter 8***

Introduction

The tallest living things in the world are the giant redwood trees in California. These trees can reach heights of over 110 meters, equivalent to a 30-story building! How does the giant redwood supply its uppermost leaves and branches with water? Part of the answer lies in tiny (0.1-mm diameter) tube-shaped cells found in the trunk of the tree. These tube cells can move water over a great vertical distance through a process called capillary action, which is the drawing up of a liquid into a narrow tube or space.

Capillary action depends partially on the polarity of the molecules of the liquid and of the material that forms the tube or space into which the liquid rises. Polar molecules such as water are asymmetrical and have polar bonds. A polar attraction between the material of the tube and the molecules of a polar liquid causes the liquid to rise into the tube. As one molecule moves up, it attracts neighboring molecules which, in turn, attract their neighbors. Once the upward attractive force is equal to the downward force of gravity, the liquid stops rising. An extreme example of this phenomenon occurs in giant trees like the redwoods. It is estimated that these large trees move about 2000 liters of water each day from their roots to their uppermost leaves.

In this investigation, you will measure the capillary action of various liquids. By observing the height that different liquids reach in a capillary tube, you will be able to estimate the relative polarity of each liquid. Also, you will investigate how the polarity of a mixture of water and ethanol changes when the proportion of the two liquids is varied.

Pre-Lab Discussion

Read the entire laboratory investigation and the relevant pages of your textbook. Then answer the questions that follow.

1. What molecular features affect the polarity of molecules? _____
   _____

2. How does the polarity of molecules affect the force of attractions
   between them? _____
   _____

3. Predict how the polarity of a liquid will affect the height to which
   that liquid can rise in a capillary tube. _____
   _____

4. What is the main hazard in working with capillary tubes and what precautions should you follow? _____

_____

_____

5. Why must there be no flames in the laboratory during this investigation? _____

Problem

How is the polarity of a liquid related to capillary action?

Materials

chemical splash goggles
laboratory apron
well plate
8 glass capillary tubes
metric ruler
5 micropipets, each containing
    one of the following liquids:

water
ethanol
ethylene glycol
propylene glycol
glycerol
paper towels
marking pen

Safety

Wear your goggles and lab apron at all times during the investigation. Glass capillary tubes are fragile and may cause cuts when broken. Handle them very gently and dispose of broken ones in the container provided by your teacher. Ethanol, ethylene glycol, and propylene glycol are toxic. If any of these chemicals come in contact with your skin, wash with plenty of water. Ethanol is flammable. Be sure all lab burners are extinguished. Note the caution alert symbols here and with certain steps of the Procedure. Refer to page *xi* for the specific precautions associated with each symbol.

Procedure

Part A

 1. Put on your goggles and lab apron. Obtain a well plate, eight capillary tubes, and a micropipet containing water.

 2. Place a few drops of water into the middle of one of the wells of the well plate. With one end of a capillary tube, touch the water. **CAUTION:** *Capillary tubes are fragile and can cause cuts if broken. Handle them gently and dispose of broken tubes in the container provided by your teacher.* The top end of the tube must be open. Note that water rises inside the tube, above the outside water level. Leave the tip of the capillary tube in contact with the water in the well plate for at least 15 seconds.

3. Once the water stops rising, gently withdraw the capillary tube from the well and use a metric ruler to measure the height of the column of water. Record the value in Data Table 1.

4. Drain the capillary tube by touching its tip to a tissue or soft paper towel.

5. Repeat Steps 2–4 four more times. If air bubbles develop, use a fresh tube.

 6. Repeat Steps 2–5 using each of the liquids provided. **CAUTION:** *Some of these liquids and their vapors are toxic. Care should be taken not to inhale the fumes. Do not let the liquids touch your skin.* Be sure to use a different well and a new capillary tube for each liquid. (Note: Glycerol requires more time to reach its final height than the other liquids do.)

Part B

  7. Label three dry wells on the well plate with the numbers 1–3. Place the following in the appropriate well: well 1: 12 drops water and 4 drops ethanol; well 2: 8 drops water and 8 drops ethanol; well 3: 4 drops water and 12 drops ethanol. **CAUTION:** *Ethanol and its fumes are toxic. Avoid inhaling its vapors. Be sure there are no open flames in the laboratory.*

8. Repeat the procedure from Part A for the three mixtures of ethanol and water. Record the values in Data Table 2.

 9. Dispose of the capillary tubes in a container provided by your teacher. Rinse excess liquids in the well plate down the drain. Clean up your work area and wash your hands before leaving the laboratory.

Observations

DATA TABLE 1   Capillary Action of Several Liquids

	Height of Column (mm)					
Liquid	**1**	**2**	**3**	**4**	**5**	**Average**
H_2O						
ethanol						
ethylene glycol						
propylene glycol						
glycerol						

Name_____

DATA TABLE 2   Capillary Action of Water/Ethanol Mixtures

Liquid	Height of Column (mm)					Average
	1	2	3	4	5	
pure water*						
Mixture 1						
Mixture 2						
Mixture 3						
pure ethanol*						

*Note: Use the values for pure water and pure ethanol from Part A.

Critical Thinking: Analysis and Conclusions

1. Calculate the average heights for all the liquids tested in Part A and enter these values in Data Table 1. Based on your data, list the liquids from the most polar to the least polar. (*Making comparisons*) _____

_____

2. Study the molecular structures of the liquids shown in Figure 23–1. Discuss how the number of oxygen atoms in the molecule might be related to the polarities of these molecules. (*Making inferences*)

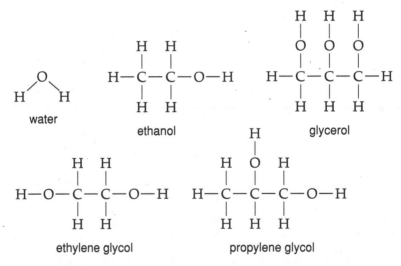

Figure 23–1

_____

_____

_____

_____

3. Calculate the average heights for all the mixtures tested in Part B and enter these values in Data Table 2. Make a graph of the data from Part B with average height (mm) on the vertical axis and percent water in the water/ethanol mixture on the horizontal axis. Describe how the polarity of water appears to change when it is mixed with ethanol. *(Interpreting diagrams and data)* _____

_____

_____

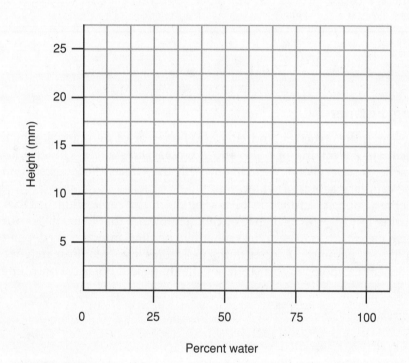

Figure 23–2

Critical Thinking: Applications

1. In addition to polarity, density affects the height a liquid may reach in a capillary tube. Heavy water containing the heavier hydrogen isotope, deuterium, is chemically identical to water, but has a higher molar mass (20.0 g/mole) and density (1.11 g/ml). How would you expect the height of heavy water in a capillary tube to compare to your data for water? *(Developing hypotheses)* _____

_____

_____

Name_____

2. Plastic capillary tubes are nonpolar. If plastic capillary tubes with the same diameter were substituted for the glass tubes, how would you expect the height of the liquids in the capillary tubes to be affected? Explain your answer. *(Making predictions)* _____

_____

_____

3. Sponges and fabrics absorb and hold water by capillary action. Some sponge materials and fabrics, like cotton, hold more water and dry more slowly than others. Relate the ability of these materials to hold water to the polarity of their molecules, and think of an example where this property is not desirable. *(Applying concepts)* _____

_____

_____

_____

Going Further

1. Research the structure and chemical behavior of detergents, which facilitate the mixing of polar and nonpolar substances. Under your teacher's supervision, experiment with the effects of detergents on the capillary action of water.
2. Nerve action, the function of hemoglobin, the replication of DNA during mitosis, the resiliency of cell membranes that helps give your flesh its texture, and countless other biochemical interactions depend on the shapes and polarities of the molecules involved. Research one biochemical molecule. Find out how its shape and polarity contribute to its function.

Exploring Dyes

Lab **24**
APPLICATION

Text reference: **Chapter 8**

Introduction

The synthetic dye industry began with a serendipitous discovery. In 1856, eighteen-year-old William Perkin, a student at the Royal College of Chemistry in London, England, was trying to synthesize quinine, a drug used to treat malaria. What he got was a vibrant purple solution that easily colored silk. The dye was called mauve. It quickly became a commercial success and by 1870, cloth could be made in more colors than had ever been possible with dyes produced from natural sources such as flowers and vegetables.

In this investigation, you will explore the importance of molecular structure and polarity in the commercial world of dyes. Some natural fibers, such as silk and wool, are essentially protein molecules. Since proteins are made from amino acids, which have many polar sites on them, they have a strong affinity for dyes that are either polar or ionic. On the other hand, nylon has no polar sites at all except at the ends of its molecular chain (which is hundreds or even thousands of atoms long) so it is very resistant to dye. In between these extremes are fabrics such as dacron and rayon, each with only a few polar sites. As you might predict, they show intermediate attractions for dyes.

In order to dye the low-polarity fabrics, a process called mordanting can be used. The term comes from the Latin word *mordant*, which means "bite." In a sense, the dye can "bite into" the fabric. The process of mordanting alters the molecular structure of the fabric by affixing metal ions to it. These ions then bind the dye to the fabric.

In this lab, you will dye a strip made of six different fabrics with two different dyes. The fabric strip that you will use is composed of (in order) wool, orlon, dacron, nylon, cotton, and acetate rayon. You will determine the attraction of each material for dye by measuring the intensity of color—the darker the color, the stronger the attraction. From your results, you will determine which end is the wool. You will then determine the extent to which mordanting improves the dye-holding capability of the six fibers tested.

Pre-Lab Discussion

Read the entire laboratory investigation and the relevant pages of your textbook. Then answer the questions that follow.

1. What materials were used to dye fabric before synthetic dyes?

_____

2. What is polarity? _____

_____

3. Why do natural fabrics, such as wool, take up dye better than do synthetic fabrics? _____

4. What is a mordant? What does a mordant do? _____

_____

_____

5. Why is it necessary to use a mordant on some fabrics? _____

_____

_____

6. Why is it necessary to wear latex gloves during this investigation?

_____

7. What is meant by the term *colorfast*? _____

_____

Problem

How is the polarity of a fabric related to its dye-holding capacity?

Materials

chemical splash goggles   paper towels
laboratory apron   soap
latex gloves   mordanting bath: iron(II) sulfate
test fabric strips   tongs
dye baths:
  methyl orange
  malachite green

Safety

Wear your goggles, gloves, and lab apron at all times during the investigation. The beakers containing the dye and mordanting baths are hot. Clean up any spills with plenty of cold water. Note the caution alert symbols here and with certain steps of the Procedure. Refer to page *xi* for the specific precautions associated with each symbol.

Procedure

Part A: Direct Dyeing

1. Put on your goggles, gloves, and lab apron. Using your tongs, immerse a strip of test cloth for seven minutes in the methyl orange dye bath set up by your teacher. Make sure the dye bath solution is near boiling temperature. **CAUTION:** *Beakers are hot. Use tongs or hot pads if you need to touch them.*

2. Remove the strip, allowing as much of the dye solution as possible to drain back into the bath. Rinse off excess dye with water. Place the strip on a paper towel to dry. Move fabrics carefully to avoid splashes.

3. Repeat Steps 1 and 2 with another strip of test cloth, using the malachite green dye bath. Record your observations.

4. After the fabric is dry, test it for colorfastness by cutting the strip in half and washing one half with soap. Allow the fabric to dry and compare the two halves. Staple the fabric to a sheet of paper and label the process you used on each sample.

 5. If you are not continuing on to Part B, turn off the hot plate. Clean up your work area and wash your hands before leaving the laboratory.

Part B: Mordants

 6. Put on your goggles, gloves, and lab apron. Using your tongs, soak another fabric strip in one of the mordanting baths for at least 25 minutes. **CAUTION:** *Beakers are hot. Use tongs or pads if you need to touch them.* Wring the fabric strip out over the mordanting bath.

7. Dye the strip in either malachite green or methyl orange, following the procedure in Part A. Test the fabric strip for colorfastness. Turn off the hot plates.

8. Staple the fabric to a sheet of paper and label as before. Observe and compare this strip with the untreated dyed cloths.

9. Dispose of all your solutions as directed by your teacher. Clean up your work area and wash your hands before leaving the laboratory.

Observations
DATA TABLE

Dye Type	Observations	Colorfast?
methyl orange		
malachite green		
mordant and methyl orange		
mordant and malachite green		

Name _____

Critical Thinking: Analysis and Conclusions

1. What is the source of ions in the mordant? *(Making inferences)* _____

_____

2. Compare your fabric strips with those of your classmates. List three variables that could account for the differences in your results. *(Interpreting data)* _____

_____

_____

3. How do the colors of the mordanted fabrics compare with the colors produced without mordanting? *(Making comparisons)* _____

_____

4. How did the mordanted fabrics compare to the untreated ones with respect to being colorfast? *(Making comparisons)* _____

_____

Critical Thinking: Applications

1. Why do you think it was necessary for the dye bath to be so hot? *(Developing hypotheses)* _____

_____

2. During the 1970s, many of the popular clothing styles included nylon shirts that had brightly colored patterns printed on one side only. Why were the colors not dyed into the shirts? *(Applying concepts)*

_____

_____

3. Silk blouses and shirts can be purchased in many intense colors. How does the nature of silk allow for a variety of intense dyes? *(Applying concepts)* _____

_____

4. Washing instructions for clothing often state "wash in cold water only." What might happen if you washed this type of clothing in hot water? *(Making predictions)* _____

_____

Going Further

1. Bring in some of your own swatches of fabric and test them under your teacher's supervision.
2. Research and report on the many dyes and mordants that are available from natural sources.

Equation Writing and Predicting Products

Small Scale Lab 25

Text reference: **Chapter 9**

Introduction

If you examine a car that has been in a junkyard for a while, you will notice that it has rusted. Rusting is a slow chemical reaction of the iron in the car with oxygen gas. If sodium is put into water, a much more rapid chemical reaction occurs. Sodium reacts with water to produce sodium hydroxide and hydrogen gas. During this reaction, enough heat is liberated to ignite the hydrogen gas, causing it to explode.

Chemists observe what is happening in a chemical reaction and try to describe it in language that is simple and clear. A chemical equation uses formulas and symbols to describe the substances involved in a reaction, the physical state of the substance, the use of a catalyst (a substance that speeds up a reaction but is not used up in the process), and relative proportions. The general form of an equation is:

Reactants → Products

In this investigation you will perform a series of reactions and make careful observations of the changes that occur. Using simple tests and your knowledge of chemistry, you will determine the identity of the products. With this information, you will write chemical equations to describe the reactions.

Pre-Lab Discussion

Read through the entire lab investigation and the relevant pages of your textbook. Then answer the questions that follow.

1. What constitutes a positive test for each of the following gases?

   a. oxygen _____

   b. hydrogen _____

   _____

   c. carbon dioxide _____

   _____

   d. water vapor _____

   e. ammonia _____

2. What is the proper way to smell a substance in the lab? Why should care be taken when smelling a gas such as ammonia? _____

   _____

   _____

3. What is the role of a catalyst in a reaction? How can you tell when a substance serves as a catalyst? _____

_____

_____

4. One way to identify limestone ($CaCO_3$) is to drop a small amount of hydrochloric acid (HCl) on it. A positive test results in a fizz of carbon dioxide being produced. Write out in words the information represented by the following balanced chemical equation and give the molar ratio of the compounds.

$$CaCO_3(s) + 2\ HCl(aq) \rightarrow CaCl_2(aq) + H_2O(l) + CO_2(g)$$

_____

_____

_____

Problem

How can chemical equations be used to describe what happens in chemical reactions?

Materials

chemical splash goggles
laboratory apron
2 pieces of magnesium ribbon
tongs
lab burner
matches
watch glass
6 test tubes
graduated cylinder
hydrochloric acid (HCl), 2.0 M
test-tube rack
test-tube holder
3 wooden splints
copper foil
file
spatula

ammonium carbonate
   (($NH_4)_2CO_3$)
cobalt chloride paper
hydrogen peroxide (H_2O_2),
   3% solution
manganese(IV) oxide, (MnO_2)
potassium iodide (KI), 0.1 M
well plate
lead nitrate ($Pb(NO_3)_2$), 0.1 M
copper carbonate ($CuCO_3$)
limewater ($Ca(OH)_2$ solution)
one-hole rubber stopper
glass tube elbow
glycerin
rubber tubing

Safety

Wear your goggles and lab apron at all times during the investigation. Avoid looking at the burning magnesium. The bright light could seriously damage your eyes. Tie back loose hair and clothing when working with a flame. Hydrochloric acid is corrosive. Avoid any direct contact with it. Ammonia is a skin and respiratory irritant, so avoid inhaling it deeply. Lead compounds are poisonous, so be sure to avoid contact with skin. If contact occurs with any of these chemicals, immediately wash the affected area with plenty of water and inform your teacher. Clean up all spills immediately. Lead and copper compounds should be collected in designated waste containers. Glass tubing breaks easily. Exercise caution when working with it. Note the caution alert symbols here and with certain steps of the Procedure. Refer to page *xi* for the specific precautions associated with each symbol.

Procedure

 1. Put on your goggles and lab apron. For each of the reactions, record in the Data Table observations such as the appearance of the reactants; evidence that a chemical reaction has taken place; the results of tests performed on any gases produced; the appearance of the products; and any other relevant data.

 2. Obtain a piece of magnesium ribbon. Light the lab burner. Holding the magnesium with your tongs, carefully place it in the lab burner flame. Hold the burning magnesium over a watch glass to catch any debris. **CAUTION:** *Tie back loose hair and clothing. The tongs will be hot. Do not touch them for at least 5 minutes. Do not look directly at the magnesium while it burns.* When the magnesium is finished burning, place the remains on the watch glass. Turn off the burner.

 3. Place a test tube in the test-tube rack. Have a second test tube ready in a test-tube holder. Add 5–10 mL of 3.0 *M* HCl to the first test tube. Drop a 2-cm piece of magnesium ribbon into the acid. **CAUTION:** *Hydrochloric acid is corrosive. Avoid spills and splashes. If you do spill acid, immediately rinse the area with plenty of cold water and report the spill to your teacher.*

 4. Invert the second test tube over the mouth of the first test tube, as shown in Figure 25–1. When the reaction appears to have ended, light a wood splint and quickly test the collected gas for flammability by holding the burning wood splint near the mouth of the second test tube. **CAUTION:** *The gas in the test tube will make a popping sound. Do not be startled.*

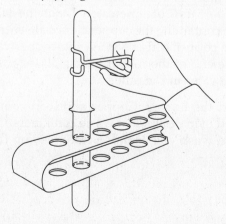

Figure 25–1

5. Light the lab burner. Grasp a small piece of copper foil with your tongs and heat it in the burner flame until it is red hot. Remove it from the flame and allow it to cool. Scratch the surface of the metal with a sharp object (such as a file).

6. Carefully place about one spatula of ammonium carbonate ((NH$_4$)$_2$CO$_3$) into a test tube. Holding the test tube with a test-tube holder, heat the solid gently by holding the test tube in the flame for a few seconds, then removing it for a few seconds. Continue heating in this manner for 1 minute. As you heat the solid, carefully waft the air toward your nose to detect any odor. **CAUTION:** *When heating the test tube, point the open end away from yourself and anyone nearby. The gas coming from the tube is a skin and respiratory irritant, so avoid inhaling it deeply.* Continuing to heat the solid, place a burning splint at the mouth of the test tube. Finally, as heating continues, place a piece of blue cobalt paper just inside the mouth of the test tube. Put the test tube in the rack to cool. Turn off the burner.

7. Place approximately 10–15 mL of hydrogen peroxide, H$_2$O$_2$, into a test tube. Have a wooden splint and matches ready. Add a very small amount (about the tip of a spatula) of manganese(IV) oxide, MnO$_2$, to the hydrogen peroxide. As the reaction occurs, light the splint and allow it to burn freely for 5 seconds. Blow the flame out and place the glowing splint halfway into the test tube.

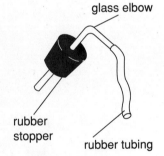

glass elbow

rubber stopper

rubber tubing

Figure 25–2

8. Place a drop of potassium iodide solution, KI, in one well of a well plate. Add a drop of lead nitrate solution, Pb(NO$_3$)$_2$. **CAUTION:** *Lead compounds are poisonous, so be sure to avoid contact with skin. If contact occurs, immediately wash the affected area with plenty of water and inform your teacher. Clean up all spills immediately.*

9. Assemble the stopper, glass elbow, and rubber tubing as shown in Figure 25–2. Place a small amount (about one spatula) of copper carbonate, CuCO$_3$, in a test tube. **CAUTION:** *Glass tubing breaks easily. Exercise caution when working with it.* Place the stopper assembly into the test tube. Prepare another test tube with about 10–15 mL of limewater. Light the lab burner. Holding the tube containing the copper carbonate with a test-tube holder, heat the copper carbonate. As the copper carbonate is heated, push the end of the rubber tubing all the way to the bottom of the limewater in the other tube.

10. Turn off the burner. Copper and lead compounds should be disposed of in designated waste containers. Clean up your work area and wash your hands before leaving the laboratory.

Observations

Reaction	Observations
burning Mg	
Mg and HCl	
heating Cu	
heating $(NH_4)_2CO_3$	
H_2O_2 and MnO_2	
KI and $Pb(NO_3)_2$	
heating $CuCO_3$	

Critical Thinking: Analysis and Conclusions

1. Write a balanced equation for each of the reactions performed. Include the physical state of each substance. *(Making inferences)*

_____

_____

_____

_____

_____

_____

2. Classify each of the reactions as direct combination, decomposition, single replacement, or double replacement. *(Classifying)* _____

_____

_____

_____

3. Limewater is an aqueous solution of $Ca(OH)_2$. Speculate on the identity of the cloudy white precipitate that forms with CO_2 gas. Write a chemical equation for this reaction that is consistent with your observations. *(Making inferences)* _____

_____

Name _____

4. A positive test for hydrogen was the "pop" test. What chemical reaction was occurring? Write a balanced equation representing this reaction. *(Making inferences)* _____

_____

Critical Thinking: Applications

1. For each of the following situations, determine the identity of the gas produced from the information given and write a balanced chemical equation that represents the reaction. *(Applying concepts)*

   a. When potassium bromate ($KBrO_3$) is heated, it decomposes into potassium bromide (KBr) and a gas that supports the combustion of a glowing splint. _____

   b. Sodium metal reacts violently with water to produce sodium hydroxide (NaOH) and a gas that "pops" in the presence of a burning splint. _____

   c. The recipe for the volcanic eruption used in many science projects is the reaction of baking soda ($NaHCO_3$) and vinegar (CH_3COOH). When these compounds are mixed together, the salt sodium acetate ($NaCH_3COO$) is formed as well as a gas that extinguishes a burning flame and a substance that turns blue cobalt chloride paper pink. _____

   _____

2. Cobalt chloride is a hydrated salt used for making humidity gauges. The formula of the hydrated form is $CoCl_2 \cdot 2H_2O$. What color is associated with the hydrated form of cobalt chloride? How might it be used to predict weather changes? *(Developing models)* _____

   _____

   _____

Going Further

1. Earth's long-term carbon cycle involves the recycling of carbon through the ecosystems over thousands of years. Many scientists believe that the cycling of carbon from carbonate rock to the atmosphere was an important factor in the development of Earth's climate. Investigate the long-term carbon cycle and its role in maintaining Earth's climate. Describe how the carbon cycle relates to the carbonate reactions in this investigation.

2. Manganese(IV) oxide (MnO_2) is considered to be a catalyst in the decomposition of hydrogen peroxide. Design an experiment to demonstrate this point. Have your teacher approve your experimental design before you begin. Perform the experiment only under a teacher's supervision.

Bags of Reactions

Introduction

"Plop, plop, fizz, fizz, oh, what a relief it is," claims an old television ad for a popular antacid. Just what is in the tablet that is relieving the upset stomach? What reaction is causing the fizzing? Can you write a chemical equation for this process? With a bit of investigating, you will be able to discover answers to all these questions.

As you learned in Chapter 2, Antoine Lavoisier, in the eighteenth century, formulated the law of conservation of mass, which states that matter can neither be created nor destroyed. During a chemical reaction, the bonds of the reactants are broken and rearranged to form new substances. Because matter must be conserved, these new substances, or products, must contain the same number and type of atoms as the reactants.

In this investigation, you will first verify the law of conservation of mass. Then in the second part, you will be given some known compounds to react. You will write and balance a chemical equation for the reaction.

Pre-Lab Discussion

Read the entire laboratory investigation and the relevant pages of your textbook. Then answer the questions that follow.

1. Define *reactants*. _____
   _____

2. Define *products*. _____
   _____

3. How can you tell when a chemical reaction has happened? _____
   _____
   _____

4. What is the point of using a resealable bag? _____
   _____

5. What is the density of water? _____

6. What is the common name for sodium hydrogen carbonate? _____
   _____

Problem

Can equations be written and balanced for chemical reactions?

Name_____

Materials

chemical splash goggles
laboratory apron
graduated cylinder, 50-mL
2 resealable plastic bags, 1-L
laboratory balance
antacid tablet

scoopula or teaspoon
calcium chloride, $CaCl_2$
sodium hydrogen carbonate,
    $NaHCO_3$
phenol red indicator

Safety

Wear your goggles and lab apron at all times during the investigation. Note the caution alert symbols here and with certain steps of the Procedure. Refer to page *xi* for the specific precautions associated with each symbol.

Procedure

Part A

1. Put on your goggles and lab apron. Measure 25 mL of tap water into a resealable plastic bag. Flatten the air out of the bag and seal it. Record its mass in Data Table 1.

2. Record the mass of the antacid tablet in Data Table 1.

3. Tip the bag sideways, and while holding the bag this way, add the tablet so that the tablet and water do not mix. Do not trap any extra air in the bag. Refer to Figure 26–1. Reseal the bag.

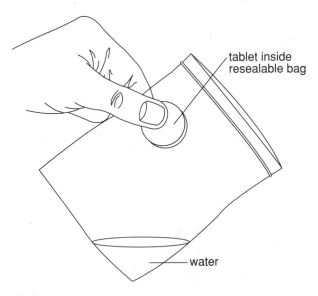

Figure 26–1

4. Let the tablet drop into the water. Observe the reaction until it comes to a complete stop. Record your observations.

5. When the reaction is complete, record the mass of the bag and its contents in Data Table 1.

Part B

6. Add 2 scoops of calcium chloride, $CaCl_2$, to the second plastic bag.

7. Add 1 scoop of sodium hydrogen carbonate, $NaHCO_3$, to the bag, and shake gently to mix.

8. Determine the mass of the bag and its contents. Record this value in Data Table 2.

9. Measure 25 mL of water into the graduated cylinder. Add 5 drops of phenol red indicator to the water.

10. Tip the bag sideways, and while holding the solids in the upper part of the bag, pour the water into the bag so that the water and solids do not mix.

11. Keeping the trapped air to a minimum, reseal the bag. Hold the bag and let the liquid move from one end of the bag to the other until the contents are mixed.

12. Observe the reaction until it comes to a complete stop. Record your observations.

 13. Record the mass of the unopened bag in Data Table 2. Clean up your work area and wash your hands before leaving the laboratory.

Observations

DATA TABLE 1   Antacid Tablet and Water

		Write observations here:
mass of bag and water		
mass of tablet		
mass of bag and reactants		
mass of bag and products		

DATA TABLE 2 $CaCl_2$, $NaHCO_3$, and Water

		Write observations here:
mass of bag and dry reactants		
volume of water		
mass of water		
total mass of bag and reactants		
mass of bag and products		

Calculations

1. Calculate the total mass of the bag and reactants in each reaction and record these values in the appropriate Data Table.

2. Using the formula for the density of water, calculate the mass of the water. Record the results in Data Table 2.

Name _____

Critical Thinking: Analysis and Conclusions

1. How do the values for total mass before and after each reaction demonstrate the law of conservation of mass? *(Interpreting data)*
   _____

2. What were at least five observations you made that indicated a reaction had occurred in Part A? *(Giving examples)* _____
   _____
   _____
   _____

3. Write an equation in words and then with formulas for the reaction that occurred in the bag in Part B. The products are sodium chloride, calcium hydroxide, and carbonic acid. *(Applying concepts)* _____
   _____
   _____
   _____

Critical Thinking: Applications

1. An indicator changes color when the acidity of a solution changes. What evidence is there that such a change occurred in Part B? *(Applying concepts)* _____

2. Judge whether the reaction mixture in Part B became more acidic or more basic. Explain. *(Making predictions)* _____
   _____

3. Carbonic acid immediately decomposes into water and carbon dioxide. Write the balanced equation for this reaction. *(Applying concepts)* _____

4. What gas was produced in Part A? *(Making predictions)* (Hint: sodium hydrogen carbonate is an active ingredient in the antacid.) _____
   _____

Going Further

1. Under the supervision of your teacher, test reactions between the following pairs of reactants to determine whether they follow the law of conservation of mass. Predict the products of the reactions and balance the equations: acetic acid (vinegar) and baking soda; zinc and hydrochloric acid.

Double Replacement Reactions

Small Scale
Lab 27

Text reference: **Chapter 9**

Introduction

As you may have read in Chapter 9 of your textbook, antacid tablets contain the compound calcium carbonate, $CaCO_3$. This compound reacts with the hydrochloric acid, HCl, in your stomach in the following way:

$$CaCO_3(aq) + 2HCl(aq) \rightarrow CaCl_2(s) + H_2CO_3(aq)$$

This reaction is an everyday example of a double replacement reaction.

A double replacement reaction usually takes place between two ionic compounds that are dissolved in water. The cation of one compound replaces the cation in another compound to produce two new compounds. The new combination of cations and anions yields a product that may be a precipitate, a gas, or water. Precipitates are solids that form from the reaction between compounds that are soluble in water.

In this investigation you will mix several pairs of aqueous solutions and ionic compounds. You will observe which combinations of solutions result in the formation of a precipitate, and you will write balanced equations for the reactions.

Pre-Lab Discussion

Read the entire laboratory investigation and the relevant pages of your textbook. Then answer the questions that follow.

1. What is a double replacement reaction? _____

   _____

   _____

   _____

2. What evidence indicates that a double replacement reaction has oc-curred between two dissolved compounds? _____

   _____

   _____

3. What type of evidence will you be looking for in this investi-gation? _____

4. What hazards are associated with using silver nitrate, and what precautions should you take in this investigation? _____

   _____

   _____

Name_____

Problem

Which combinations of ionic solutions form precipitates that indicate a double replacement reaction has occurred?

Materials

chemical splash goggles
laboratory apron
latex gloves
marking pen
well plate
sheet of white paper
beaker to hold micropipets
dropper (for cleanup)

7 micropipets, each filled with
    one of the following 0.1 M
    solutions:
silver nitrate ($AgNO_3$)
iron(III) nitrate ($Fe(NO_3)_3$)
copper(II) nitrate ($Cu(NO_3)_2$)
sodium phosphate (Na_3PO_4)
sodium sulfate (Na_2SO_4)
sodium hydroxide ($NaOH$)
sodium chloride ($NaCl$)

Safety

Wear your goggles and lab apron at all times during the investigation. Wear gloves when handling silver nitrate as it is toxic and can cause stains to skin and clothing. Handle all chemicals with care; avoid spills and contact with your skin. If contact occurs, wash with plenty of cold water and tell your teacher.

Note the caution alert symbols here and with certain steps of the Procedure. Refer to page *xi* for the specific precautions associated with each symbol.

Procedure

1. Put on your goggles, gloves, and lab apron. Label the wells of the well plate as shown in Figure 27–1. Place the well plate on the sheet of white paper. Use a micropipet to place five drops of silver nitrate solution, $AgNO_3$, into each of wells A1 through A4. **CAUTION:** *Silver nitrate is poisonous. Be careful not to get it on your skin or clothing, as it will produce a stain that is hard to remove. If any spills occur, ask your teacher how to clean up safely.*

2. Place five drops of iron(III) nitrate solution, $Fe(NO_3)_3$, into each of wells B1 through B4. Then place five drops of copper(II) nitrate solution, $Cu(NO_3)_2$, into each of wells C1 through C4.

3. Now you will add a different ionic compound to each column of wells. To avoid contamination of the ionic solution in the micropipet, do not let its tip touch the solutions that are already in the wells. Add five drops of sodium phosphate solution, Na_3PO_4, to each of the solutions in wells A1, B1, and C1. Observe whether or not a precipitate forms in each well and record your observations in the Data Table. If a precipitate forms, record the color. If a precipitate does not form, write *NR* for *No Reaction*.

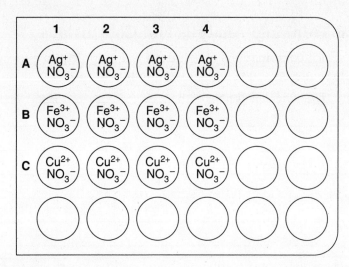

Figure 27–1

4. Add five drops of sodium sulfate solution, Na_2SO_4, to each of the solutions in wells A2, B2, and C2. Record your observations in the Data Table.

5. Add five drops of sodium hydroxide solution, NaOH, to each of the solutions in wells A3, B3, and C3 and record your observations. **CAUTION:** *Sodium hydroxide solution is caustic. Avoid spilling it on your skin or clothing. Wash spills with plenty of cold water.*

6. Add five drops of sodium chloride solution, NaCl, to the solutions in wells A4, B4, and C4 and record your observations.

7. Use a dropper to pull up the silver solutions in the row A wells of the well plate and deposit the material into the container provided by your teacher. Any silver nitrate solution left in a micropipet should be disposed of in a similar manner. Wash the sodium hydroxide down the drain with plenty of water. Clean up your work area and wash your hands before leaving the laboratory.

Observations
DATA TABLE

	Ionic Solutions	1 Na^+ PO_4^{3-}	2 Na^+ SO_4^{2-}	3 Na^+ OH^-	4 Na^+ Cl^-
A	Ag^+ NO_3^-				
B	Fe^{3+} NO_3^-				
C	Cu^{2+} NO_3^-				

Name _____

Critical Thinking: Analysis and Conclusions

1. For which combinations of solutions did no precipitate form? Based on these observations, which compounds are soluble in water? Explain. *(Drawing conclusions)* _____

   _____

   _____

   _____

   _____

   _____

   _____

2. Based on your observations, which positive ion reacts to form the greatest number of precipitates: Ag^+, Fe^{3+}, or Cu^{2+}? Explain. *(Interpreting data)* _____

   _____

   _____

3. Use a solubility table to determine the identity of the precipitates that formed in the wells in column 1. Then write the balanced equation for the reactions, including the symbols for phase, *(s)* and *(aq)*. *(Interpreting data)*

   _____

   _____

   _____

Critical Thinking: Applications

1. Write the equation for the reaction that takes place when a solution of silver nitrate is added to a solution of sodium chloride. *(Applying concepts)* _____

2. Sodium hydrogen carbonate, $NaHCO_3$, and sodium chloride, NaCl, are both soluble in water. Will a double replacement reaction take place if a solution of sodium hydrogen carbonate is added to a solution of sodium chloride? Explain. *(Making inferences)* _____

   _____

   _____

Going Further

1. Given a solution that contains one or more of the compounds used in this investigation, explain how you could identify the unknown compound or compounds. Use a chart to show your scheme.

Molar Volume of Hydrogen Gas

Small Scale Lab 28

Text reference: **Chapter 10**

Introduction

How would you measure the mass and volume of a gas? This is actually quite a difficult problem because gases often seem to lack definitive properties. If you filled a balloon with hydrogen gas and then tried to measure the combined mass of the hydrogen and the balloon, you would obtain an inaccurate measurement because of the buoyancy of the surrounding air. You could try to measure the volume of the hydrogen, but gas volume changes with variations in temperature or pressure. If you placed hydrogen gas in a rigid container, it would expand to fill the entire volume of the container regardless of the amount of hydrogen present. Also, gases can be produced or absorbed by chemical and physical changes of solids or liquids, as in some decompositions or in evaporation and condensation.

The mystery of gas properties was a major stumbling block to the development of modern chemistry. A solution to this mystery was found when scientists discovered that the changes in gas volume caused by pressure and temperature variations could be mathematically predicted. Another pivotal discovery was the realization that the mass of a gas can be determined by measuring the change in mass of the solid or liquid that produced the gas.

In 1811, Avogadro published his hypothesis that equal volumes of different gases at a given temperature and pressure contain identical numbers of gas particles. This hypothesis led to the idea that a mole of a given gas (6.02×10^{23} particles) occupies the same volume as a mole of any other gas, as long as the temperature and pressure are the same.

In this investigation you will determine an experimental value for the molar volume of hydrogen gas. You also will see if your results confirm the accepted molar volume of 22.4 liters per mole at a temperature of 0°C and a pressure of 760 mm Hg (one atmosphere). To make your results comparable, you will keep the gas as close as possible to 0°C and do a calculation to adjust for differences in pressure.

Pre-Lab Discussion

Read the entire laboratory investigation and the relevant pages of your textbook. Then answer the questions that follow.

1. Why is this investigation carried out in a basin of ice water that is at or near 0°C? _____

_____

_____

Name _____

2. Write the balanced equation for the reaction that occurs between magnesium and hydrochloric acid. _____

3. How is the volume of gas collected at room temperature adjusted to standard pressure? _____

_____

4. What happens to the acid that is placed in the graduated cylinder at the start of the experiment? How might this pose a safety hazard? _____

_____

_____

Problem

What is the molar volume of hydrogen gas?

Materials

chemical splash goggles   magnesium strip (Mg)
laboratory apron   scissors
latex gloves   plastic micropipet, long-stem
plastic basin   hydrochloric acid (HCl), 3.0 M
ice   graduated cylinder, 10-mL
tap water   plastic wrap, 5 × 5 cm
metric ruler   rubber band
Celsius thermometer   pin
barometer

Safety

Wear your goggles, gloves, and lab apron at all times during the investigation. The hydrochloric acid is corrosive. If you spill any, wash the affected area with lots of cold running water and report the spill immediately to your teacher. To protect your hands, be careful when rinsing out the micropipet and other equipment.

Note the caution alert symbols here and with certain steps of the Procedure. Refer to page xi for the specific precautions associated with each symbol.

Procedure

1. Put on your goggles, gloves, and lab apron. Fill the plastic basin one-third full of ice. Add tap water to a depth of 5–10 cm. Place a Celsius thermometer in the basin. Add more ice if necessary until the temperature is 0°C. Use a barometer to measure the atmospheric pressure in the laboratory. Record the temperature and pressure in the Data Table.

2. Obtain a strip of magnesium that is about 1.0 cm long. With scissors, trim the cut edges so that they are straight across, rather than diagonally cut. Measure the length of the strip to the nearest 0.02 cm and record the length in the Data Table.

3. Use the micropipet to dispense approximately 3 mL of 3.0 M HCl into the bottom of an empty 10-mL graduated cylinder. Insert the micropipet into the center of the cylinder to avoid getting acid on the sides of the cylinder. **CAUTION:** *Hydrochloric acid is corrosive. Avoid spills and splashes. If you do spill some, rinse the affected area with water and immediately inform your teacher.*

4. Rinse out the micropipet. Fill the rest of the graduated cylinder with tap water using the micropipet. Drip the water down the inside surface of the cylinder to prevent mixing the acid with the water. The water should overfill the cylinder top slightly to form a smooth curved surface.

5. Roll or fold the magnesium and place it carefully onto the surface of the water in the cylinder. It should float. Quickly cover the cylinder with a square of plastic wrap, stretch the plastic tight, and secure it with a rubber band. Make sure that there are no air bubbles trapped under the plastic wrap. See Figure 28–1.

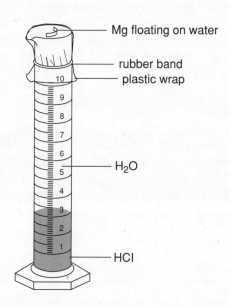

Figure 28–1

6. With a pin, poke a tiny hole in the plastic over the cylinder mouth. Holding the cylinder by the base (to avoid heating it), immediately invert it in the basin of ice water. Hold the inverted cylinder vertically with its mouth submerged. Do not block the pin hole. See Figure 28–2.

7. The magnesium will react with the acid, producing hydrogen gas that collects in the cylinder. When the reaction is complete, chill the gas by submerging the cylinder completely in the ice water for about one minute, tipping it at a slight angle if necessary.

Name_____

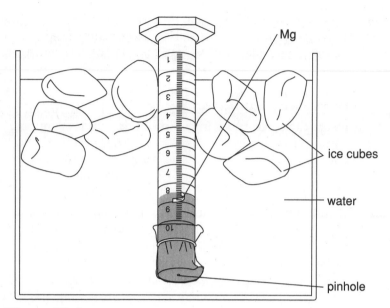

Figure 28–2

8. To read the volume of hydrogen gas in the cylinder, lift the cylinder vertically until the liquid level inside the cylinder matches the level of the water in the basin. This equalizes the gas pressure in the cylinder with the atmospheric pressure outside the cylinder. Record the volume of hydrogen gas in the Data Table.

9. If time permits, carry out a second trial by repeating Steps 2 through 8.

 10. When you are finished, rinse the diluted acid in the basin down the drain. **CAUTION:** *Hydrochloric acid is corrosive. Avoid spills and splashes. If you do spill some, rinse the affected area with water and immediately inform your teacher.* Clean up your work area and wash your hands before leaving the laboratory.

Observations
DATA TABLE

	Trial 1	Trial 2
length of Mg strip (cm)		
volume of hydrogen collected (mL)		
temperature of water in basin (°C)		
atmospheric pressure (mm Hg)		

Calculations

1. Find the mass of magnesium used in each trial, using the following formula and the mass-to-length ratio provided by your teacher:

mass (g) = mass/length ratio (g/cm) × Mg length (cm)

2. Use the equation you wrote in Question 2 of the Pre-Lab Discussion to identify the number of moles of hydrogen produced per mole of magnesium. Then calculate the number of moles of hydrogen produced during the investigation. _____

_____

3. Find the volume of hydrogen at standard pressure used in each trial, using the following formula:

$$\text{volume} = \text{measured volume (L)} \times \frac{\text{atmospheric pressure (mm Hg)}}{760 \text{ mm Hg}}$$

Critical Thinking: Analysis and Conclusions

1. Based on your data, calculate the molar volume of hydrogen (liters H_2/moles H_2) and compare to the accepted value of 22.4 L/mole by computing the percent error. (*Making comparisons*)

2. How would you explain the percent error for your calculation of molar volume? (*Interpreting data*) _____

_____

_____

_____

3. How would you redesign this experiment to reduce the percent error? (*Designing experiments*) _____

_____

_____

4. Why do you think the graduated cylinder was inverted in the ice water bath rather than being held right side up? (*Making inferences*)

_____

_____

5. What type of chemical reaction—single replacement, double replacement, decomposition, or direct combination—occurred between the magnesium and the hydrochloric acid? (*Classifying*) _____

_____

Name _____

Critical Thinking: Applications

1. How do you think each of the following factors would affect the accuracy of your results when compared with the accepted volume of 22.4 liters per mole at 0°C and 760 mm Hg? *(Making predictions)*

   a. Gas temperature higher than 0°C. _____

   _____

   b. Evaporation of water vapor into the collected hydrogen. _____

   _____

   c. Using a longer strip of magnesium. _____

   _____

   _____

   _____

2. Since gases change volume with changes in pressure and temperature, explain why it is not immediately obvious how much gas is in a propane gas tank. What is the minimum information you need to compare suppliers of propane gas for refilling barbecue propane

   tanks? *(Evaluating)* _____

   _____

   _____

   _____

   _____

Going Further

1. Design an experiment in which you can generate and collect a measurable volume of another gas, for example carbon dioxide. Under your teacher's supervision, conduct the experiment and determine the molar volume of the gas. Analyze and report on your results.

Molar Mass of Butane

Lab 29
APPLICATION

Text reference: **Chapter 10**

Introduction

Every pure substance is composed of a distinct combination of atoms and is identified by its own molecular formula. The sum of the atomic masses of the atoms in this molecular formula is the substance's formula mass. The same number, measured in grams, is the substance's molar mass.

Butane, with the molecular formula C_4H_{10}, is a gas at normal room conditions. It can be liquefied by placing it under pressure, as in a disposable butane lighter. When the valve is opened the liquid butane quickly escapes and changes into a gas. Butane also is extremely insoluble in water, so it can be bubbled through water with very little of it going into solution. Because of these properties, a refill cylinder for a butane lighter is a good source of butane gas, and water displacement is a good method of collecting a measurable sample of it.

In this investigation you will collect some butane gas in a container by means of water displacement. You will determine the volume of the gas collected and, from that volume, the number of moles of butane. The mass of the gas collected will be obtained by taking the difference between the mass of the refill cylinder before and after butane is released from it. From the mass and the number of moles of the gas collected you can then calculate the mass of one mole, or the molar mass, of butane.

Pre-Lab Discussion

Read the entire laboratory investigation and the relevant pages of your textbook. Then answer the questions that follow.

1. What is the difference between the formula mass and the molar mass of a substance? Include the appropriate units for each. _____

_____

_____

_____

2. Describe the procedure known as water displacement. When is it used? _____

_____

_____

3. Why should there be no flames in the laboratory when this investigation is being done? _____

_____

Name _____

4. Describe the piece of equipment known as a pneumatic trough. What is its purpose during the investigation? _____

_____

_____

_____

_____

5. Why is the insolubility of butane important in this investigation?

_____

_____

6. Why is it important to make sure that the flask is filled to the very top with water before it is turned upside down? _____

_____

_____

7. What is the volume occupied by one mole of any gas at STP? Do you think the volume would be larger or smaller at laboratory conditions? _____

_____

_____

Problem

How can you determine the molar mass of butane gas?

Materials

safety goggles	2 pieces rubber tubing
laboratory apron	pneumatic trough
laboratory balance	flask, 500-mL
butane refill cylinder	glass square

Safety

Wear your goggles and lab apron at all times during the investigation. Butane is very flammable, so make certain there are no open flames or matches in the laboratory.

Note the caution alert symbols here and with certain steps of the Procedure. Refer to page *xi* for the specific precautions associated with each symbol.

Procedure

 1. Put on your goggles and lab apron. This investigation requires you to work carefully with your partner. Decide now which one of you will handle the flask and which one will handle the butane cylinder.

2. Determine the mass of a dry butane refill cylinder. Record the mass in your Data Table.

3. Fill the pneumatic trough with water to a level about 2 cm above the shelf. Connect one piece of rubber tubing to the overflow spout of the trough, and place the other end of it in the sink. (See Figure 29–1.)

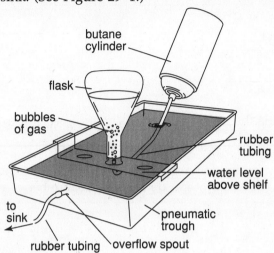

Figure 29–1

4. Fill a 500-mL flask completely (to the very top) with water. Cover the mouth of the flask with a glass square, carefully invert the flask, and place it in the trough so the mouth is under water, pointing down. Make sure that there are no air bubbles in the flask. Remove the glass square from the mouth of the flask and set the flask over one of the holes in the shelf. One student should hold the flask vertical and steady while the other handles the butane cylinder.

5. Connect one end of the second piece of rubber tubing to the butane refill cylinder and insert the other end of the tubing a few centimeters into the neck of the flask, so that the gas will rise into the flask when the valve is opened. **CAUTION:** *Butane is highly flammable. Do not bring any flames into the laboratory, or use any electrical equipment, during this investigation.*

6. Holding the gas refill above the trough, press the valve of the cylinder to release the butane, and fill the round portion of the flask with gas exactly to the 500-mL mark. Make sure not to release any of the gas outside of the flask.

7. When the flask is filled, release the valve and carefully disconnect the rubber tubing from it.

8. Lift the flask off the shelf in the pneumatic trough, and place the glass square over its mouth. Turn the flask right side up and carry it to the fume hood. Remove the glass square and stand the flask upright.

9. Making sure that the butane cylinder is dry, measure its mass on the same balance used previously. Record the value in your Data Table. Clean up your work area and wash your hands before leaving the laboratory.

Name _____

Observations

DATA TABLE

initial mass of butane cylinder	
final mass of butane cylinder	
mass of butane gas	
volume of butane	

Calculations

1. Determine the mass of butane used and record it in the Data Table.

2. Using the molar volume given to you by your teacher for the conditions in your laboratory, determine the number of moles of butane gas collected.

3. From the mass and the number of moles of butane gas collected, calculate the mass per mole of butane—its molar mass.

Critical Thinking: Analysis and Conclusions

1. Calculate the formula mass of butane (C_4H_{10}) using a chart of atomic masses. *(Applying concepts)*

2. Determine your percent error *(Interpreting Data)*.

3. If a small air bubble had been in the flask before you filled it with butane, how would it have affected your results? Explain. *(Making predictions)* _____

_____

_____

4. What other sources of experimental error might have affected your results in this investigation? How? *(Interpreting data)* _____

_____

_____

5. Why were you unable to use the standard molar volume (22.4 L/mol) in this investigation? *(Making comparisons)* _____

_____

_____

_____

Critical Thinking: Applications

1. How would you alter this investigation to determine the molar volume of a gas that is soluble in water? *(Designing experiments)* _____

_____

2. Propane gas tanks for barbecues are filled by weight. Can you expect a fair measurement this way? Explain. *(Making judgments)* _____

_____

Going Further

1. Under your teacher's supervision, determine experimentally the molar mass of another gas, for example, propane. Report your findings.

Stoichiometry Using Copper   Lab 31

Text reference: ***Chapter 11***

Introduction

Have you ever noticed how many different uses copper has? The first things that come to mind are probably coins and electrical wires. How many others can you think of? Why is copper so useful?

Copper is widely distributed in Earth's crust. It is commonly found in sulfides, carbonates, and as uncombined metal. It is a relatively soft metal, reddish in color, and similar in many ways to another metal in Group 1B, silver. It is an excellent conductor of electricity and heat, second only to silver. Like silver, it maintains its integrity through a series of chemical reactions and has the advantage of being relatively inexpensive.

In this investigation, you will perform a series of chemical reactions involving copper and copper compounds. The equations for the reactions are listed here in unbalanced form.

$$Cu + HNO_3 \rightarrow Cu(NO_3)_2 + NO_2 + H_2O$$
$$Cu(NO_3)_2 + NaOH \rightarrow Cu(OH)_2 + NaNO_3$$
$$Cu(OH)_2 \rightarrow CuO + H_2O$$
$$CuO + H_2SO_4 \rightarrow CuSO_4 + H_2O$$
$$CuSO_4 + Zn \rightarrow Cu + ZnSO_4$$

Beginning with a sample of copper of known mass, you will perform a series of reactions, eventually recovering the copper at the end. You will then analyze your quantitative data to see what percentage of the copper was recovered.

Pre-Lab Discussion

Read the entire laboratory investigation and the relevant pages of your textbook. Then answer the questions that follow.

1. What are some properties of copper metal? _____

   _____

2. Balance the first two equations given in the Introduction.

   _____

   _____

3. What safety hazards are associated with dissolving copper in nitric acid? What precautions should be taken? _____

   _____

   _____

Name_____

4. How will copper(II) sulfate be prepared in the investigation? _____

_____

5. In which step of this investigation is the initial copper recovered?

_____

6. What method will be used to dry the final amount of copper produced? _____

Problem

How is copper affected by a series of chemical reactions?

Materials

Part A

chemical splash goggles
laboratory apron
latex gloves
laboratory balance
copper wire
beaker, 250-mL
graduated cylinder,
    50- or 100-mL

nitric acid (HNO₃), 6.0 *M*
watch glass
beaker, 600-mL
ice
tap water
sodium hydroxide (NaOH),
    6.0 *M*
pH paper

Part B

hot plate
stirring rod
beaker tongs
sulfuric acid (H₂SO₄), 3.0 *M*

zinc granules
evaporating dish
weighing paper

Safety

Wear your goggles, gloves, and lab apron at all times during the investigation. Both 6.0 *M* nitric acid and 3.0 *M* sulfuric acid are corrosive and should be handled with care. The 6.0 *M* sodium hydroxide is caustic. If you spill any of these solutions on your skin, wash the spill with plenty of water and notify your teacher.

    Part A must be performed in a fume hood.

    Note the caution alert symbols here and with certain steps of the Procedure. Refer to page *xi* for the specific precautions associated with each symbol.

Procedure

Part A

1. Put on your goggles, gloves, and lab apron. Find the mass of the copper wire and record it in Data Table 1. Place the copper wire in a 250-mL beaker.

2. In a fume hood, slowly add 25 mL of 6.0 *M* nitric acid, HNO₃, to the beaker and cover it with a watch glass. The reaction produces nitrogen dioxide, NO₂. **CAUTION:** *Do not inhale NO₂ fumes.* When the copper has completely dissolved and the reddish-brown color of NO₂ can no longer be seen, record your observations in Data Table 2.

3. Put some ice and water into a 600-mL beaker until the beaker is about half full. Place the smaller beaker in the ice bath to keep the reaction mixture cool.

 4. Obtain 25 mL of 6.0 *M* sodium hydroxide, NaOH, in a graduated cylinder and test its pH with pH paper. Slowly add the NaOH solution to the 250 mL beaker and test the reaction mixture's pH until it is at pH 13. Record your observations in Data Table 2. If Part B will be done on another day, clean up your work area and wash your hands before leaving the laboratory.

Part B

5. Put on your goggles, gloves, and lab apron. To the reaction mixture from Part A, add 50 mL of water. Using a hot plate, gently heat the mixture to a boil. Stir while heating for approximately 5 minutes. **CAUTION:** *Stir the mixture continuously; otherwise the beaker could break or the mixture could foam out of the top.* Record your observations in Data Table 2.

 6. Remove the beaker from the hot plate using beaker tongs and allow the solution to cool for approximately 5 minutes. Turn off the hot plate. Decant (pour off) the liquid from the beaker into the sink with the water running. While stirring, add 50 mL of water to the precipitate in the beaker, let it settle, and decant the liquid. Repeat this process. It is important that the precipitate remain in the beaker.

 7. To the precipitate from Step 6, slowly add 50 mL of 3.0 *M* sulfuric acid, H₂SO₄, while stirring. Record your observations in Data Table 2.

8. Add approximately 10 grams of zinc to the solution from Step 7. Cover the beaker and swirl gently until all of the blue color disappears from the solution. Do this for a minimum of 10 minutes. Record your observations in Data Table 2.

 9. Since there will be excess zinc remaining in the beaker, add 30 mL of 3.0 *M* H₂SO₄ and swirl. The bubbles indicate the evolution of hydrogen gas from the reaction mixture. When the evolution of gas ceases, add an additional 20 mL of H₂SO₄. When no further evidence of the evolution of gas is present, add 50 mL of water and decant the liquid.

10. Find the mass of the evaporating dish and record the value in Data Table 1. Transfer the solid remaining in the beaker to the evaporating dish. Set up a steam bath as shown in Figure 31–1 and evaporate the remaining liquid from the copper precipitate. Do not overheat the copper.

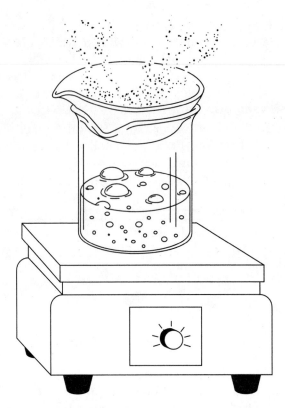

Figure 31–1

11. Remove the evaporating dish from the steam bath and let it cool. Find the combined mass of the copper and the evaporating dish and record it in Data Table 1.

 12. Dispose of the recovered copper as directed by your teacher. Clean up your work area and wash your hands before leaving the laboratory.

Observations

DATA TABLE 1   Quantitative Data

initial mass of copper	
mass of evaporating dish	
mass of evaporating dish and copper	
mass of recovered copper	

DATA TABLE 2   Qualitative Data

Reaction	Observations
$Cu + HNO_3$	
$Cu(NO_3)_2 + NaOH$	
$Cu(OH)_2$	
$CuO + H_2SO_4$	
$CuSO_4 + Zn$	
$Zn + H_2SO_4$	

Calculations

1. Calculate the final mass of copper and record it in Data Table 1.

2. Calculate the final number of moles of copper.

3. Calculate the initial number of moles of copper.

4. Calculate the percentage of copper recovered.

Critical Thinking: Analysis and Conclusions

1. Why is the product of the reaction between copper and nitric acid in Step 2 placed on ice? *(Making inferences)* _____

   _____

2. What type of chemical reaction—single replacement, double replacement, decomposition, or direct combination—occurred in each of Steps 4, 7, and 9? *(Classifying)*

   Step 4: _____

   Step 7: _____

   Step 9: _____

3. The reaction of excess zinc with sulfuric acid is a critical step in this investigation. Write the balanced equation for this reaction. What problems would arise from an incomplete reaction? *(Making predictions)* _____

_____

4. Account for any difference in mass between the initial amount of Cu used and the amount of Cu reclaimed. Would you expect this?

(Making inferences) _____

_____

_____

_____

Critical Thinking: Applications

1. How many grams of each of the following chemicals would be formed from your initial mass of copper? *(Applying concepts)*

   a. $Cu(NO_3)_2$

   b. $Cu(OH)_2$

   c. $ZnSO_4$

2. Recovery of metals from industrial processes, both from waste water and from sediments, is an important environmental issue. How does an investigation like the one just performed relate to such activities?

   (Applying concepts) _____

   _____

   _____

Going Further

1. Recycling is a focus of great environmental interest. Group 1B in the periodic table contains copper, silver, and gold. Use the library and contact photography labs and metal platers. Then write a short description of the recovery of silver from solutions.

Zinc Thickness in Galvanized Iron

Introduction

How much water can a rusty bucket hold? None. When a bucket gets rusty, the rust flakes off, leaving holes and leaks behind. The corrosion, or rusting, of iron has had great economic impact on the construction and automotive industries. A number of methods have been developed to prevent rust formation. The most expensive is the alloying of nickel and chromium with iron to make rust-resistant stainless steel. Other methods use a series of nonmetallic coatings to slow the formation of rust. These methods are widely used in the manufacture of automobiles. Another method that has been in use for a long time is galvanization, or coating of iron with a thin layer of zinc. Since zinc is oxidized more easily than iron, it forms zinc oxide, which stays firmly in place and continues to protect the iron for a long time. Unfortunately, even galvanized iron eventually disintegrates, so that the bucket eventually rusts and leaks despite this preventive effort.

Since zinc is more expensive than iron, it is cost effective to use the thinnest coating of zinc possible. How much zinc is involved in such a process? In this investigation, you will determine the thickness of the zinc coating on a piece of galvanized iron. You will start by determining the mass of the zinc on a piece of iron. You will then calculate the thickness of its coating.

Pre-Lab Discussion

Read the entire laboratory investigation and the relevant pages of your textbook. Then answer the questions that follow.

1. What is meant by the term corrosion of metals? _____

   _____

2. What is galvanized iron? _____

3. How will the thickness of the zinc coating be determined in this experiment? _____

   _____

   _____

4. What precautions must be taken in performing this experiment and why? _____

   _____

   _____

Problem

How do you determine the thickness of zinc on a piece of galvanized iron?

Materials

chemical splash goggles
laboratory apron
rectangular piece of galvanized
    iron
laboratory balance
metric ruler

latex gloves
beaker, 250-mL
hydrochloric acid (HCl), 6.0 *M*
tap water
paper towel

Safety

Wear your goggles and lab apron at all times during the investigation. Hydrochloric acid is corrosive and can give off hydrogen chloride fumes when heated. Use in a well-ventilated area, preferably under a hood. Wear gloves when using 6.0 *M* hydrochloric acid. Note the caution alert symbols here and with certain steps of the Procedure. Refer to page *xi* for the specific precautions associated with each symbol.

Procedure

1. Put on your goggles and lab apron. Determine the mass of a piece of galvanized iron and record it in the Data Table.

2. Measure the width and length of the galvanized iron and record these values in the Data Table.

 3. Put on your gloves. Work in a fume hood. Place the galvanized iron in the 250-mL beaker and cover with 30 mL of 6.0 *M* hydrochloric acid (HCl). **CAUTION:** *Hydrochloric acid is corrosive and can give off hydrogen chloride fumes when heated.* When the rapid evolution of gas stops, add water to the beaker and then pour off the liquid into a beaker your teacher has provided. Rinse the remaining metal with tap water and dry it with a paper towel.

4. Determine the mass of the remaining metal and record it.

 5. Clean up your work area and wash your hands before leaving the laboratory.

Name_____

● **Observations**

DATA TABLE

mass of galvanized iron (g)	
mass of remaining iron (g)	
mass of zinc (g)	
length of metal, l (cm)	
width of metal, w (cm)	

▦ **Calculations**

1. Find the area of iron covered by zinc (remember zinc covers both sides of the piece).

2. Find the mass of the zinc coating.

3. Given the density of zinc as 7.14 g/cm³, find the volume of zinc.

4. Find the thickness of the zinc coating.

5. Given the diameter of the zinc atom as 2.66×10^{-8} cm, find the thickness of the zinc coating in atoms.

6. How many moles of zinc are in the coating?

Critical Thinking: Analysis and Conclusions

1. Write the balanced equation for the reaction of zinc with hydrochloric acid. (*Applying concepts*) _____

2. How did you know that the zinc had fully reacted with the acid? (*Interpreting data*) _____ _____

_____

3. What are the major sources of error in this investigation? *(Drawing conclusions)* _____

_____

Critical Thinking: Applications

1. What does the thickness of the zinc coating indicate about the effectiveness of zinc in protecting iron? *(Drawing conclusions)* _____

_____

_____

Going Further

1. Obtain from your teacher strips of metals such as aluminum, copper, magnesium and zinc. Devise an experiment to test the reactivity of these metals in acidic and basic mediums. Conduct the experiment under your teacher's supervision. Report on whether or not corrosion problems are related to the presence of acids and bases.

Limiting Reactants in Brownies

Lab 33
APPLICATION

Text reference: **Chapter 11**

Introduction

Have you ever made a dip for a party and found that you were low on one ingredient you needed? Could you still make the dip? How much dip could you make? The same situation exists for chemical reactions. How do you determine how much product will come out of a chemical process? First, you have to know the balanced equation for the reaction. Then you need to know how much of each starting reactant you have. Next you need to determine which reactant is the limiting quantity, given the molar ratios of all the reactants. Finally, you must use the quantity of the limiting reactant to determine how much product you will get.

When you use recipes in the kitchen, the same process takes place. Nothing made in a chemistry lab can be eaten, so you will do this investigation at home. You will be given a list of ingredients. By comparing this list to the standard recipe, you will determine which ingredient is present in a different amount. You will calculate the quantities of materials you need based on the concept of limiting reactants, and then bake a batch of brownies according to your new recipe. It is important that you keep careful records of your procedure and the amounts of your materials. Your results will then be compared to those of your classmates.

Pre-Lab Discussion

Read the entire laboratory investigation and the relevant pages of your textbook. Then answer the questions that follow.

1. Will the results always be identical if you mix the same ingredients in exactly the same proportions every time? _____

_____

_____

2. What is the importance of having a procedure and following it precisely? _____

3. How does the quantity of a chemical in a reaction determine the outcome of an experiment in the kitchen? In the chemistry lab?

_____

_____

_____

4. What safety precautions should you observe in the kitchen? _____

_____

5. If 16.5 grams of aluminum are reacted with 39.2 grams of chlorine gas, then aluminum chloride is formed.

   a. Which reactant is the limiting reactant? _____

   b. Calculate the mass of aluminum chloride produced.

Problem

How can the concept of limiting reagents be applied to a cooking recipe?

Materials

index card with instructions
kitchen, equipped with measur-
    ing cups, measuring spoons,
    pot holders, mixer, oven,
    and pan
ingredients for brownie recipe:
    1/3 cup shortening
    2 squares unsweetened
        chocolate (2 oz.)

1 cup sugar
2 eggs
1 teaspoon vanilla
3/4 cup flour
1/2 teaspoon baking powder
1/2 teaspoon salt

Safety

Do not work in the kitchen without adult supervision. Wash your hands with soap and water before beginning this investigation. Wear an apron. Ovens and pans are hot. Use pot holders when removing pans from the oven. Let the brownies cool before cutting them. Note the caution alert symbols here and with certain steps of the Procedure. Refer to page *xi* for the specific precautions associated with each symbol.

Procedure

Part A: At Home

1. Wash your hands with soap and water. Wear an apron. Work under adult supervision. Calculate the amount of each ingredient you will use, based upon the information on the index card you received from your teacher. List these amounts in Data Table 1.

2. Gather the ingredients and other materials you will need. Explain to your family what you are doing and how this investigation relates to what you are studying in chemistry.

3. Mix the ingredients, making careful notes of measurements, the order of adding the ingredients, and other factors that you think might affect the results. If you have a thermometer in your oven, record the actual temperature of the oven.

 4. Bake at 350°F for approximately 30 minutes (record the actual time). **CAUTION:** *Use pot holders to remove the pan from the oven.*

5. Let the pan cool completely. Cut the brownies into 30 equal-sized pieces. Clean up completely before leaving the kitchen.

Part B: In Class

6. On the day specified by your teacher, bring your experimental results to class to be tested. Arrange the experiments so that everyone can observe and then taste the brownies.

7. Make a Data Table using sample Data Table 2 as a guide. Fill in the table for dimensions, color, texture, and taste for every type of brownie.

Observations

DATA TABLE 1

Ingredient	Amount	Order of Mixing
shortening		
unsweetened chocolate		
sugar		
eggs		
vanilla		
flour		
baking powder		
salt		

DATA TABLE 2

	Brownie Ratings			
Name or Group #	Dimensions	Color	Texture	Taste

Name _____

Critical Thinking: Analysis and Conclusions

1. Interview the classmate who made what you consider to be the best brownie in each category (color, texture, taste). Record the order of mixing, time of baking, brand of ingredients, etc. Try to identify what factor(s) may have contributed to the success of the recipe. *(Drawing conclusions)* _____

   _____

2. Were all the brownies the same size? If not, what affected the size? *(Drawing conclusions)* _____

   _____

3. Were all the brownies of the same consistency (chewy, moist, etc.)? If not, what affected the consistency? *(Making comparisons)* _____

   _____

   _____

4. Write the procedure for making what you thought was the best brownie. *(Developing models)* _____

   _____

   _____

5. What effect did the lack of a written procedure have? *(Developing hypotheses)* _____

   _____

6. Why are the ratios of ingredients important in a brownie recipe? *(Drawing conclusions)* _____

Critical Thinking: Applications

1. Can the amounts of the ingredients in a brownie recipe vary without ruining the product? If so, which ones do you think you could use more or less of? What would be the results if you did vary the amounts? *(Interpreting data)* _____

   _____

   _____

2. If you wanted to make a brownie with fewer calories but good texture, what changes would you try? *(Designing experiments)*

   _____

   _____

Going Further

1. Look up an example of a commercial product in which limiting reactants play an important role in the manufacturing process. Prepare an oral report on this product.

Simulating the Flameless Ration Heater

Lab 35
APPLICATION

Text reference: **Chapter 12**

Introduction

Picture yourself out on military maneuvers in a desolate area. You're very hungry, but making a fire or setting up a stove would take too much time and could be very dangerous. In order to make hot meals available to its troops, the U.S. Army worked with private industry to develop the Meal Ready to Eat (MRE) and a device called a Flameless Ration Heater (FRH).

The MRE is an aluminum-foil and plastic pouch containing a main course, condiments, or dessert. The FRH consists of a long plastic sleeve containing a small, porous cardboard envelope. Inside the envelope are heat-generating chemicals that react exothermically when water is present. The food pouch is placed inside the sleeve and water is added. As the heat-generating chemicals begin to react, the MRE is heated. See Figure 35–1.

In Investigation 16, you observed the reactivity of two alkaline earth metals, magnesium and calcium. The reaction of calcium with water was both very rapid and very exothermic. The reaction of magnesium was much slower. In fact, the rate of heat release was so slow that it was difficult to tell if the reaction was even exothermic. Yet the Flameless Ration Heater uses magnesium as the major fuel to provide heat. What

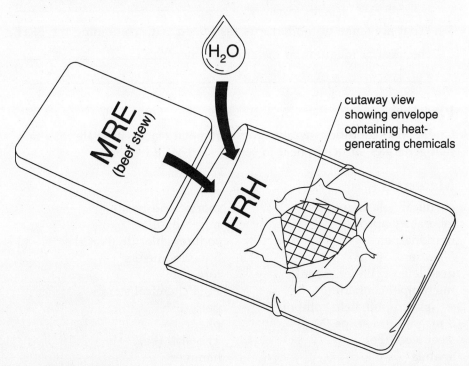

cutaway view showing envelope containing heat-generating chemicals

Figure 35–1

Name _____

is it about the reaction of the FRH that is different from the magnesium reaction from Investigation 16? The answer lies in the other ingredients that are present.

In this investigation, you will vary the reaction ingredients and the method of combination of the ingredients in order to determine the effect of the FRH reaction.

Pre-Lab Discussion

Read the entire laboratory investigation and the relevant pages of your textbook. Then answer the questions that follow.

1. Why isn't calcium metal used as one of the FRH heat-generating chemicals? _____

   _____

2. What does the pink color of phenolphthalein indicate? _____

   _____

3. Are the following reactions endothermic or exothermic? What is the standard change in enthalpy for each?
   a. $Mg(s) + 2H_2O(l) \rightarrow Mg(OH)_2(aq) + H_2(g) + 84$ kcal
   b. $2Fe(s) + O_2(g) \rightarrow 2FeO(s) + 130$ kcal
   c. $2Mg(s) + O_2(g) \rightarrow 2MgO(s) + 290$ kcal

   _____

4. What would be a disadvantage in using any of the reactions in Pre-Lab Question 3 as a source for heat generation? _____

   _____

5. What are some of the hazards associated with combining the FRH chemical or magnesium metal with water? _____

   _____

Problem

Under what conditions will magnesium metal react with water at a rate that generates sufficient heat to serve as an MRE heater?

Materials

chemical splash goggles
laboratory apron
marking pen
5 beakers, 50-mL
graduated cylinder, 50-mL
micropipet containing
    phenolphthalein solution
8 magnesium strips (Mg)
steel wool (Fe)
spatula
iron powder (Fe)

mortar and pestle
microspatula
sodium chloride (NaCl)
5 thermometers
forceps
FRH chemical sample
petri dish
pliers
iron slab (Fe)
hammer
iron filings (Fe)

Safety

Wear your goggles and lab apron at all times during the investigation. The FRH chemicals are poisonous and should be handled with the forceps. The solutions produced in this investigation are caustic and contact with your skin should be avoided. Note the caution alert symbols here and with certain steps of the Procedure. Refer to page *xi* for the specific precautions associated with each symbol.

Procedure

Part A

1. Put on your goggles and lab apron.
2. Using a marking pen, label five beakers *1–5*. Put 25.0 mL of water, as measured in a graduated cylinder, and three or four drops of phenolphthalein solution into each beaker.
3. Polish four magnesium strips with steel wool until they are shiny. Place a spatula of iron powder into a mortar. Feed in a strip of magnesium, grinding the two metals together with the pestle. When the entire length of the magnesium strip has been ground together with the iron, turn it over and repeat the process.
4. Repeat Step 3 with another strip of magnesium. Set both strips aside.
5. To beakers 4 and 5 add a microspatula of sodium chloride (NaCl).
6. Using the thermometers, measure the temperature of the water in each beaker. Record the values in Data Table 1.

7. **CAUTION:** *The FRH chemicals are poisonous and should be handled only with the forceps.* To each beaker add the following:

> Beaker 1: FRH chemical sample
> Beaker 2: Magnesium strip
> Beaker 3: Magnesium/iron strip
> Beaker 4: Magnesium strip
> Beaker 5: Magnesium/iron strip

Make sure the metal strips are completely submerged in the water.

8. After waiting 10–15 minutes to be sure the reactions are complete, record the final temperature, the final color, the relative rates of the reactions, and any other observations of note for each beaker.

9. Dispose of the liquid contents of the beakers by rinsing them into the labeled container provided by your teacher. The solid magnesium strips can be rinsed, dried, and cleaned, if necessary, with steel wool. Wash, rinse, and dry the beakers as well.

10. If you are not going directly on to Part B, clean up your work area and wash your hands before leaving the laboratory.

Name _____

Part B

11. Put on your goggles and lab apron. Polish four more magnesium strips with steel wool.

12. Place a spatula of iron powder in the inverted top of a petri dish and pinch the iron powder and one of the magnesium strips together with a pair of pliers. Continue for the entire length of the strip. Repeat for the other side of the strip. See Figure 35–2.

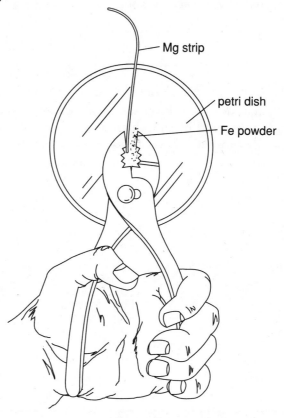

Figure 35–2

13. Place a spatula of iron powder on an iron slab, push the second magnesium strip into the powder, and strike the magnesium with a hammer as the strip is fed through the powder. Repeat for the other side of the strip.

14. Place a spatula of iron filings into a mortar. Repeat the treatment performed in Step 3.

15. Wrap a strip of magnesium with strands of steel wool. Roll the strip into a loose ball.

16. Label four beakers *1–4* and add 25.0 mL water, three or four drops of phenolphthalein, and a microspatula of sodium chloride to each.

17. In Data Table 2, record the initial temperature of the water in each beaker. To each beaker add the following:

   Beaker 1: magnesium/iron pinched with pliers
   Beaker 2: magnesium/iron hammered together

Beaker 3: magnesium/iron filings
Beaker 4: magnesium/steel wool strands

Make sure the metal strips are completely submerged in the water.

18. After waiting 10–15 minutes to be sure the reactions are complete, record the final temperature, the final color, the relative rates of the reactions, and any other observations.

19. Dispose of the liquid contents of the beakers by rinsing them into the labeled container provided by your teacher. Clean up your work area and wash your hands before leaving the laboratory.

Observations

DATA TABLE 1

Beaker	Initial Temp. (°C)	Final Temp. (°C)	Final Color	Rate of Reaction	Other Observations
1					
2					
3					
4					
5					

DATA TABLE 2

Beaker	Initial Temp. (°C)	Final Temp. (°C)	Final Color	Rate of Reaction	Other Observations
1					
2					
3					
4					

Lab 35
APPLICATION

Critical Thinking: Analysis and Conclusions

1. Rank the rate of reaction for the materials in each beaker in Parts A and B on a scale of 1 to 5 with 1 being the fastest. Write your determinations in the Data Tables. *(Making comparisons)*

2. Did any of your observations suggest that the heat-generating chemical became very hot? *(Making inferences)* _____

_____

3. What is the most likely composition of the layer of material you removed from the magnesium metal with the steel wool? Why was it important to remove this material? *(Making inferences)* _____

_____

_____

4. Compare the reaction rates of the magnesium metal strips in beakers 4 and 5 of Part A. How does sodium chloride affect the rate of the reaction? *(Interpreting data)* _____

_____

5. Describe the conditions you observed in Part A that favored the greatest rate of reaction of magnesium metal with water. What does this indicate about the reaction ingredients? *(Interpreting data)*

_____

_____

6. Did any of the beakers from Part B have a peak temperature as high as Beaker 1 from Part A? Describe the conditions that favored the highest peak temperature in Part B. *(Making comparisons)* _____

_____

_____

Critical Thinking: Applications

1. Given the hazards associated with the FRH, would it make a good "instant hot pad" to use for applying heat to a sore or stiff body part? Explain. *(Evaluating)* _____

_____

_____

2. Some of the iron, magnesium, and sodium chloride will remain exposed to atmospheric oxygen when the FRH is used as directed. Give balanced chemical equations, including values for changes in enthalpy, that describe any additional reactions that could be occur-

© Prentice-Hall, Inc.

ring. How might these reactions affect the heat production of the FRH? *(Making predictions)* _____

_____

_____

3. Hand-warming devices are available that generate heat by exposing a package of dry, inert vermiculite particles, iron powder, and table salt to the atmosphere. No water is added to this type of warmer. State the chemical equation that describes the most likely reaction for generating the heat. Refer to the thermodynamics tables in chemistry reference material or your textbook to find the change in enthalpy for this reaction. *(Applying concepts)* _____

_____

Going Further

1. Devise an experiment with a procedure similar to the one used in this investigation that will test the heat-generating capacity of iron metal powder and salt in water without magnesium. Under your teacher's supervision, perform the experiment and report your findings to the class.
2. Devise an experiment that will test the heat-generating capacity of a commercial hand warmer. You may wish to try to simulate the efficiency of a commercial hand warmer with one that you devise. Under your teacher's supervision, perform the experiment and report your findings to the class.
3. Devise a procedure that uses a double-walled calorimeter and some FRH heat-generating chemicals to find the heat generated per gram of FRH chemicals. Under your teacher's supervision, perform the experiment and report your findings to the class.
4. Using a computer with a temperature probe, produce a temperature versus time graph of several of the beakers. Discuss the significance of any differences you observe.

Determining Heat Capacity

Text reference: **Chapter 12**

Introduction

In the Middle Ages, defenders of a castle sometimes poured hot liquids down onto invaders who tried to storm the fortress walls. The liquid of choice was usually any available oil. What properties of oil do you think prompted this choice? This investigation will allow you to discover a chemical principle that has had many practical applications over the centuries, although today we look upon some of them as less than exemplary.

You know from experience that it takes much longer to heat a large kettle of water to boiling than it does a small pan of water. You reason that there is more water to be heated in the larger sample, and that is correct. You also know that the longer heating time involves a larger amount of heat. We say that the larger sample has a larger heat capacity. The heat capacity of anything—whether solid, liquid, or gas—depends on the amount of the material in the sample as well as its chemical composition. For example, every gram of water requires the same amount of heat on warming from room temperature to 100°C. It follows that the larger the sample, the greater is the amount of heat needed to reach the boiling point.

In this investigation you will find the heat capacity of a lead sinker. You will do this by finding the mass of the sinker, warming it to the boiling point of water, placing it in a sample of room-temperature water in a calorimeter, and measuring the temperature change of the water sample. From the data collected you will then calculate the heat lost by the sinker to the water and thus the lead sinker's heat capacity.

Pre-Lab Discussion

Read the entire laboratory investigation and the relevant pages of your textbook. Then answer the questions that follow.

1. What quantities do you need to know in order to determine the amount of heat released by the lead sinker in cooling to the final temperature? _____

   _____

2. What important assumption have you made in Question 1 in determining the amount of heat released by the lead sinker? _____

   _____

   _____

Name _____

3. How is each quantity in Question 1 obtained? _____

_____

_____

_____

4. What quantities do you need to know in order to determine the heat capacity of the lead sinker? _____

_____

5. How is each quantity in Question 4 obtained? _____

_____

_____

_____

6. How is the heat capacity of the lead sinker determined? _____

_____

_____

7. Why should you not use the thermometer as a stirring rod? _____

_____

_____

Problem

How can the heat capacity of a lead sinker be determined?

Materials

chemical splash goggles   2 beakers, 250-mL
laboratory apron   hot plate
lead sinker   graduated cylinder, 100-mL
laboratory balance   stirring rod
string, 20-cm   thermometer
plastic foam cup, 8-oz.

Safety

Wear your goggles and lab apron at all times during the investigation. Use caution when working with the hot plate. Never touch it with bare skin. Note the caution and alert symbols here and with certain steps of the Procedure. Refer to page *xi* for the specific precautions associated with each symbol.

Procedure

 1. Put on your goggles and lab apron.

2. Obtain a lead sinker from your instructor and find its mass. Record the mass in the Data Table. Attach a piece of string to

© Prentice-Hall, Inc.

the brass loop in the top of the sinker. The string is to be used in moving the sinker.

3. Place a plastic foam cup inside a 250-mL beaker. This will serve as your calorimeter.

 4. On a hot plate, heat to boiling about 100 mL of water contained in another 250-mL beaker. Carefully rest the sinker in the boiling water bath and leave it there for at least three minutes. The string should be left hanging outside the beaker. **CAUTION:** *The hot plate and water are very hot. Avoid touching them with bare skin.* Measure and record the temperature of the boiling water to the nearest 0.2°C.

5. Place 50.0 mL of room-temperature water in the calorimeter. Record the temperature of the water to the nearest 0.2°C. Keep the thermometer in the calorimeter for the remainder of the investigation.

6. Carefully remove the sinker from the boiling water bath and place the sinker into the water in the calorimeter.

7. Gently stir the calorimeter water with the stirring rod while continuously observing the temperature change. Record the maximum temperature to the nearest 0.2°C.

 8. When the final temperature reading has been taken, return the sinker to your instructor. Turn off the hot plate. Clean up your work area and wash your hands before leaving the laboratory.

Observations

DATA TABLE

mass of lead sinker	
volume of room-temperature water	
initial temperature of water	
final temperature of water	
temperature of boiling water	

Calculations

1. Determine the change in temperature of the water in the calorimeter.

2. Determine the heat absorbed by the 50.0 mL of water in the calorimeter in warming to the final temperature.

Name _____

3. Determine the change in temperature of the lead sinker in cooling to its final temperature.

4. Calculate the amount of heat released by the lead sinker for each one-degree Celsius change in temperature. This is the heat capacity of the sinker.

Critical Thinking: Analysis and Conclusions

1. What scientific law accounts for the assumption that the heat gained by the water in the calorimeter is equal to the heat lost by the lead sinker? *(Applying concepts)* _____
_____

2. If you had a lead sample that was double the mass of the sinker you used in the investigation, what would be the heat capacity of the heavier sample? Give the reason for your answer. *(Making comparisons)*
_____
_____
_____
_____
_____

3. What is the relationship between the specific heat of a substance and the heat capacity of a sample of that substance? *(Applying concepts)* _____
_____
_____
_____

4. Given the mass of your lead sample, calculate *c*, the specific heat of lead. *(Applying concepts)*

5. Determine the percent error for the specific heat calculated in Question 4 if the accepted value for the specific heat of lead is 0.159 J/g•°C. *(Applying concepts)*

6. Predict whether or not the values for the heat capacity of the sinkers used by your classmates will be the same as the value you obtained for your sinker. *(Making predictions)* _____

_____

_____

_____

Critical Thinking: Applications

1. The specific heat of most oils is about 2 J/g•°C, compared to a value of 4.18 J/g•°C for water. Why do you now think oil, rather than water, was the liquid of choice used by castle defenders against invading forces? *(Making comparisons)* _____

_____

_____

_____

_____

_____

2. A disc of wax has several hot metal samples placed on it. The samples are of different metals. They are all at the same temperature and have the same mass and contact area with the wax. How will the heat capacity of each metal sample affect the rate at which it melts the wax? *(Making predictions)* _____

_____

_____

Going Further

1. The procedure used in the investigation is commonly utilized in determining the specific heat of a solid or the heat capacity of a sample of a solid. Suggest a method for determining either value for a liquid.

The Ideal Gas Constant

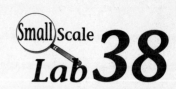

Small Scale Lab 38

Text reference: **Chapter 13**

Introduction

The ideal gas law is represented by the formula $PV = nRT$, where R is the ideal gas constant. In this laboratory investigation you will experimentally determine the value of R. To do this, you must first determine the values of the other variables in the ideal gas equation. You will generate and collect a sample of hydrogen gas and determine its volume, temperature, pressure, and the number of moles produced under laboratory conditions.

The hydrogen gas is generated in a graduated cylinder from the reaction between magnesium and hydrochloric acid. By wrapping the magnesium ribbon in a copper wire cage, you can ensure that the magnesium will remain in the acid environment. Hydrochloric acid is in excess in the reaction so that the moles of hydrogen gas produced may be determined from the moles of magnesium that react.

Pre-Lab Discussion

Read the entire laboratory investigation and the relevant pages of your textbook. Then answer the questions that follow.

1. Describe how the values for P, V, n, and T are obtained in this investigation. _____

   _____

   _____

   _____

   _____

2. Why do you think copper wire is used to make the cage for the magnesium ribbon in this reaction? _____

   _____

3. When the graduated cylinder is inverted, why does the acid flow downward? _____

4. Why is it important to tap the side of the graduated cylinder before reading the volume of gas collected? _____

   _____

5. How can you protect yourself from the hazards of working with 3 M HCl? _____

   _____

Name _____

Problem

What is the value of the ideal gas constant?

Materials

chemical splash goggles
laboratory apron
metric ruler
1.0 cm or less of magnesium
    ribbon
25 cm thin-gauge copper wire
one-hole rubber stopper to fit
    graduated cylinder
graduated cylinder, 10-mL
beaker, 400-mL

tap water
latex gloves
micropipet
3.0 M hydrochloric acid (HCl)
wash bottle
thermometer
table of vapor pressures of
    water

Safety

Wear your goggles and lab apron at all times during the investigation. Hydrochloric acid (HCl) is corrosive. Avoid spills and contact with your skin and clothing. If HCl comes in contact with your skin or clothing, inform your teacher and flush the acid with large quantities of water. Neutralize any acid spills on the work surface with baking soda.

When inserting the stopper into the graduated cylinder, tap it down gently to avoid breaking the top of the cylinder. Note the caution alert symbols here and with certain steps of the Procedure. Refer to page *xi* for the specific precautions associated with each symbol.

Procedure

1. Put on your goggles and lab apron.

2. Using a metric ruler, measure and record the exact length of the piece of magnesium (Mg) ribbon provided by your teacher. The ribbon should be no longer than 1.0 cm.

3. Your teacher will give you the mass of 100.0 cm of Mg ribbon. Record this mass, which will be used as a conversion factor to determine the mass of your piece of Mg ribbon.

4. Wrap the copper wire around the magnesium ribbon, making a cage that surrounds the ribbon, as shown in Figure 38–1 (left). Leave a handle of copper wire approximately 6 cm long.

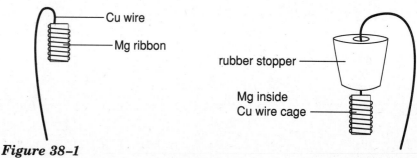

Figure 38–1

5. Insert the handle end of the copper wire into the one-hole rubber stopper as shown in Figure 38–1 (right). When the stopper is inserted into the graduated cylinder, the copper wire cage and Mg ribbon will be inside the cylinder.

6. Fill the 400-mL beaker or other container approximately half full with water.

7. Put on latex gloves. Use a dropper or micropipet to add approximately 3 mL of 3.0 *M* hydrochloric acid (HCl) to the graduated cylinder. **CAUTION:** *Hydrochloric acid is corrosive. Avoid contact with skin or clothing. Flush any spills with water and notify your teacher.*

8. Using the wash bottle, gently fill the graduated cylinder by drizzling water down the cylinder's inner side to avoid mixing. Because HCl has a greater density than water, the acid will remain at the bottom of the cylinder.

9. Insert the stopper into the graduated cylinder by tapping gently so as to avoid cracking the cylinder. The copper wire cage should be suspended at the top of the cylinder. Holding your finger over the hole in the rubber stopper, quickly invert the cylinder into the beaker of water. When the top of the cylinder is underwater you may remove your finger. Rest the cylinder in the beaker.

10. Notice the appearance of the acid solution inside the cylinder. Record any indication of a chemical reaction.

11. When the Mg ribbon is no longer reacting, tap the side of the cylinder to release any trapped bubbles.

12. Let the cylinder sit for 5 minutes. Using the thermometer, read and record the temperature in the beaker.

13. Determine and record the atmospheric pressure in the lab. Determine the water vapor pressure from a reference table.

14. Lift the graduated cylinder slightly until the levels of water inside and outside the cylinder are the same. See Figure 38–2.

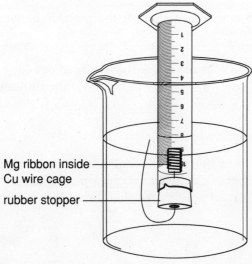

Mg ribbon inside
Cu wire cage

rubber stopper

Figure 38–2

Name_____

15. Read and record the volume of gas in the cylinder. Remember that you are reading an inverted cylinder.

16. After reading the volume of gas, remove the cylinder from the beaker and dispose of the contents of the beaker by pouring it down the drain. Turn the cylinder right side up, remove the stopper holding the copper cage, and dispose of any remaining liquid down the sink. Note the appearance of the copper wire.

 17. Clean up your work area and wash your hands before leaving the laboratory.

Observations

length of Mg ribbon   _____

mass of 100.0 cm Mg ribbon   _____

temperature of the reaction system   _____

atmospheric pressure   _____

water vapor pressure at system temperature   _____

volume of gas produced   _____

Calculations

1. Calculate the number of moles of Mg that reacted, using the length of Mg ribbon you used, the mass of 100.0 cm Mg ribbon provided by your teacher, and the molar mass of Mg.

                              moles Mg = _____

2. Write the balanced equation for the reaction between Mg and HCl.

   _____

3. Determine the value of n. Use the balanced equation and the number of moles of Mg that reacted to calculate the moles of H_2 produced.

                              n = _____

4. Determine the value of P. Calculate the pressure of the H_2 gas collected by subtracting the water vapor pressure from the atmospheric pressure. Convert your pressure units from mm Hg to atmospheres.

                              P = _____

5. Determine the value of *V*. Calculate the volume of gas collected in liters. Remember that you must read the bottom of the meniscus, but that the scale is inverted. Then convert the volume units from mL to L.

$$V = \text{_____}$$

6. Determine the value of *T*. Convert the temperature units of the gas collected from °C to kelvins.

$$T = \text{_____}$$

7. Using the pressure, volume, temperature, and moles of H_2, calculate the value of the gas constant where $R = PV/nT$. Include all units in your answer.

$$R = \text{_____}$$

Critical Thinking: Analysis and Conclusions

1. Why is it necessary to subtract the value for water vapor pressure from atmospheric pressure to determine the pressure of the H_2 gas? *(Interpreting data)* _____

_____

_____

2. What evidence of a chemical reaction did you observe? *(Making inferences)* _____

_____

3. At the end of the reaction, how did the appearance of the copper wire compare with that of the magnesium ribbon? What can you conclude about the effect of HCl on copper wire? *(Making comparisons, drawing conclusions)* _____

_____

4. Using the accepted value for the ideal gas constant, determine the percent deviation of the value you calculated. Then explain the possible sources of experimental error in this investigation. *(Interpreting data)*

_____

_____

_____

_____

Name_____

Critical Thinking: Applications

1. What is the importance of your choice of units in expressing the value of the ideal gas constant? *(Making judgments)* _____
   _____

2. Convert the pressure of dry H_2 gas to kilopascals and calculate the value of R in kPa-L/mol-K. *(Applying concepts)*

3. If all other conditions remained the same, how would the value of R change if your investigation made use of a gas other than hydrogen? Explain. *(Making predictions)* _____
   _____
   _____
   _____

4. How could you demonstrate that the copper wire did not participate in the chemical reaction? *(Designing experiments)* _____
   _____
   _____

Going Further

1. Under the supervision of your teacher, try this experiment with other metals, such as iron, aluminum, or zinc. Before you begin, find out the safety precautions you must follow.

2. Use the experimental value you found for R to calculate the molar volume of a gas at STP. Compare your calculation to the accepted value.

Diffusion of Two Gases

Small Scale Lab 39

APPLICATION

Text reference: **Chapter 13**

Introduction

Have you ever noticed how quickly a helium balloon deflates? A common latex balloon filled with helium will lose much of its gas overnight, yet the same balloon filled with air will remain inflated for several days. Why is this so? The kinetic-molecular theory states that gases consist of tiny particles in constant rapid motion. These particles have mass, and they frequently make elastic collisions with each other and the walls of their container. Different gases, however, differ in the rate at which they are able to move among each other (diffusion) or through tiny openings (effusion), such as a hole in a balloon.

Thomas Graham recognized that the different rates of movement of gas particles at constant temperature are related to the molar masses of the gases. Graham's law compares the rates of diffusion or effusion of any two gases as follows: Under constant temperature and pressure, the rate of diffusion or effusion of two gases is inversely proportional to the square roots of their molar masses. Mathematically, Graham's law may be expressed as a ratio:

$$\frac{r_a}{r_b} = \frac{\sqrt{\mathcal{M}_b}}{\sqrt{\mathcal{M}_a}}$$

In this formula, r_a is the rate of diffusion (or effusion) of a gas and r_b is the rate of diffusion (or effusion) of a second gas. Similarly, $\mathcal{M}_a$ and $\mathcal{M}_b$ are the respective molar masses of the two gases.

In this laboratory investigation, you will compare the rates of diffusion of ammonia (NH_3) gas and hydrogen chloride (HCl) gas. These two gases react chemically to form tiny white ammonium chloride (NH_4Cl) crystals that appear as an aerosol, or suspension, in the air. In Part A of the investigation, you will observe the results of the reaction between NH_3 and HCl. In Part B, you will place solutions containing these gases at different locations in a reaction tube. By measuring where in the tube the aerosol forms, you will be able to use Graham's law to find the relative rates of diffusion of the gases.

Pre-Lab Discussion

Read the entire laboratory investigation and the relevant pages of your textbook. Then answer the questions that follow.

1. In Part A, why is it important to use drops of HCl and NH_3 that are small enough to avoid drips or runs when the petri dish is

    inverted? _____

    _____

    _____

Lab 39
APPLICATION

Name_____

2. In Part A, what is the purpose of repeatedly turning the petri dish over? _____

_____

3. What are the hazards of working with concentrated solutions of HCl and NH_3, and what precautions should you follow? _____

_____

_____

_____

4. How will you know when gaseous NH_3 and HCl molecules have made contact with each other?_____

5. Using the molar masses of the gases and Graham's law, calculate the ratio of the diffusion rate of NH_3 to the diffusion rate of HCl that you expect to find in Part B of this investigation.

6. Predict whether the NH_4Cl crystals will form in Part B closer to the source of NH_3 or HCl gas. _____

_____

Problem

Will two gases of differing molar mass diffuse toward each other at different rates?

Materials

Part A

chemical splash goggles
laboratory apron
2 micropipets
tap water
petri dish
tissues

latex gloves
black paper
HCl solution, 6.0 *M*
NH_3 solution, 6.0 *M*
wash bottle

Part B

chemical splash goggles
laboratory apron
latex gloves
2 clear plastic straws
scissors
clear adhesive tape
2 cotton swabs

marking pen
beaker, 100- or 250-mL
tap water
micropipet containing
    concentrated HCl
micropipet containing
    concentrated NH_3

210

© Prentice-Hall, Inc.

Safety

Wear your goggles and lab apron at all times in the laboratory. Gaseous ammonia (NH_3) and hydrogen chloride (HCl) molecules are irritating to skin, nasal passages, and eyes. Hydrochloric acid solution is corrosive. Wear gloves. Do not sniff these solutions. Do not let these solutions contact your skin or clothing. When the pipets containing these solutions are no longer needed, return them to the container from which they were obtained. At the end of Part A, flush these solutions from the petri dish with a stream of water from a wash bottle.

Do Part B in a fume hood. Before discarding the cotton swabs, place them in a small beaker of water to dilute the hydrochloric acid and ammonia solutions. If these solutions contact your skin or clothing, flush these areas with great quantities of water and notify your teacher.

Note the caution alert symbols here and with certain steps of the Procedure. Refer to page *xi* for the specific precautions associated with each symbol.

Procedure

Part A

1. Put on your goggles and lab apron. Using a micropipet, place a small drop of water on the inner surface of the top plate of the petri dish. The drop needs to be small enough that it does not run or drip when the plate is turned over.

2. Practice placing one drop of water on the inside of the top plate and one on the bottom plate, closing the petri dish, and flipping it over several times until you can size the drops small enough that they remain in place. Dry the petri dish with tissue paper.

3. Put on latex gloves. Place the petri dish on the piece of black paper. Remove the top plate and hold it open side up.

4. Place a half drop of 6.0 *M* hydrochloric acid solution (HCl) about 1 cm from the center on the inside of the plate. Very carefully turn the plate back over without allowing the drop of acid to run. Set the top plate near the bottom half of the dish. **CAUTION:** *Hydrochloric acid is corrosive to skin and clothing and its vapors are irritating to lungs and eyes. Avoid contact with the solution and inhaling its vapors. If contact occurs, flush with plenty of cold water and notify your teacher.*

5. Place a half drop of 6.0 *M* ammonia solution (NH_3) about 1 cm from the center of the bottom plate. **CAUTION:** *Ammonia solution is irritating to skin, lungs, and eyes. Avoid contact with the solution and inhaling its vapors. If contact occurs, flush with plenty of cold water and notify your teacher.*

6. Immediately place the top plate over the bottom plate so that the drops of solution do not line up, as shown in Figure 39–1. Observe the reaction and record your observations.

7. Without opening the petri dish, rotate the top plate slowly. Observe and record your observations.

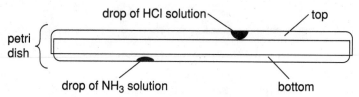

Figure 39–1

8. Invert the closed petri dish. Note whether the relative position of the drops has any effect on the reaction.

9. Bring the petri dish back to the original position. Try to determine whether the reaction seems to occur nearer to the surface of the drop of HCl solution or the drop of NH_3 solution. Continue to turn the petri dish over and back until you have completed your observations.

10. Place the pipets containing the HCl and NH_3 solutions back in the containers where you obtained them.

11. With the wash bottle, rinse the drops of solution from the petri dish. Dry the dish with tissue paper.

Part B

12. Put on your goggles and lab apron. Splice the two straws into one tube as follows. Using the scissors cut a small slit (about 7 mm) in the end of one straw. Push the cut end into one end of the other straw. Secure the straws together with a piece of clear adhesive tape, as shown in Figure 39–2.

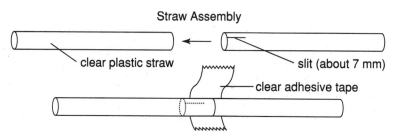

Figure 39–2

13. Place a cotton swab into each end of the straw tube. Using a marking pen, mark the tube at the points where the swabs have penetrated, as shown in Figure 39–3. These marks represent the starting points from which the gases will diffuse. Measure and record the total distance between these two marks.

14. Use the marking pen to mark one of the cotton swabs. This swab will be used for the hydrochloric acid (HCl).

15. Half fill a small beaker with water and set it aside for use in Step 19.

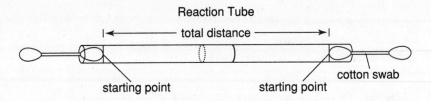

Reaction Tube

|← total distance →|

starting point   starting point

cotton swab

Figure 39–3

 16. Put on latex gloves. Using a thin-stem or micropipet labeled "conc. HCl," place 2 drops of concentrated hydrochloric acid solution on the marked swab. Using a micropipet labeled "conc. NH₃," place 2 drops of concentrated ammonia solution on the other swab. **CAUTION:** *Work under a fume hood. Concentrated HCl and NH₃ are toxic and irritating to eyes and nasal passages. HCl is corrosive to skin and clothing. Avoid contact with the solutions and their vapors.*

17. While one person holds the straw tube steady, another person should simultaneously insert the two wet swabs in opposite ends of the tube. The swabs should penetrate to the points you previously marked.

18. Watch for the formation of a white aerosol ring inside the tube. The ring consists of tiny crystals of ammonium chloride (NH₄Cl). Measure and record the distance traveled by the HCl gas from its initial mark to the point where the ring forms. Do the same for the NH₃ gas.

 19. Remove the wet swabs and immediately place them in the beaker of water you prepared in Step 15. This precaution will minimize the escape of HCl and NH₃ gases into the laboratory. It will also dilute the concentrated solutions and allow them to neutralize each other.

20. Rinse the beaker and swabs thoroughly with water and discard the swabs as directed by your teacher. Rinse the straw tube with water from the wash bottle and discard as directed by the teacher.

21. Clean up your work area and wash your hands before leaving the laboratory.

Observations

Part A
DATA TABLE

Step	Observation
6	
7	
8	
9	

Part B

total distance between the marks _____

distance traveled by the HCl gas _____

distance traveled by the NH$_3$ gas _____

Critical Thinking: Analysis and Conclusions

1. Write a balanced chemical equation to describe the reaction you observed. Include the states of the reactants and products. *(Interpreting data)* _____

2. Give a possible reason for your observations of the location of the NH$_4$Cl crystals that formed in Part A. *(Making inferences)* _____

   _____

   _____

   _____

3. Calculate the ratio (d_{NH_3}/d_{HCl}) of the distances traveled by the gases in Part B. How does your experimental ratio compare to the diffusion ratio you calculated in Pre-Lab question 5? *(Making comparisons)*

   _____

4. Calculate the percent error of the experiment.

5. Are the results of your investigation consistent with Graham's law? Explain. *(Drawing conclusions)* _____

   _____

   _____

Critical Thinking: Applications

1. Suppose the distance between the solutions in the straw tube is 40.0 cm. Use Graham's law to calculate the distance the NH$_3$ and HCl gases would travel before they collide. *(Making predictions)*

2. Consider the latex balloon described in the Introduction to this investigation. Explain why the balloon deflates more quickly if it is filled with helium than if it were filled with air. *(Developing hypotheses)*

   _____

   _____

3. Suppose you had an unknown gas. How could you use Graham's law to design an experiment that would help you determine the identity of the gas? *(Designing experiments)* _____

_____

_____

_____

_____

Going Further

1. Two gases at the same temperature have the same kinetic energy. Use the formula $KE = \frac{1}{2}Mv^2$ to derive Graham's law for two gases.

2. Research how Graham's law was applied during World War II to extract uranium-235 for use in nuclear reactions.

3. Compare the rates of loss of helium from a Mylar balloon and a latex balloon. Research possible reasons for differences you observe.

How Many Drops Can You Pile on a Penny?

Small Scale Lab **40**
APPLICATION

Text Reference: **Chapter 14**

Introduction

Have you ever seen how water striders can walk across the surface of a pond, or how a mosquito can land on a puddle of water without sinking? Although the strider's weight pushes down on the water, forces within the water create a "skin" that supports the strider on the water's surface. This phenomenon is called surface tension.

The forces within water that are responsible for surface tension originate at the molecular level. As you know, a water molecule is polar. The oxygen atom has a partial negative charge, and each hydrogen atom has a partial positive charge. As a result, electrical attractions occur between the oxygen atom of one molecule and the hydrogen atom of another molecule, as illustrated in Figure 40–1. These intermolecular attractive forces are called hydrogen bonds (H-bonds).

water molecule

hydrogen bonding between
water molecules

Figure 40–1

Surface tension can be affected by substances dissolved in water. If a substance interferes with hydrogen bonding, the surface tension of water decreases. If a substance enhances hydrogen bonding, the surface tension of the water increases. In this investigation, you will observe the effects of several solutes in water. The ionic or molecular structures of the solutes you will be using are illustrated in Figure 40–2 on the next page. You will use your knowledge of molecular geometry and the behavior of molecular dipoles to make predictions about the effects of these solutes on the surface tension of water.

In Part A, you will investigate the surface tension of water by seeing how many drops of water can be piled on top of a penny. You will observe the shape and behavior of the water as surface tension holds the drops of water together. In Part B, you will design your own experiment to determine the effects of three substances on the surface tension of water: liquid detergent, sodium chloride (NaCl), and sodium carbonate (Na_2CO_3).

Name _____

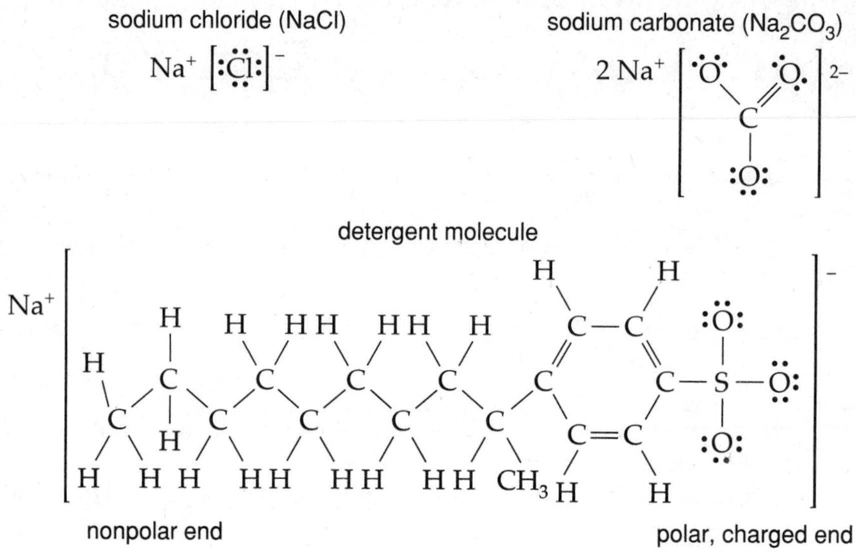

sodium chloride (NaCl)

Na⁺ [:C̈l:]⁻

sodium carbonate (Na₂CO₃)

2 Na⁺ [structure]²⁻

detergent molecule

[molecular structure diagram]

nonpolar end   polar, charged end

Figure 40–2

Pre-Lab Discussion

Read the entire laboratory investigation and the relevant pages of your textbook. Then answer the questions that follow.

1. Explain how the intermolecular forces between water molecules act to create the "skin" or surface tension upon which water striders can walk. _____

    _____

    _____

2. What causes water molecules to be polar? _____

    _____

    _____

3. Which part of a detergent molecule allows it to dissolve in water? Which part of a detergent molecule allows it to dissolve in oily substances? _____

    _____

    _____

4. Predict whether the nature of detergent molecules would increase or decrease hydrogen bonding in water. Explain. _____

    _____

    _____

5. What is viscosity? How is viscosity related to the surface tension of a liquid? _____

    a liquid? _____

Problem

What effects do chemicals have on the surface tension of water?

Materials

Part A

chemical splash goggles
laboratory apron
micropipet

tap water
clean, dry penny
paper towel

Part B

3 micropipets
3 beakers, 100-mL
graduated cylinder, 10-mL
10 mL liquid detergent solution
10 mL saturated sodium chlo-
    ride (NaCl) solution

10 mL saturated sodium carbon-
    ate (Na_2CO_3) solution
tap water

Safety

Wear your goggles and lab apron at all times during the investigation.
Sodium carbonate is irritating to the skin. Do not let this material come
in contact with your skin. Note the caution alert symbols here and with
certain steps of the Procedure. Refer to page *xi* for the specific precautions
associated with each symbol.

Procedure

Part A

 1. Put on your goggles and lab apron. Obtain one micropipet and
    a penny from your teacher.

 2. Fill the micropipet with water.

3. Place drops of water on top of the penny. Be sure to hold the
    micropipet vertically. Do not touch the penny or the water that
    is accumulating there.

4. Count the number of drops you can add before the water flows
    off the penny. Record the total.

5. Dry the penny and repeat Steps 3 and 4 two more times, or
    until you get consistent results.

Part B

6. You will be given three solutions: sodium carbonate (Na_2CO_3),
    sodium chloride (NaCl), and 1% liquid detergent. Your task is

to design and carry out an experiment to determine their effect on the surface tension of water. Write your plans on a separate piece of paper.

7. Design a procedure for your test that includes (a) a control, (b) steps that will ensure that the results are reliable (or reproducible), and (c) your predictions of the effect of each solute.

8. Create a table that will organize your data clearly.

9. Obtain the necessary materials and run the experiment.

 10. Clean up your work area and wash your hands before leaving the laboratory.

Observations

Part A

Number of drops of water observed:

Trial 1 _____

Trial 2 _____

Trial 3 _____

Average _____

Critical Thinking: Analysis and Conclusions

1. Compare the average number of drops placed on your penny with the results of your classmates. What might account for any differences? *(Making comparisons)* _____

_____

2. What happened when the water finally flowed off the penny? Explain in terms of the chemical and physical forces involved. *(Drawing conclusions)* _____

_____

_____

_____

3. In Part B, what were your predictions for the effect of each solute on the surface tension of water? *(Making predictions)* _____

_____

4. What was the control in your procedure? *(Designing experiments)*

_____

5. What steps did you include in your procedure to increase the reliability or reproducibility of your results? *(Designing experiments)*

_____

_____

6. Do the results of your investigation agree with your hypotheses? *(Drawing conclusions)* _____

7. Is it correct to say that the addition of salts to water will always increase the surface tension of water? Explain. *(Drawing conclusions)*

_____

_____

8. What effect, if any, did the detergent have on surface tension? Why? *(Interpreting data)* _____

_____

_____

Critical Thinking: Applications

1. State any questions or projects for further investigation that surfaced as a result of your investigation. *(Developing models)* _____

_____

2. Make judgments about the hypotheses made by the class, and be ready to discuss your opinions. *(Making judgments)* _____

_____

3. People usually think of water as being wet. If water alone is used to wash clothing, however, it doesn't penetrate the fabric very well. How does the addition of detergent make water "wetter", that is, more capable of penetrating the pores of fabric? *(Applying concepts)*

_____

_____

_____

_____

4. There are a lot of cleaners and detergents on the market that contain sodium carbonate (Na_2CO_3). It is known that sodium carbonate neutralizes odors. Based upon the results of your experiment, does sodium carbonate play another role as well? *(Applying concepts)*

_____

_____

5. When you read the contents of some cleaning powders or liquids, they often list anionic surfactants. Predict what these anionic surfactants might be and how they might act. *(Making predictions)* _____

_____

_____

Name _____

6. Viscosity is a property described as a measure of the resistance of a liquid to flow. This resistance is affected by the same intermolecular forces as is surface tension. Which of the liquids you tested for surface tension in Part B of this investigation do you predict will exhibit the greatest relative viscosity and the least relative viscosity? *(Making predictions)* _____

_____

_____

Going Further

1. Investigate the effect of temperature on the surface tension of a liquid. First, hypothesize how varying the temperature of a liquid might affect its surface tension. Then design an experiment to test your hypothesis, taking into consideration any safety precautions you must follow. Under the supervision of your teacher, perform the experiment and present your findings to the class.

Melting Points of Common Substances

Small Scale Lab 42

Text reference: **Chapter 14**

Introduction

A solid substance melts when it absorbs enough energy for its particles to overcome the attractive forces that lock them together. The particles then can slide around and about each other randomly, giving the substance fluid properties. Nearly all pure substances have distinct melting points that are determined by the strength of attractions between their particles. The greater the attractive forces are, the more energy is needed to overcome them.

Molecular compounds have melting points considerably lower than those of ionic compounds, which contain strong electrostatic attractions between their ions. Among molecular compounds, differences in melting points depend on the degree of intermolecular forces that occur. These forces include dipole-dipole forces, dispersion forces, and hydrogen bonding.

In this investigation, you will determine the melting points of four molecular substances by heating small amounts of each substance in capillary tubes immersed in oil. You will also compare the structural formulas of the substances and determine what factors might account for the similarities and differences in the melting points that you find.

Pre-Lab Discussion

Read the entire laboratory investigation and the relevant pages of your textbook. Then answer the questions that follow.

1. What is a polar bond? A polar molecule? _____
    _____
    _____
    _____
    _____
    _____

2. What causes dipole-dipole interactions? _____
    _____
    _____

3. What are dispersion forces and what causes them? _____
    _____
    _____
    _____

Name _____

4. How is molar mass related to the dispersion forces in a nonpolar substance? _____

_____

_____

5. What effect would hydrogen bonding have on the melting point of a substance? _____

_____

_____

6. Look at the structural formulas of the substances in Figure 42–1. Determine whether they are polar or nonpolar, and predict how their melting points will compare. (Hint: Look for the presence of polar bonds arranged in such a way that their effects do not cancel out.)

_____

_____

7. Why must naphthalene (moth balls) be kept in a tightly capped container and stored under a fume hood? _____

_____

_____

_____

8. Why is a mineral oil bath used instead of a water bath? _____

_____

_____

benzoic acid

naphthalene

sucrose

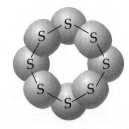
sulfur-8

Figure 42–1

© Prentice-Hall, Inc.

9. Why must the mineral oil in the beaker be changed after each determination? _____

_____

Problem

What factors affect the melting point of a molecular substance?

Materials

chemical splash goggles
laboratory apron
latex gloves
4 capillary tubes
beaker tongs
matches
lab burner
spatula
4 pieces of glassine paper
small amounts (a few crystals) of
    benzoic acid ($C_6H_5CO_2H$)
    sulfur (S_8)
    naphthalene ($C_{10}H_8$)
    sucrose ($C_{12}H_{22}O_{11}$)

ring stand
clamp
iron ring
wire gauze
beaker, 150-mL
mineral oil
4 rubber bands
thermometer, 0°–250°C, with
    one-hole stopper
hot pads

Safety

Wear your goggles and lab apron at all times while you are in the laboratory. When you seal one end of a capillary tube, hold the tube with beaker tongs, and hold the open end of the tube away from you. Wear gloves while filling the capillary tubes. Keep naphthalene and sulfur away from burner flames, as they are flammable. The vapors of naphthalene are toxic. Keep it in a tightly capped container and use only in a fume hood. Do not breathe its vapors. Use hot pads for handling the beaker of hot mineral oil.

Note the caution alert symbols here and with certain steps of the Procedure. Refer to page *xi* for the specific precautions associated with each symbol.

Procedure

Part A

1. Put on your goggles and laboratory apron.

 2. Light the burner. Seal one end of each of four capillary tubes by holding the end of the tube in the tip of the blue flame of a lab burner. Allow the tubes to cool. **CAUTION:** *Tie back loose hair and clothing. Capillary tubes are fragile. Handle gently. Use tongs to hold the capillary tube when heating, and point the open end of the tube away from you.* Turn off the burner.

Name_____

3. Put on gloves. Using a clean spatula, obtain a small amount (a tipful) of one solid to be tested and place it on a sheet of glassine paper. Tap the open end of a capillary tube in the solid to capture a few crystals. Turn the tube over and gently tap against the counter to shake the crystals to the bottom. Continue this process until the tube has about 1 cm of crystals. Tape the tube to a sheet of paper and label it. Repeat this procedure for each of the other three compounds. **CAUTION:** *Naphthalene should be used in a fume hood. Do not breathe its vapors. Wear gloves to protect your hands from corrosive substances.*

4. Fill the beaker half full with mineral oil. Set up the apparatus as diagramed in Figure 42–2, using a ring stand, iron ring, wire gauze, clamp, and burner.

5. Secure the capillary tube to the thermometer with a rubber band so that the bulb of the thermometer is even with the sealed end of the capillary tube. Clamp the stopper that contains the thermometer to the ring stand so that the mouth of the capillary tube is above the surface of the mineral oil and the solid in the tube is completely immersed.

6. Light the burner. Heat the oil slowly so that the temperature rises only about 2–3 C° per minute. Keep a close watch on the solid in the tube. Record the temperature at which the solid is completely melted. **CAUTION:** *Keep hair and clothing away from burner flames. The oil will become very hot. Do not touch the beaker with your bare hands. Use tongs or a hot pad.*

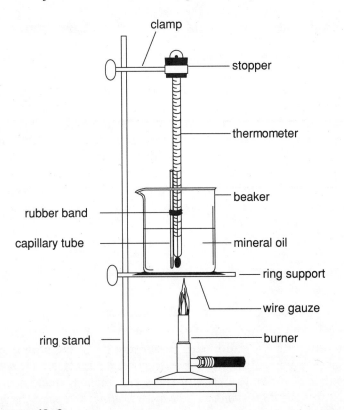

Figure 42–2

7. Carefully remove the beaker with the hot oil from the apparatus and pour the hot oil into a receptacle marked for this purpose. Refill the beaker with unheated oil. Discard the capillary tube in the container marked for glass disposal.

8. Repeat Steps 6 and 7 with the remaining three substances.

 9. Clean up your work area and wash your hands before leaving the laboratory.

Observations

DATA TABLE 1

Substance	Melting Point (°C)	Molar Mass (g/mol)
benzoic acid		
naphthalene		
sucrose		
sulfur		

Critical Thinking: Analysis and Conclusions

 1. Calculate and compare the molar masses of the substances tested. Write the values in Data Table 1. *(Making comparisons)* _____

_____

2. Rank the substances in order from lowest to highest melting point in the following table. Look back at your answers to Pre-Lab Question 6 and write the polarity of each substance on the appropriate line. *(Making comparisons)*

DATA TABLE 2

Substance	Melting Point (°C)	Polarity

3. Describe the relationship between a substance's polarity and its melting point, using an example from your data. *(Drawing conclusions)*

_____

_____

Name _____

4. What factor could account for the conclusion you formed in Pre-Lab Question 1? *(Making inferences)* _____

_____

_____

5. What factor could account for the difference in melting points between the two nonpolar substances or between the two polar substances? Explain. *(Making inferences)* _____

_____

_____

_____

_____

6. How do the predictions you made in Pre-Lab Question 6 compare to the actual results of your experiment? *(Drawing conclusions)*

_____

Critical Thinking: Applications

1. What is the freezing point of each substance tested in the investigation? Explain. *(Applying concepts)* _____

_____

_____

_____

2. Does the nature of intermolecular forces change when a substance goes from a solid to a liquid? Explain. *(Applying concepts)* _____

_____

_____

_____

3. Water is polar and contains hydrogen bonds, while sulfur is nonpolar and does not contain hydrogen bonds. Explain why water melts at a temperature below the melting point of sulfur. *(Developing hypotheses)*

_____

_____

Going Further

1. Make a list of the types of substances whose melting points could not be determined by the procedure used in this investigation. Explain why the procedure would not work, and give at least one example of each type of substance.

T-Shirt Chromatography

Lab 43
APPLICATION

Text reference: **Chapter 15**

Introduction

Have you ever been caught in the rain on your way home from school and gotten your notebooks all wet? If your notes were written in water-soluble ink, they would be turned into a colorful blur, which would not be much help if you had a quiz scheduled for the next day. This everyday occurrence is an example of a process called chromatography.

In chromatography, solutes are distributed along a medium by a moving solvent. In this way, a liquid or gaseous mixture is separated into its components. The term *chromatography* comes from two ancient Greek words, *chroma* meaning "color" and *graphein* meaning "to write." The molecules of the solutes have different masses, and so they travel along a medium—such as paper as it becomes wet—at different rates. Lighter molecules travel faster than heavier molecules. The resulting pattern is called a chromatogram.

In this investigation, you will be separating a familiar mixture—indelible ink—into its constituent compounds. Indelible ink is a nonpolar compound and is insoluble in a polar solvent such as water. Therefore, a solvent such as 2-propanol, which is only slightly polar, must be used. Figure 43–1 shows the structure of 2-propanol, commonly known as rubbing alcohol or isopropyl alcohol. When indelible ink is placed on a medium, such as cotton cloth, and 2-propanol is added slowly, the ink separates as each component is carried along by the traveling solvent.

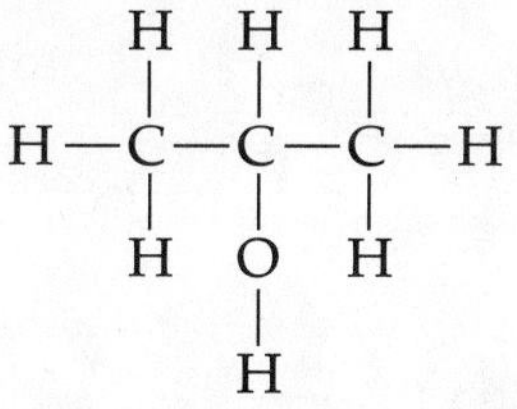

Figure 43–1

Pre-Lab Discussion

Read the entire laboratory investigation and the relevant pages of your textbook. Then answer the questions that follow.

1. How would you define *chromatography?* _____

_____

_____

2. What is a solute? What is the solute in this investigation? _____

_____

3. What is a solvent? What is the solvent in this investigation? _____
_____
_____

4. Why is a medium necessary in chromatography? What medium is used in this investigation? _____
_____

5. Why is 2-propanol used instead of water in this investigation?
_____
_____

6. What makes 2-propanol slightly polar? _____
_____

7. Why should you take care not to expose the 2-propanol to heat or flames? _____

8. Why do you think the ink will separate into its component compounds? _____
_____
_____

Problem

How can you separate a mixture using chromatography?

Materials

chemical splash goggles
laboratory apron
white cotton T-shirt, prewashed
   without fabric softener
large can or jar
elastic band

5 permanent felt-tip markers,
   different colors
2-propanol
dropper
large plastic bag

Safety

Wear your goggles and lab apron at all times during the investigation. Make sure there are no open flames in the lab, because 2-propanol is flammable.

    Note the caution alert symbols here and with certain steps of the Procedure. Refer to page *xi* for the specific precautions associated with each symbol.

Procedure

1. Put on your goggles and lab apron. Stretch a single thickness of cloth of the T-shirt over the open top of the can or jar. Pull the cloth taut and secure it with an elastic band placed around the outside of the can or jar. See Figure 43–2.

Name _____

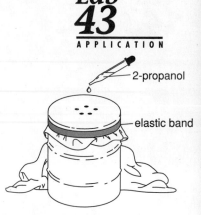

2. Select a marker and make a 5-dot circle that is about the size of a quarter at the center of the stretched fabric.

 3. Fill a dropper with 2-propanol and slowly drip it onto the center of the circle, as shown in Figure 43–2. **CAUTION:** *Make sure there are no open flames in your lab because 2-propanol is flammable.* Continue dripping the 2-propanol onto the cloth until the solvent has spread to the edges of the can or jar.

4. Allow the wet section of the T-shirt to dry.

5. Repeat Steps 1–4 with each of the other markers, using a different color marker each time to make another set of dots or to make creative patterns. Record your observations.

6. If desired, repeat Steps 1–5 on a new section of the T-shirt.

7. After all the chromatography patterns have developed, allow the T-shirt to dry completely. Place the dry T-shirt in a plastic bag to bring home.

 8. Dispose of any excess 2-propanol as directed by your teacher. Rinse out the can or jar and the dropper with water. Clean up your work area and wash your hands before leaving the laboratory.

9. At home, you can iron the T-shirt to help set the inks. For the first machine washing, wash the T-shirt by itself in case any of the inks run.

Figure 43–2

Observations

DATA TABLE

Color Trial	Observations
1	
2	
3	
4	
5	

Critical Thinking: Analysis and Conclusions

1. Why was it necessary to stretch the cloth taut? What do you think would have happened if the cloth had remained loose? (*Making inferences*) _____

_____

2. Which marker contained the greatest number of compounds? The fewest? How were you able to tell? (*Interpreting data*) _____

_____

_____

3. What differences were there between your results and the predictions you made in the Pre-Lab Discussion? *(Making comparisons)* _____

_____

_____

4. Explain how the components of each ink separate. What can you infer about the molecules making up the color that travels the greatest distance? The least distance? *(Making inferences)* _____

_____

_____

Critical Thinking: Applications

1. Predict what would have happened in the investigation if a polar solvent had been used. *(Making predictions)* _____

_____

_____

2. Are "permanent" markers truly permanent? Explain. *(Applying concepts)* _____

_____

_____

3. Chromatography is often used to identify unknown compounds. Explain how this might be done. *(Applying concepts)* _____

_____

_____

_____

_____

Going Further

1. Cotton was used in this investigation. Find out if other fabrics work equally well. With the approval and supervision of your teacher, try this investigation using swatches of rayon, wool, or polyester.
2. Redesign this investigation so that it works with water-soluble inks.
3. Research the uses of chromatography in measuring and monitoring pollutants in air and water. Prepare an oral report to present to your class.

Boiling Points of Solutions   Lab 44

Introduction

You may know that the boiling and freezing points of a solution are different from the boiling and freezing points of a pure solvent. Adding a solute to a solvent elevates the boiling point and depresses the freezing point. There are many everyday examples of this chemical principle. Antifreeze is added to the water in automobile radiators to prevent both boiling over in hot weather and freezing in cold weather. Saltwater harbors may freeze during prolonged cold spells, but only when the temperature of the salt water is much lower than 0°C. Adding table salt to cooking water is probably the most familiar example of a solute elevating the boiling point of a solution.

When antifreeze is added to a car radiator there are well-defined mixing directions to be followed. As with all other solutions, the molality of the antifreeze-water mixture determines the temperature at which the solution will boil. When one mole of particles is dissolved in one kilogram of solvent (a one molal solution), the boiling point is elevated by a precise amount depending on the solvent. If the solvent is water, the increase will be $K_b = 0.52$°C for a one molal solution. (This figure is a constant.) For nondissociating solutes, there is no change in the number of particles as the solute dissolves, so the temperature change for the solution is determined by multiplying the molality by the solvent constant, according to the following formula:

$$\Delta T_b = K_b m$$

As ionic solids dissolve, they dissociate, resulting in at least two moles of particles in solution for each mole of crystalline solute. The molal concentration of the ions in solution increases—doubling, tripling, and so on. Accordingly, the change in temperature for a solvent's boiling point is two, three, or more times the value of the solvent constant.

In this investigation, you will find the boiling points of distilled water, a urea-water solution, and a salt-water solution. Temperature readings will be taken for the samples as each is heated from room temperature to the boiling point. The time and temperature data will be plotted on a single graph. From the graph you can compare the boiling points of the different samples. Where the boiling points of the samples differ, you can suggest reasons for the differences based on an examination of the chemical formulas of the solutes.

Pre-Lab Discussion

Read the entire laboratory investigation and the relevant pages of your textbook. Then answer the questions that follow.

1. What is the molality of a solution if 0.0300 moles of nonionizing solute dissolve in 15.0 mL of water?

2. What is the concentration of the particles in solution in Question 1?

   _____

   _____

3. Calculate the concentration of particles in solution if 0.0300 moles of an ionic solid such as $CaCl_2$ dissolve in 15.0 mL of water. _____

   _____

4. How many grams of urea (NH_2CONH_2) equal 0.0300 moles of urea?

   _____

5. How many grams of sodium chloride (NaCl) equal 0.0300 moles of sodium chloride? _____

   _____

6. How should the test tube be heated so that the temperature increases continuously but not rapidly? _____

   _____

7. What precautions should you take when using the burner? _____

   _____

Problem

What effect do solutes have on the boiling point of a solvent?

Materials

chemical splash goggles
laboratory apron
graduated cylinder, 100-mL
distilled water
large test tube
boiling chips
thermometer
#2 cork stopper, cutaway
ring stand
ring

test-tube clamp
wire gauze square
lab burner
watch or clock with a second
   hand
urea (NH_2CONH_2)
laboratory balance
stirring rod
sodium chloride (NaCl)

Safety

Wear your goggles and lab apron at all times during the investigation. Tie back loose hair and clothing to avoid any fire hazard. Always point the open end of a test tube away from yourself and others when heating a substance. Since glass retains heat without looking hot, heated glassware should be given ample time to cool before it is handled.

Note the caution alert symbols here and with certain steps of the Procedure. Refer to page *xi* for the specific precautions associated with each symbol.

Procedure

1. Put on your goggles and lab apron.

2. Precisely measure out 15.0 mL of distilled water and pour it into the test tube. Put two or three boiling chips into the test tube.

3. Carefully insert the thermometer into the cutaway cork stopper, positioning it so the calibrations are fully visible. Place the thermometer in the test tube so that the bulb of the thermometer is about 1 cm above the bottom of the test tube.

4. Set up the ring stand and attach the ring and test-tube clamp. Place the wire gauze on the ring. Adjust the height of the ring so that the burner will fit underneath it. Put the test tube into the test-tube clamp and position it so that the bottom of the test tube just rests on the wire gauze. Rotate the clamp and test tube away from the ring.

5. Light the burner and adjust the flame to a medium setting. **CAUTION:** *Tie back loose hair and clothing to avoid any fire hazard.* Move the burner underneath the wire gauze and adjust the height of the ring so the inner cone of the burner flame just hits the gauze. Readjust the position of the test tube if necessary. Preheat the wire gauze for a minute or two without the test tube in place.

6. Find the initial temperature of the water and record it in the Data Table. Turn the clamp back so the test tube again rests on the wire gauze. The test tube should be slightly off to the side rather than directly over the flame. Record time and temperature readings at 30-second intervals. Continue until the temperature remains constant for three or four readings. If necessary, change the position of the burner so the temperature of the water increases continuously but not rapidly. **CAUTION:** *Always point the open end of a test tube away from yourself and others when heating a substance.*

7. Turn off the burner. Remove the thermometer, rinse it, and set it aside for the next trial. Keeping the hot test tube in the clamp, carefully remove the clamp and test tube from the ring stand. Pour the water in the sink and rinse out the test tube. Discard the boiling chips. **CAUTION:** *Since glass retains heat without looking hot, heated glassware should be given ample time to cool before it is handled.*

8. Using the calculations from Pre-Lab Discussion Question 4, obtain 0.0300 moles of urea and record its mass to the nearest 0.01 g. Place the urea and 15.0 mL of distilled water into the test tube. Stir gently with the stirring rod until the urea dissolves. Put two or three boiling chips into the solution.

9. Repeat Steps 3–7 for the urea-water solution.

10. Using the calculations from Pre-Lab Discussion Question 5, obtain 0.0300 moles of sodium chloride and record its mass. Place the sodium chloride and 15.0 mL of distilled water into the test tube. Stir gently with the stirring rod until the sodium chloride dissolves. Put two or three boiling chips into the solution.

11. Repeat Steps 3–7 for the sodium chloride–water solution.

12. Clean up your work area and wash your hands before leaving the laboratory.

Observations
DATA TABLE

Time (min)	Temperature (°C)		
	Distilled Water	Urea-Water	Salt-Water
0.0			
0.5			
1.0			
1.5			
2.0			
2.5			
3.0			
3.5			
4.0			
4.5			
5.0			
5.5			
6.0			
6.5			

Calculations

1. Predict the new boiling point for the urea-water solution.

2. Predict the new boiling point for the sodium chloride–water solution.

Critical Thinking: Analysis and Conclusions

1. Construct a boiling-point graph using only the data collected for temperatures above 80°C, plotting temperature as a function of time. Plot the data for all three samples—the distilled water, the urea-water solution, and the sodium chloride–water solution—on the same graph. Use different symbols or colors to differentiate among the data points for each of the three samples. Draw best-fit curves for all three sets of data points. *(Interpreting data)*

2. Examine the graph. Do you see any pattern in the boiling points of the two solutions compared to the boiling point of the distilled water?

   (Making comparisons) _____

   _____

   _____

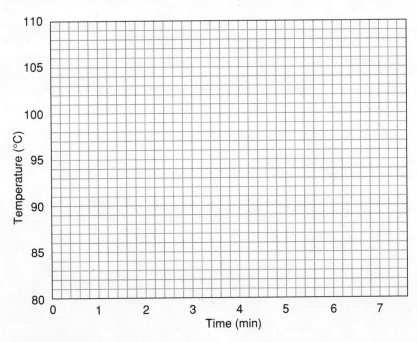

Figure 44–1

3. Examine the formulas for the two solutes, urea (NH_2CONH_2) and sodium chloride (NaCl). What inferences can you make about the effects of each of these two solutes on the boiling point of water? *(Making inferences)* _____

_____

4. Compare the boiling points of the two solutions from your graph to the predicted values from Calculations 1 and 2. Do the experimental and predicted values match? If they differ, how might you account for the differences? *(Making comparisons)* _____

_____

_____

_____

_____

_____

Critical Thinking: Applications

1. What do you think would happen to the temperature of either solution if you kept heating it? Explain. *(Making predictions)* _____

_____

_____

_____

2. In terms of particles, explain why the boiling points of the solutions are higher than the boiling point of distilled water. *(Developing models)* _____

_____

_____

_____

Going Further

1. Predict the boiling point for a 2.00 molal solution of aluminum chloride ($AlCl_3$). Under the supervision of your teacher, conduct an investigation to test your prediction. Report your findings.

Observing Chemical Equilibrium

Lab 46

Introduction

Some types of eyeglasses get darker when light shines on them. This is because a silver compound (AgCl) present in the lenses undergoes a chemical reaction when exposed to light. The products of the reaction (silver and chlorine atoms) are more opaque than the reactant. The reaction can be reversed by decreasing the amount of light, returning the sunglasses to a lighter tint:

$$AgCl(s) + light \rightleftharpoons Ag°(s) + Cl°(s)$$
$$\text{(transparent)} \qquad\qquad \text{(dark)}$$

This reaction is an example of an equilibrium reaction since, assuming the amount of light remains constant, the rate of the forward reaction is equal to the rate of the reverse reaction. In this example, light energy is considered to be a reactant.

In this investigation, you will examine three other examples of equilibrium reactions. In each case, you will establish equilibrium in the system. Then you will disturb the equilibrium by changing either the concentration of a reactant, the acid/base level, or the temperature. The effects on the equilibrium of each system will be observed.

Pre-Lab Discussion

Read the entire laboratory investigation and the relevant pages of your textbook. Then answer the questions that follow.

1. What is meant by the statement "The reaction is in equilibrium"?

   _____

2. How can equilibrium be compared to passengers entering and leaving an elevator as it changes floors? _____

   _____

   _____

3. What is meant by the term *dynamic equilibrium*? _____

   _____

   _____

4. What are some safety hazards associated with sodium hydroxide solutions? _____

   _____

Lab 46

Problem

What are some of the factors that affect the equilibrium of a chemical system?

Materials

chemical splash goggles
laboratory apron
2 beakers, 600-mL
hot plate
graduated cylinder, 10-mL
sodium chloride (NaCl)
laboratory balance
3 test tubes
3 stoppers to fit the test tubes
test-tube rack
5 micropipets, containing the following solutions:

hydrochloric acid (HCl), 1.0 M
bromthymol blue indicator
hydrochloric acid (HCl), 0.1 M
sodium hydroxide (NaOH), 0.1 M
copper(II) sulfate ($CuSO_4$), 0.1 M
marking pen
distilled water

Safety

Wear your goggles and lab apron at all times during the investigation. Hot plates get very hot, so do not touch them with bare hands. Hydrochloric acid and sodium hydroxide solutions are irritating to skin and will damage clothing. If you spill any of these, immediately wash the area with plenty of cold water and notify your teacher. Copper(II) sulfate is poisonous. Avoid contact with it.

Note the caution alert symbols here and with certain steps of the Procedure. Refer to page *xi* for the specific precautions associated with each symbol.

Procedure

Part A

 1. Put on your goggles and lab apron. Place a beaker containing about 300 mL of water on a hot plate. Set the hot plate to a moderate setting. You do not want the water to boil. **CAUTION:** *The water and hot plate will become very hot. Do not touch them with bare hands.* Go on to the next steps while you are waiting for the water to heat.

 2. Put 10.0 mL of water into a test tube. Create a saturated solution of sodium chloride by adding 4.0 g NaCl to the test tube, inserting a stopper, and shaking. Remove the stopper, allow the solution to rest for 1 minute, and then, using a micropipet, add 1.0 M HCl a few drops at a time. **CAUTION:** *Hydrochloric acid is corrosive. Avoid spilling it on your skin or clothing.* Keep adding drops until you observe a change. Record your observations.

3. Rinse the contents of the tube down the drain with plenty of water. Set the tube upside down in the test-tube rack to drain.

Part B

4. Label three test tubes *1–3*. Half-fill them with distilled water. Add three drops of bromthymol blue indicator solution to each tube. Insert stoppers into each tube and shake.

 5. Add two drops of 0.1 *M* HCl to test tube 1. Observe and record.

 6. Add two drops of 0.1 *M* NaOH to test tube 2. **CAUTION:** *Sodium hydroxide is caustic. Avoid spilling it on your skin or clothing.* Observe and record.

 7. Add two drops of 0.1 *M* HCl to test tube 3. Then add two drops of 0.1 *M* NaOH to the test tube. Observe and record.

8. Rinse out the test tubes with plenty of water.

Part C

 9. Place 3.0 mL 0.1 *M* copper(II) sulfate solution in each of two test tubes. Add an equal number of drops of 0.1 *M* NaOH to each test tube until a thick blue-white precipitate forms.

10. Place one of the tubes into the hot-water bath. After four minutes, observe and record any changes. Use the other tube for comparison.

11. Rinse the test tubes out with plenty of water. Turn off the hot plate. Clean up your work area and wash your hands before leaving the laboratory.

Observations

HCl added to saturated NaCl solution _____

0.1 *M* HCl added to bromthymol blue _____

0.1 *M* NaOH added to bromthymol blue _____

0.1 *M* HCl then 0.1 *M* NaOH added to
bromthymol blue _____

0.1 *M* NaOH added to 0.1 *M* CuSO$_4$
in hot water _____

Critical Thinking: Analysis and Conclusions

1. Write a chemical equation showing solid sodium chloride in equilibrium with aqueous sodium and chloride ions. *(Making inferences)*

_____

2. In Part A, how did the addition of HCl change the concentration of ions in solutions? Speculate on the identity of the white precipitate.

(Making inferences) _____

_____

3. Write a rule that describes how the equilibrium of a system is shifted when the concentration of a substance in the reaction is increased. *(Drawing conclusions)* _____

_____

_____

4. In Part B, does the NaOH counteract the effects of the HCl? Explain.

   (Interpreting data) _____

   _____

5. Write the chemical equation showing the reaction in Part C. Include heat as a term in the equation. Is this an exothermic or endothermic

   reaction? *(Making inferences)* _____

   _____

   _____

6. Write a rule that describes how the equilibrium is shifted when the temperature of an endothermic reaction, such as this, is increased. (Hint: Look at the answer to Analysis and Conclusions Question 3.)

   (Drawing conclusions) _____

   _____

Critical Thinking: Applications

1. Write a rule that describes the effect on the equilibrium of a system when the concentration of a substance in the reaction is decreased.

   (Making predictions) _____

   _____

2. Are the rates of the forward and reverse reactions still equal immediately after a disturbance is introduced to a system at equilibrium?

   Explain. *(Applying concepts)* _____

   _____

   _____

3. Write a general rule covering all of the types of disturbances to equilibrium observed in this investigation. *(Developing hypotheses)*

   _____

   _____

Going Further

1. Investigate and report on the effect of pressure on a system in which gases are involved in a chemical reaction. Give examples of equilibrium systems that would be affected by pressure.

2. Equilibrium can be shifted by decreasing the concentration of a substance. Suggest how this might be done. Devise an experiment to test your idea. Have your teacher approve your experimental design before you begin. Perform the experiment only under your teacher's supervision.

Le Chatelier's Principle

Introduction

Most chemical reactions that you have studied so far appear to proceed to completion or until one of the reactants is used up. For example, a piece of magnesium, ignited in oxygen, burns until all of the magnesium has reacted to form magnesium oxide. In other reactions, however, the products have enough energy to react to form the reactants again in the reverse reaction. When the rate of the forward and reverse reactions are equal, a state of equilibrium exists. Both reactions continue to occur, but there is no net change in the concentrations of reactants or products.

Le Chatelier's principle enables you to predict the effect of a stress placed on an equilibrium system. Stresses include changes in the concentrations of reactants or products, or in the temperature of the system. Le Chatelier's principle can be stated as follows: If a system in equilibrium is put under a stress, the system will respond by shifting to reduce the stress. For example, adding a reactant to a system in equilibrium will cause the system to shift to the right, thereby reducing the amount of reactant.

In this investigation, you will examine the equilibrium system represented by the following net ionic equation:

$$\underset{\text{pink}}{Co(H_2O)_6^{2+}} + 4Cl^- \rightleftharpoons \underset{\text{blue}}{CoCl_4^{2-}} + 6H_2O$$

You will subject the system to various stresses and observe the effects on the equilibrium.

Pre-Lab Discussion

Read the entire laboratory investigation and the relevant pages of your textbook. Then answer the questions that follow.

1. State Le Chatelier's principle. _____

   _____

2. Explain what happens when equilibrium is reached. _____

   _____

3. List the stresses that will be studied in this experiment. _____

   _____

   _____

   _____

Small Scale Lab 47

4. The formula for solid cobalt(II) chloride is $CoCl_2 \cdot 6H_2O$. What is the name given to compounds such as this, which have water as part of their crystal structure? _____

5. What safety precautions must be observed with hydrochloric acid (HCl)? With silver nitrate ($AgNO_3$)? _____

_____

_____

6. Predict the effect on the following equilibrium system if you: (a) add HCl; (b) add H_2O; (c) add NaOH.

$$2CrO_4^{2-} + 2H^+ \rightleftharpoons Cr_2O_7^{2-} + H_2O$$

_____

_____

_____

Problem

What are the effects of stressing a system at equilibrium?

Materials

chemical splash goggles
laboratory apron
latex gloves
2 beakers, 250-mL
tap water
hot plate
marking pen
well plate, 24-well
1 sheet of white paper
4 micropipets containing the
    following liquids:
      cobalt chloride ($CoCl_2$),
      0.2 M

hydrochloric acid (HCl),
    12.0 M
distilled water
silver nitrate ($AgNO_3$), 0.1 M
petri dish
plastic toothpick
paper towel
small test tube
ice cubes

Safety

Wear your goggles and lab apron at all times during the investigation. Hot plates get very hot; use caution when working with them. Hydrochloric acid is extremely corrosive. It will irritate skin and damage clothing. Wear gloves when working with it. If you spill any acid, immediately wash the area with plenty of cold water and notify your teacher. Cobalt chloride and silver nitrate are toxic, and silver nitrate will stain skin and clothing; avoid contact with them. Do not put your fingers in your mouth at any time during the investigation. Note the caution alert symbols here and with certain steps of the Procedure. Refer to page *xi* for the specific precautions associated with each symbol.

Procedure

1. Put on your goggles and lab apron. Place a beaker containing about 100 mL of water on a hot plate. Set the hot plate to a moderate setting; you do not want the water to boil. **CAUTION:** *The water and hot plate will become very hot.* Go on to the next steps while you are waiting for the water to heat.

2. Using the marking pen, label a well plate from left to right along the top with the numbers 1–6. Down the left side, label the rows of wells A–D. Place the well plate on a sheet of white paper.

3. Put on latex gloves. Obtain four micropipets labeled as follows: *Co* (CoCl₂ solution), *HCl* (hydrochloric acid), *H₂O* (distilled water), and *Ag* (AgNO₃ solution). Place them upside down in an inverted petri dish cover. **CAUTION:** *Be careful not to spill any CoCl₂, HCl, or AgNO₃ solution. Wear gloves when working with 12.0 M hydrochloric acid. If spillage does occur, wash with plenty of water and inform your teacher.* Use these micropipets to fill the wells of the labeled well plate as indicated in Steps 4–8.

4. Place five drops of CoCl₂ solution in each of the 24 wells of the labeled well plate on the white sheet of paper. **CAUTION:** *Be careful not to ingest any CoCl₂ or spill any on your skin.*

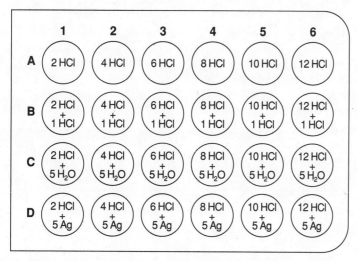

All wells contain 5 drops of CoCl₂ solution.

Figure 47–1

5. As shown in Figure 47–1, add two drops of HCl to the CoCl₂ solution in wells A1, B1, C1, and D1. Similarly, place four drops of HCl in each well in column 2, six drops in each well in column 3, eight drops in each well in column 4, ten drops in each well in column 5, and 12 drops in each well in column 6. Mix the contents of each well with the plastic toothpick. Rinse the toothpick with water and set it aside on a paper towel. **CAUTION:** *12.0 M hydrochloric acid is extremely corrosive. Avoid spilling it on your skin or clothing.* Record the color of the solution in each well of row A in the Data Table. Row A will be your control.

6. In row B, add one more drop of HCl to each well and stir thoroughly with the toothpick. Rinse the toothpick with water and set it aside on a paper towel. Record the colors of row B in the Data Table.

7. Add five drops of distilled water to each well in row C. Stir thoroughly with the toothpick. Rinse the toothpick with water and set it aside on a paper towel. Record the colors of row C in the Data Table.

 8. Add five drops of AgNO₃ solution to each well in row D and stir thoroughly with the toothpick. Discard the toothpick. **CAU-TION:** *Be careful not to ingest any AgNO₃ or spill any on your skin.* Record any color changes and precipitate formation in the Data Table.

 9. Place 5 mL of the cobalt solution in a test tube. Add just enough distilled water to get a purple color half-way between blue and pink. Place the test tube in the beaker of hot water from Step 1 until a color change occurs. **CAUTION:** *The water and hot plate are hot. Do not touch them with bare hands.* Record your observations. Turn off the hot plate.

10. Prepare an ice bath by placing ice cubes in a 250-mL beaker and adding water. Place the test tube in the ice bath until a color change occurs. Record your observations.

11. Dispose of all chemicals according to your teacher's instructions. Clean up your work area and wash your hands before leaving the laboratory.

Observations

DATA TABLE

	1	2	3	4	5	6
A						
B						
C						
D						

CoCl₂ at room temperature: _____

CoCl₂ in hot water: _____

CoCl₂ in cold water: _____

Critical Thinking: Analysis and Conclusions

1. Refer to the net ionic equation below or in the Introduction to answer the following questions. *(Interpreting data)*

$$Co(H_2O)_6{}^{2+} + 4Cl^- \rightleftharpoons CoCl_4{}^{2-} + 6H_2O$$

In what direction was the equilibrium shifted by

a. the addition of HCl? _____

_____

b. the addition of water? _____

_____

c. the addition of $AgNO_3$? _____

_____

d. increasing the temperature? _____

_____

e. decreasing the temperature? _____

_____

2. How do you explain the results described in answers 1a and 1b? *(Making inferences)* _____

_____

_____

_____

_____

3. Explain the results observed when $AgNO_3$ was added. *(Making inferences)* _____

_____

_____

_____

_____

4. Is the reaction shown in the Introduction exothermic or endothermic? How do you know? *(Drawing conclusions)* _____

_____

_____

5. Write the equilibrium expression for the system studied. *(Applying concepts)*

Critical Thinking: Applications

1. Predict how the addition of sodium chloride would affect the equilibrium. Explain your prediction in terms of Le Chatelier's principle. *(Making predictions)* _____

_____

_____

2. Rewrite the net ionic equation including the energy term where appropriate. The ΔH for this reaction is $+50$ kJ/mol. *(Applying concepts)* _____

3. Silver chloride (AgCl) is a white solid. For the equilibrium reaction

$$Ag^+(aq) + Cl^-(aq) \rightleftharpoons AgCl(s)$$

$K_{eq} = 6 \times 10^9$. At equilibrium, would you expect to have more silver and chloride ions or more solid silver chloride? Explain. *(Making predictions)* _____

_____

_____

Going Further

1. Design an experiment to test the hypothesis that the effects observed in row B were due to added H^+ rather than Cl^-. Under your teacher's supervision, perform the experiment and report the results to your class.

2. Use a solution of $CaCl_2$ to further verify the role of Cl^- in the changes observed in row B. Under your teacher's supervision, perform the experiment and report the results to your class.

Shifting Equilibria in Plant Tissues

Lab 48
APPLICATION

*Text reference: **Chapter 16***

Introduction

The variety and beauty of the colors of flowers have touched human emotions and sparked the imagination of poets for centuries. What makes flowers so colorful? Even the fruits and leaves of some plants appear unusually rich in colors. The reason you see such a wealth of colors in plants is that they possess a variety of pigments. Pigments are compounds that give color to the cells in leaves, stems, fruits, and flowers. Two examples of these pigments are carotenoids and anthocyanins. Carotenoids, found in such plants as carrots and tomatoes, cause plant parts to appear yellow to orangish red. Anthocyanins cause fruits and flowers to appear red, blue, violet, or creamy yellow.

Some of these pigments are sensitive to certain air pollutants and will undergo equilibrium reactions in their presence. Consider the following example. When gaseous sulfur dioxide (SO_2) invades leaves or flower petals and dissolves in the water surrounding the cells, it reacts to form sulfurous acid (H_2SO_3), which in turn dissociates into hydrogen (H^+) and hydrogen sulfite (HSO_3^-) ions.

$$SO_2(g) + H_2O(l) \rightleftharpoons H_2SO_3(aq)$$
$$H_2SO_3(aq) \rightleftharpoons H^+(aq) + HSO_3^-(aq)$$

The hydrogen sulfite ions react with pigments in the plant cells to form a colorless compound. A simplified description of the reaction is shown by the following equation, where Pgm represents a plant pigment.

$$Pgm^+ + HSO_3^- \rightleftharpoons Pgm\text{-}SO_3^- + H^+$$

(color)   (colorless)

As you can tell from the equation, the presence or absence of pigment color indicates shifts in the equilibrium reaction.

In this investigation you will see Le Chatelier's principle in action. First, you will generate sulfur dioxide gas in a petri dish containing samples of plant tissue and observe the color changes. Then you will cause a shift in equilibrium by adding sulfuric acid (H_2SO_4) to the mixture. You will be able to observe and analyze the shift by the appearance or disappearance of the color in the plant tissue.

Pre-Lab Discussion

Read the entire laboratory investigation and the relevant pages of your textbook. Then answer the questions that follow.

1. How can Le Chatelier's principle help explain a shift in the equilibrium of a reversible reaction? _____

_____

_____

Name _____

2. In this investigation, you will generate SO_2 gas by reacting a solution of sodium sulfite (Na_2SO_3) with sulfuric acid (H_2SO_4). Also formed are sodium sulfate and water. Write the balanced equation for this

   reaction. _____

3. What is the source of HSO_3^- ions in this investigation? _____

   _____

4. What ions are introduced to the system by the addition of more H_2SO_4 in Step 6? (Hint: Study the equation for the dissociation of

   sulfurous acid (H_2SO_3) given in the Introduction.) _____

5. What are some of the hazards associated with the generation of sulfur dioxide gas (SO_2) in this investigation? How can you avoid

   these hazards? _____

   _____

   _____

   _____

6. How are the acids in the petri dish neutralized before cleanup?

   _____

Problem

How can the reactions of certain plant pigments serve as indicators of an equilibrium reaction?

Materials

chemical splash goggles
laboratory apron
plastic petri dish with
   access port
sheet of white paper
single-hole paper punch
piece of red cabbage leaf
cotton swab
tap water
pen or pencil
petals from each of the
   following flowers:
      red petunia
      orange lily
      yellow lily
      blue hydrangea

scissors
3 micropipets, containing the
   following solutions:
      sodium sulfite (Na_2SO_3),
         0.5 M
      sulfuric acid (H_2SO_4),
         2.0 M
      ammonia ($NH_3(aq)$),
         2.0 M
wash bottle
paper towel

Safety

Wear your goggles and lab apron at all times during the investigation. Sulfuric acid is corrosive. Ammonia and its fumes are caustic and irritating to eyes and nasal passages. Wash any skin or clothing that comes into contact with these substances with large quantities of water.

Sulfur dioxide gas forms a corrosive acid when it dissolves in the eyes and nasal passages. If you are allergic to sulfites, report your allergy to your teacher before the investigation. Once the reaction begins, open and close the petri dish only according to directions.

Note the caution alert symbols here and with certain steps of the Procedure. Refer to page *xi* for the specific precautions associated with each symbol.

Procedure

1. Put on your goggles and lab apron. Place the bottom plate of the petri dish on the white paper.

2. Using the single-hole paper punch, carefully punch two small circular pieces from the red cabbage leaf. Place what is left of the cabbage leaf aside for later color comparison.

3. Using a moistened cotton swab, pick up the circular pieces of cabbage leaf and position them opposite each other in the bottom plate of the petri dish as shown in Figure 48–1. Notice that the samples should be placed about the same distance from the center of the dish as the access port in the lid. Lift the dish and write labels on the white paper corresponding to the position of the cabbage circles in the petri dish. Replace the dish.

4. If the flower petals are sufficiently large, punch out two pieces of each of the flower types and place them opposite each other in the petri dish. If the leaf is fragile you can use scissors to cut small squares from the petal. If the petals are tiny, simply use the whole petal. As with the cabbage samples, label the flower types on the white paper. Place what is left of the flower samples aside for later color comparison. The first column of the Data Table lists the type and original color of each sample.

5. Generate SO_2 gas by placing two drops of 0.5 M Na_2SO_3 in the center of the petri dish and then adding two drops of 2.0 M H_2SO_4. Immediately cover the bottom half of the petri dish with the lid. Observe for 5 minutes and record any color changes that occur during that time. **CAUTION:** *Sulfuric acid is corrosive. If you spill any on your skin or clothing, rinse it off immediately with lots of cold water. Do not breathe the sulfur dioxide gas produced.*

6. Peel back the piece of clear adhesive tape from the access port. Rotate the lid so that the access port is over the left side of the petri dish and introduce one drop of 2.0 M H_2SO_4 onto each sample on that side of the dish. Record any color changes that occur.

Lab 48
APPLICATION

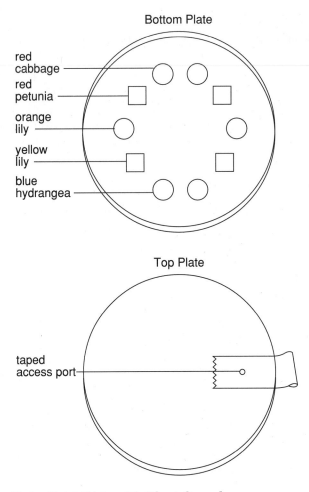

Bottom Plate

red cabbage

red petunia

orange lily

yellow lily

blue hydrangea

Top Plate

taped access port

Figure 48–1 *Petri Dish with Plant Samples*

 7. When all observations are completed, terminate the production of SO$_2$ gas by adding a few drops of 2.0 *M* NH$_3$(*aq*) to the dish through the access port. Note the color changes that occur. **CAUTION:** *Ammonia is caustic. If you spill any on your skin, rinse it off immediately with plenty of cold water. Do not breathe the ammonia fumes.*

 8. Wait about 5 minutes. Open the petri dish and use a wash bottle to flush the plant samples and solution from the bottom of the dish into the container provided by your teacher. Rinse the petri dish well with tap water and dry it with a paper towel. Clean up your work area and wash your hands before leaving the laboratory.

Observations

DATA TABLE   Color Changes in Plant Pigments

Plant Type and Original Color	SO$_2$	H$_2$SO$_4$	NH$_3$(aq)
red cabbage			
red petunia			
orange lily			
yellow lily			
blue hydrangea			

Critical Thinking: Analysis and Conclusions

1. Assume that most of the yellow and orange colors in the samples are due to carotenoids. Which category of pigments appears to be most sensitive to discoloration due to SO$_2$ gas? (*Interpreting data*)

   _____

   _____

2. Is there evidence that bleaching of the anthocyanins with the hydrogen sulfite ion is reversible? Explain. (*Interpreting data*) _____

   _____

   _____

3. Look back at the equation for the reaction between the plant pigment and HSO$_3^-$ ions given in the Introduction. In what direction would the equilibrium have to shift for the color to return? (*Making inferences*) _____

4. Look at the answer you wrote for Pre-Lab Discussion Question 4. Based on your data and keeping Le Chatelier's principle in mind, explain what caused the reaction to shift toward the re-formation of the red-colored anthocyanin molecule. (*Making inferences*) _____

   _____

   _____

   _____

5. In which direction did the addition of NH$_3$(aq) appear to shift the equilibrium? Explain your reasoning. (*Making inferences*) _____

   _____

   _____

   _____

Name _____

Critical Thinking: Applications

1. Some fresh fruits and vegetables turn brown after being cut. This effect results when the pigment melanin in the plant tissue reacts with oxygen in the atmosphere. Hydrogen sulfite ions react with browned melanin to render it colorless and prevent further browning. Considering the results of your investigation, which types of fruits and vegetables are most likely to be protected from browning without affecting their natural colors? Explain. (*Making judgments*) _____

   _____

   _____

2. Suppose you were a fruit farmer or flower grower whose business was downwind of a coal-burning power plant (a source of SO_2 gas). What pollution problems would you have to deal with? Would the problem exist only when it rained? (*Applying concepts*) _____

   _____

   _____

   _____

   _____

3. Acid-base indicators are colorful molecules that are sensitive to changes in acidity or alkalinity. They have predictably different colors at different levels of acidity values. Could anthocyanins, such as those found in red cabbage leaves, serve as indicators if they are extracted from the red cabbage tissue? Explain in light of your observations. (*Making judgments*) _____

   _____

   _____

Going Further

1. Using the procedure from this investigation, design a controlled experiment to test whether hydrogen sulfite ions will efficiently prevent the browning of freshly cut fruit. Under the supervision of your teacher, carry out the investigation and present the results to your class.

2. Because some people are allergic to sulfites, a better method for preventing the browning of fruits is to bathe the fruits with vitamin C, ascorbic acid. This chemical is sold commercially in such products as Fruit Fresh. Design an investigation to compare the effect of bathing the fruits with a solution of Fruit Fresh (according to the directions on the package) with that of introducing hydrogen sulfite ions. Under the supervision of your teacher, carry out the investigation and report on your results.

Solubility Curve of KNO₃   *Lab* **49**

Introduction

The maximum amount of solute that will dissolve in a given amount of solvent is called its solubility. What factors determine the solubility of a substance? Certainly the identity of the solute affects the amount of the substance that can dissolve. For example, sodium iodide is more soluble than sodium chloride in a given amount of water. The identity of the solvent also affects the solubility of a substance. Sodium chloride is highly soluble in water but not very soluble in ethanol. Temperature of the solvent is another factor affecting solubility. The solubility of most solids varies directly with temperature. In other words, the higher the temperature of the solvent, the more solute will dissolve—that is, the greater the solubility of the solid.

In this investigation, you will study the relationship between the solubility of potassium nitrate (KNO_3) and the temperature of the water solvent. Different amounts of KNO_3 will be dissolved in a given amount of water at a temperature close to its boiling point. You will observe each solution as it cools and note the temperature at which crystallization occurs. Crystallization indicates a saturated solution, or one that contains the maximum amount of KNO_3 in that amount of water. From this solubility data, a solubility curve for KNO_3 can be constructed.

Pre-Lab Discussion

Read the entire laboratory investigation and the relevant pages of your textbook. Then answer the questions that follow.

1. Define the following terms.

    solubility: _____

    _____

    saturated solution: _____

    unsaturated solution: _____

    _____

    supersaturated solution: _____

    _____

2. Determine the solubility of sodium sulfate, Na_2SO_4, in grams per 100 g of water, if 0.94 g of Na_2SO_4 in 20 g of H_2O results in a saturated solution.

3. Why is it necessary to warm the thermometer in Procedure Step 2 before placing it into the solutions? _____

_____

4. A student stated that the solubility of potassium chloride, KCl, at 20°C was 36 g of KCl per 100 g of solution. What is wrong with this statement? _____

_____

5. How do you know when the solid is completely dissolved? _____

_____

6. What special precautions should be taken while doing this investigation? _____

_____

Problem

How does the solubility of potassium nitrate depend on temperature?

Materials

chemical splash goggles	laboratory balance
laboratory apron	potassium nitrate (KNO$_3$)
4 test tubes, 18 mm × 150 mm	graduated cylinder, 10-mL
marking pen	distilled water
test-tube rack	utility clamp
beaker, 400-mL	ring stand
thermometer	stirring rod
hot plate	test-tube holder

Safety

Wear your goggles and lab apron at all times during the investigation. Do not touch the hot plate or heated water with your bare skin. Note the caution alert symbols here and with certain steps of the Procedure. Refer to page *xi* for the specific precautions associated with each symbol.

Procedure

1. Put on your goggles and lab apron. Label four test tubes *1–4* with a marking pen. Place them in a test-tube rack.

2. Fill a 400-mL beaker three-fourths full of tap water, place a thermometer in it, and heat the water on a hot plate until its temperature is about 90°C. **CAUTION:** *Do not touch the hot plate or heated water with your bare skin.* While you are waiting for the water to heat, go on to Steps 3 and 4.

3. Place the following masses of potassium nitrate (KNO_3) into the test tubes:

   2.0 g in test tube 1
   4.0 g in test tube 2
   6.0 g in test tube 3
   8.0 g in test tube 4

4. Add 5.0 mL distilled water to each test tube. Attach a utility clamp to a ring stand.

 5. Place test tube 1 in the clamp and lower it into the hot water bath. Stir the KNO_3 solution with the stirring rod until the solid is completely dissolved. Remove the stirring rod and rinse it off. Loosen the utility clamp and, using a test-tube holder, remove the test tube.

6. One lab partner should place the warm thermometer from the hot water bath into test tube 1 while the other repeats Step 5 for test tube 2.

7. Watch test tube 1 for the first sign of crystallization and when it occurs record the temperature in the Data Table. Remove test tube 2 from the hot water bath and repeat Steps 6 and 7.

8. Repeat Steps 5–7 for test tubes 3 and 4.

 9. Place all the test tubes back in the hot water bath and redissolve the solid. Flush the solutions down the drain with plenty of hot water. Turn off the hot plate. Clean up your work area and wash your hands before leaving the laboratory.

Observations

DATA TABLE

Test Tube #	Temperature (°C)
1	
2	
3	
4	

Name_____

Calculations

1. For each test tube, determine the solubility of KNO_3 in grams per 100 g H_2O.

   test tube 1:

   test tube 2:

   test tube 3:

   test tube 4:

Critical Thinking: Analysis and Conclusions

1. Construct a solubility curve for KNO_3 by graphing the mass of KNO_3 per 100 grams H_2O (solubility) versus temperature. Place temperature on the x-axis and solubility on the y-axis. Connect the points in a smooth curve. *(Interpreting data)*

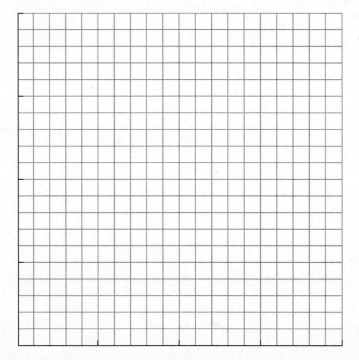

Figure 49–1

2. Describe the relationship between the solubility of KNO_3 and the temperature of the solvent. *(Interpreting diagrams)* _____

_____

3. Using your graph, determine how many grams of KNO_3 can be dissolved in 100 g of H_2O at the following temperatures: *(Interpreting diagrams)*

35°C _____

60°C _____

70°C _____

Critical Thinking: Applications

1. Using your graph, predict whether the following solutions of KNO_3 would be considered saturated, unsaturated, or supersaturated. *(Making predictions)*

75 g KNO_3/100 g H_2O at 40°C _____

_____

60 g KNO_3/100 g H_2O at 50°C _____

_____

2. Sketch the general shape for a solubility curve for a gas. *(Applying concepts)* _____

_____

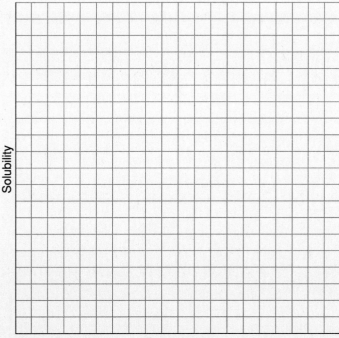

Going Further

1. Design a procedure to determine a solubility curve for lithium carbonate, one of the solutes whose solubility decreases with increasing temperature. With your teacher's supervision, conduct the experiment.

2. The dissolved oxygen content of water is extremely important to marine life. Investigate the solubility of oxygen in water in relation to temperature and relate that to the oxygen needs of various kinds of marine animals. Report your findings to the class.

Precipitates and Solubility Rules

Introduction

What do geothermal vents have in common with a bathtub ring? The vents spew clouds of mineral-rich water from deep inside Earth into the ocean near mid-ocean ridges. A bathtub ring is a deposit formed from hard water and soap. Both involve the process of precipitation, the formation of insoluble or slightly soluble solids. When oppositely charged ions come in contact, they attract each other, and if that attraction is stronger than the ions' attraction to water, they form crystalline solids.

When two different ionic solutions with concentrations below their saturation points are combined and a precipitate forms, they have undergone a double replacement reaction in which one of the products is insoluble. The reaction of aqueous solutions of calcium chloride and zinc sulfate, for example, combines Ca^{2+} ions and SO_4^{2-} ions in a concentration above the saturation point of calcium sulfate. The formation of the precipitate is described by the following equation:

$$CaCl_2(aq) \ + \ ZnSO_4(aq) \rightarrow ZnCl_2(aq) \ + \ CaSO_4(s)$$

Insoluble salts can be identified by their low K_{sp} values (equilibrium dissociation constants). The identity of precipitates can also be deduced from the results of combining pairs of salt solutions, as you will do in this investigation. A comparison of the products from the combinations allows for the identification of any precipitates that form. Trends, called solubility rules, can also be found for some ions that tend to form precipitates more readily than others.

In this investigation, you will combine pairs of six given salt solutions and look for precipitates. After you write a chemical equation for each combination, you will attempt to deduce which products are precipitates, and also discover some common solubility rules.

Pre-Lab Discussion

Read the entire laboratory investigation and the relevant pages of your textbook. Then answer the questions that follow.

1. How many products are there in a double replacement reaction from which to choose the precipitate? _____

    _____

2. How can you recognize a precipitate when you see one? _____

    _____

3. Why is it necessary to use different micropipets for different solutions? _____

Name_____

4. Why were the solutions made with distilled water? _____

_____

Problem

What are the precipitates that form from the reactions of salt solutions?

Materials

chemical splash goggles
laboratory apron
latex gloves
6 micropipets, containing the
    following 0.1 M solutions:
        sodium carbonate
          (Na_2CO_3)
        magnesium chloride
          ($MgCl_2$)

copper(II) sulfate ($CuSO_4$)
sodium nitrate ($NaNO_3$)
silver nitrate ($AgNO_3$)
potassium phosphate
    (K_3PO_4)
well plate
marking pen
distilled water

Safety

Wear your goggles and lab apron at all times during the investigation. Silver nitrate ($AgNO_3$) causes stains to skin and clothing. Wear gloves while handling silver nitrate. Note the caution alert symbols here and with certain steps of the Procedure. Refer to page *xi* for the specific precautions associated with each symbol.

Procedure

 1. Put on your goggles and lab apron. Obtain micropipets of each solution and label them if necessary. Mark the well plates with the names of the six solutions in the manner shown in the Data Table.

 2. Put on your gloves. In the upper left well of the well plate, combine the first pair of solutions, ten drops each, using the micropipets. Note the appearance or absence of a precipitate and record your observation in the Data Table. Write *NR* if there is no reaction.

3. Continue the solution combinations (15 total) until each of the solutions has been combined with all of the others. Record the results in the Data Table.

 4. Dispose of any solutions containing silver compounds in a labeled container provided by your teacher.

 5. Wash the well plate with soapy water, then rinse with tap water and finally distilled water. Clean up your work area and wash your hands before leaving the laboratory.

Observations

DATA TABLE

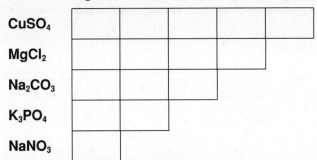

	AgNO₃	NaNO₃	K₃PO₄	Na₂CO₃	MgCl₂
CuSO₄					
MgCl₂					
Na₂CO₃					
K₃PO₄					
NaNO₃					

Critical Thinking: Analysis and Conclusions

1. Complete the double replacement reaction equations for each combination. Leave blank spaces for the phase symbols. You will fill them in for Question 2. (*Applying concepts*)

   $CuSO_4(aq) + 2AgNO_3(aq) \rightarrow$

   $MgCl_2(aq) + 2AgNO_3(aq) \rightarrow$

   $Na_2CO_3(aq) + 2AgNO_3(aq) \rightarrow$

   $K_3PO_4(aq) + 3AgNO_3(aq) \rightarrow$

   $NaNO_3(aq) + AgNO_3(aq) \rightarrow$

   $CuSO_4(aq) + 2NaNO_3(aq) \rightarrow$

   $MgCl_2(aq) + 2NaNO_3(aq) \rightarrow$

   $Na_2CO_3(aq) + NaNO_3(aq) \rightarrow$

   $K_3PO_4(aq) + 3NaNO_3(aq) \rightarrow$

   $3CuSO_4(aq) + 2K_3PO_4(aq) \rightarrow$

   $3MgCl_2(aq) + 2K_3PO_4(aq) \rightarrow$

   $3Na_2CO_3(aq) + 2K_3PO_4(aq) \rightarrow$

   $CuSO_4(aq) + Na_2CO_3(aq) \rightarrow$

   $MgCl_2(aq) + Na_2CO_3(aq) \rightarrow$

   $CuSO_4(aq) + MgCl_2(aq) \rightarrow$

2. Find those equations in Question 1 that have no precipitate in the products. The products in these equations are salts that must be soluble. Label each of these salts with (*aq*), like the reactants that are soluble. Search for these same soluble salts in the products of the reactions that did produce precipitates. Where they occur, label them (*aq*), and note that the other product must be the precipitate. Label the precipitates with the symbol (*s*) for "solid." Refer to Figure 17–9 in your text for any additional solubility rules you may need. (*Interpreting data*)

3. There should still be equations for which no precipitate has been identified. To deduce solubility rules for use in identifying precipitates in these cases, fill in conclusions for the following list based on your lab results. (*Making predictions*)

   a. List all metal ions that are not part of any precipitate.

   _____

   b. List all negative ions that are not part of any precipitate.

   _____

   c. List all metal ions that occur only in products that are precipitates.

   _____

   d. List all metal ions sometimes found in a precipitate.

   _____

   e. Use the list of generalities in a–d above to find which salts are the precipitates in the remaining cases.

   _____

Critical Thinking: Applications

1. Which metal ions of those encountered in this investigation would you expect to find contributing to precipitates formed on the ocean floor around geothermal vents? Explain your answer. (*Making predictions*) _____

   _____

2. Soaps often contain sodium stearate. (Stearate is a complex ion derived from fatty acids or fat.) If a precipitate forms when soap is dissolved in hard water (water containing Ca^{2+} and Mg^{2+} ions), what ion from the soap would you expect to find in the precipitate? Why?

   (*Making predictions*) _____

   _____

Going Further

1. Look up the K_{sp} values for the precipitates in this lab and list them from the most to the least soluble.
2. Under the supervision of your teacher, prepare a saturated solution of NaCl by placing excess salt in water and stirring periodically until no more of the salt on the bottom dissolves. Adding drops of concentrated HCl to the saturated NaCl causes a precipitate to form. The precipitate has to be NaCl. Explain.

Investigating Hardness of Water

Small Scale **Lab 51** APPLICATION

*Text reference: **Chapter 17***

Introduction

Have you ever had trouble washing your hair or clothes because of hard water? Hard water contains calcium and magnesium ions that react with compounds in soaps and detergents to form insoluble salts. These insoluble salts may be familiar to you as "ring-around-the-tub." The ions dissolved in hard water also reduce the amount of suds made by soaps and detergents, diminishing the cleansing action of these products.

In this investigation, you will determine the amount of calcium ions present in a water sample by reacting it with $EDTA^{4-}$, or ethylenediaminetetraacetate. $EDTA^{4-}$ is a large carbon-based ion that can donate six electron pairs to form coordinate covalent bonds with calcium. In a coordinate covalent bond, one atom donates both electrons.

Figure 51–1 *Lewis Dot Diagram of $EDTA^{4-}$ Ion*

The reaction of EDTA with calcium occurs best in a basic solution. The negative ion of EDTA reacts with the positive calcium ions according to the following equation.

$$EDTA^{4-} + Ca^{2+} \rightarrow [Ca \cdot EDTA]^{2-}$$

In this reaction, the negative EDTA ion surrounds the positive calcium ion to form the complex ion $[Ca \cdot EDTA]^{2-}$ shown in Figure 51–2.

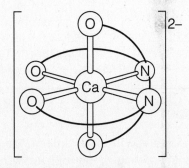

Figure 51–2 *Ball-and-Stick Model of $[Ca \cdot EDTA]^{2-}$*

Name _____

In this investigation, you will analyze various water samples and measure the amount of EDTA required to remove all of the calcium ions from each sample. (Calmagite, a dye indicator, turns from red to blue when there are no uncombined calcium ions in a solution.) You will then be able to use your data to calculate the concentration of calcium in the water.

Pre-Lab Discussion

Read the entire laboratory investigation and the relevant pages of your textbook. Then answer the questions that follow.

1. What is the purpose of the solution in well B1? _____

   _____

2. Why are three trials used for each solution? _____

   _____

3. How is the formation of bonds in a complex ion used to determine the concentration of calcium ions? _____

   _____

   _____

   _____

4. What is the purpose of the white paper? _____

   _____

5. What is a coordinate covalent bond? _____

   _____

Problem

How can the concentration of calcium ions in water be determined?

Materials

chemical splash goggles
laboratory apron
well plate
marking pen
sheet of white paper
6 micropipets, containing the
    following solutions:
      EDTA solution

distilled water
tap water with Ca^{2+} ions
Ca^{2+} solution
buffer solution
calmagite solution
plastic toothpick
wash bottle with distilled water
graduated cylinder, 10-mL

Safety

Wear your goggles and lab apron at all times during the investigation.
    If you spill EDTA or calmagite solution on your skin or clothing, rinse it off immediately with plenty of water and notify your teacher.

© Prentice-Hall, Inc.

Note the caution alert symbols here and with certain steps of the Procedure. Refer to page *xi* for the specific precautions associated with each symbol.

Procedure

1. Put on your goggles and lab apron. Using the marking pen, label the wells of the well plate from left to right along the top: *1, 2, 3, 4, 5, 6*. Down the left side, label the top two rows of wells A and B. Place the well plate on a sheet of white paper.

2. Obtain micropipets containing the six solutions needed for the investigation.

3. Place 20 drops of distilled water in well B1. Throughout this investigation, be sure to count accurately the number of drops. Hold the pipets in the same vertical position whenever you are dispensing drops.

4. Test the indicator by adding four drops of buffer solution and one drop of indicator solution to well B1 and stirring with a plastic toothpick. The solution should be blue. If not, add one drop of EDTA to well B1. Rinse the toothpick with distilled water.

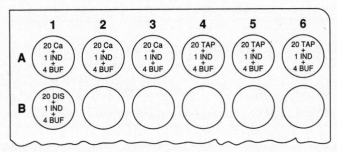

Figure 51–3

5. Place exactly 20 drops of the known Ca^{2+} solution in well A1. Record the concentration of the solution and the number of drops in Data Table 1. Then add four drops of buffer solution and one drop of indicator solution to well A1.

6. Add one drop of the EDTA solution to well A1 and stir. Continue adding EDTA one drop at a time until the solution turns the same color blue as the solution in well B1. The reaction takes time so you should add a drop, stir, and then wait a few seconds before adding another drop. In Data Table 1, record the number of drops of EDTA solution you added to well A1. Rinse the toothpick with distilled water.

7. Repeat Steps 5 and 6 using wells A2 and A3. Enter the data from these two wells in Data Table 1.

8. You will now determine the Ca^{2+} concentration in tap water. Place 20 drops of tap water in each of wells A4, A5, and A6. Record the number of drops placed in each well in Data Table 2. Add four drops of buffer solution and one drop of indicator solution to each of wells A4, A5, and A6.

Name_____

9. Add the EDTA solution one drop at a time to well A4 and stir after each drop. Stop adding drops after the solution turns the same color blue as the solution in well B1. Repeat this procedure for wells A5 and A6. In Data Table 2, record the number of drops of EDTA solution added to each well.

10. Flush all of the chemicals down the drain with large amounts of water. Clean up your work area and wash your hands before leaving the laboratory.

Observations

DATA TABLE 1 EDTA with Known Ca²⁺ Solution

	Trial 1	Trial 2	Trial 3
Concentration of Ca^{2+} (mol/L)	2.0×10^{-3}	2.0×10^{-3}	2.0×10^{-3}
Number of drops of Ca^{2+} solution	20	20	20
Number of drops of EDTA solution			
Ratio A			

DATA TABLE 2 EDTA with Tap Water

	Trial 4	Trial 5	Trial 6
Number of drops of tap water	20	20	20
Number of drops of EDTA solution			
Ratio B			

Calculations

1. For each trial, calculate the ratio of drops of EDTA solution to drops of known Ca^{2+} solution. Enter these values in Data Table 1 as Ratio A.

2. For each trial, calculate the ratio of drops of EDTA solution to drops of tap water. Enter these values in Data Table 2 as Ratio B.

3. Calculate the average ratio of drops for trials 1–3 and 4–6 respectively to obtain values for Ratio A_{avg} and Ratio B_{avg}.

    Ratio A_{avg} _____   Ratio B_{avg} _____

4. Calculate the concentration of Ca^{2+} in the tap water by using the following formula:

$$Ca^{2+}(\text{tap water}) = Ca^{2+}(\text{known solution}) \times \frac{\text{Ratio } B_{avg}}{\text{Ratio } A_{avg}}$$

280

© Prentice-Hall, Inc.

Critical Thinking: Analysis and Conclusions

1. For each trial of the solution with the known concentration of Ca^{2+} ions, calculate the percent deviation from Ratio A_{avg} using the following formula: *(Interpreting data)*

$$\text{Percent deviation} = \frac{\text{trial result} - \text{average value}}{\text{average value}} \times 100\%$$

   Trial 1 _____   Trial 2 _____   Trial 3 _____

2. For each trial of the solution with the unknown concentration of Ca^{2+} ions, calculate the percent deviation from Ratio B_{avg}. *(Interpreting data)*

   Trial 4 _____   Trial 5 _____   Trial 6 _____

3. Why are there differences in results from trial to trial? *(Making inferences)* _____

_____

4. How does the hardness of the tap water compare to that of the known solution of Ca^{2+} ions? *(Making comparisons)* _____

_____

5. Based on your data, how is the number of drops of EDTA needed for a color change related to the hardness of water? *(Making inferences)*

_____

6. Why is it possible to use the formula in Calculations Step 4 to find the concentration of Ca^{2+} ions in the tap water? *(Making inferences)*

_____

Critical Thinking: Applications

1. Design an experiment using soap or detergent to measure the hardness of water. *(Designing experiments)* _____

_____

_____

2. You have probably seen advertisements for cleaning products that remove tub and tile stains caused by hard water. What type of chemicals do you think might be in the active ingredients of these cleaners? *(Making predictions)* _____

_____

Name _____

Going Further

1. Find out how water softeners work to remove Ca^{2+} ions from hard water. Using the techniques you learned in this investigation, test the effectiveness of three different water softeners on a sample of hard water.

2. Research the occurrence of hard water in different regions of the country. Find out where hard water is most common and what geographical conditions contribute to the cause.

Properties of Acids and Bases

Lab 52

Introduction

Acids and bases are common chemicals in everyday life. Many products—from shampoos to fruit juices, from medicines to cleaning agents—derive much of their usefulness from their activity as acids or bases. Acids can be classified as substances that ionize in aqueous solutions to produce hydronium ions, H_3O^+. Acids react with metals to produce hydrogen gas and turn litmus paper red. Bases can be classified as substances that dissociate in aqueous solutions to produce hydroxide ions, OH^-. Bases turn litmus paper blue and feel slippery. The strengths of acids and bases depend on the extent to which they ionize, or dissociate. Strong acids or bases dissociate almost completely, while weak acids or bases dissociate to a lesser degree.

In this investigation you will observe some reactions of acids and bases with each other, with other compounds, and with various indicators. From your observations, you should be able to describe some of the characteristic properties of acids and bases.

Pre-Lab Discussion

Read the entire laboratory investigation and the relevant pages of your textbook. Then answer the questions that follow.

1. What is an acid? _____

   _____

2. What is a base? _____

   _____

3. What is an indicator? What indicators will you be using in this experiment? _____

   _____

   _____

4. Write balanced chemical equations for the reactions that occur when the following solutions are mixed:

   a. $HNO_3(aq) + NaOH(aq) \rightarrow$ _____

   b. $2HCl(aq) + Ca(OH)_2(aq) \rightarrow$ _____

5. What safety precautions need to be observed when handling acids and bases? _____

   _____

Name_____

6. For what gas is the reaction product being tested in Step 8? Step 10? _____

_____

7. Give an example of each of these reactions from the investigation:

a. neutralization _____

b. double replacement _____

_____

Problem

How do you observe the properties of acids and bases?

Materials

chemical splash goggles
laboratory apron
latex gloves
marking pen
well plate
hydrochloric acid (HCl), 3.0 M
   and 1.0 M
acetic acid ($HC_2H_3O_2$), 1.0 M
sodium hydroxide (NaOH),
   0.5 M
litmus paper, red and blue
pH paper
phenolphthalein
microspatula

zinc (Zn)
magnesium ribbon (Mg)
iron filings (Fe)
copper wire or sheet (Cu)
5 test tubes, 18 × 150 mm
test-tube rack
wooden splint
match
rubber stopper, 1-hole, fit with
   right-angle bend glass
   tubing
limewater
calcium carbonate ($CaCO_3$)
2 micropipets

Safety

Wear your goggles and lab apron at all times during the investigation. Acids are corrosive and bases are caustic; avoid contact with skin or clothing. Wash spills and splashes with plenty of cold water. Note the caution alert symbols here and with certain steps of the Procedure. Refer to page *xi* for the specific precautions associated with each symbol.

Procedure

Part A: Using Indicators

1. Put on your goggles and lab apron. Add five drops of each of the following solutions to separate labeled depressions in the well plate: 1.0 M HCl; 1.0 M $HC_2H_3O_2$; 0.5 M NaOH. **CAUTION:** *Handle solutions with care. Acids are corrosive and bases are caustic. They can cause serious injury if they come into contact with skin or eyes. Wash spills and splashes with plenty of water.*

2. Place a drop of each solution onto a piece of red litmus paper. Record your observations in Data Table 1. Discard the litmus paper in a solid waste container.

3. Repeat Step 2, using blue litmus paper and then pH paper. Record your observations.

4. Add one drop of phenolphthalein to each solution. Record your observations. Discard the solutions by rinsing them down the drain with plenty of water. Rinse the well plate with water and dry.

Part B: Reactions of Acids with Metals

5. To four separate, clean, labeled depressions in your well plate, add a small piece of zinc, magnesium, iron, and copper.

 6. To each of these depressions, add enough 1.0 M HCl to cover the metal. Observe and compare the relative speed of reaction of the metals with the acid. Record your observations in Data Table 2.

7. Repeat Steps 5 and 6, using clean wells but substituting 1.0 M acetic acid ($HC_2H_3O_2$) for 1.0 M HCl. Compare the reactivity of each metal with $HC_2H_3O_2$ to its reactivity with HCl. Record your observations. Discard the contents of the well plate by putting the metals into a solid waste container using the microspatula and rinsing the solutions down the drain. Rinse and dry the well plate.

8. Add a small amount of zinc to a depression in your well plate. Cover the zinc with 1.0 M HCl. As the reaction proceeds, hold an inverted test tube over the zinc for about two minutes. Without turning the test tube upright, quickly insert a burning splint into the test tube. Record your observations. Discard the contents of your well plate as you did in Step 7. Clean and dry the well plate.

Part C: Reactions of Acids with Carbonates

 9. Put on your latex gloves. Half fill a clean test tube with lime-water solution. Into a second test tube, place a small amount of calcium carbonate ($CaCO_3$). Obtain from your teacher a rubber stopper with a right-angle bend of glass tubing.

 10. Add enough 3.0 M HCl to cover the $CaCO_3$. **CAUTION:** *Acids are corrosive. They can cause serious injury if they come into contact with skin or eyes. Wash spills and splashes with plenty of water.* Insert the rubber stopper into the test tube containing $CaCO_3$ and HCl. Place the open end of the glass tubing into the lime-water. Record your observations. Discard the solutions and place any leftover $CaCO_3$ into the solid waste container. Clean the test tube.

Part D: Neutralization

 11. Using a micropipet, add ten drops of 1.0 M HCl to a clean test tube. Add one drop of phenolphthalein. Test with pH paper. Record your observations.

12. Using a second micropipet, add 0.5 M NaOH to the acid, one drop at a time. After the addition of each drop, swirl the test tube to thoroughly mix the contents. Count and record the total

Name_____

number of drops of NaOH needed to cause a permanent color change. Once the color change is observed, test the solution again with pH paper. Record your results. Pour the solution down the drain and clean the test tube.

 13. Clean up your work area and wash your hands before leaving the laboratory.

Observations

DATA TABLE 1   Reactions with Indicators

Solution	Red litmus	Blue litmus	pH paper	Phenolphthalein
1.0 M HCl				
1.0 M $HC_2H_3O_2$				
0.5 M NaOH				

DATA TABLE 2   Speed of Reaction with Metals

Metal	1.0 M HCl	1.0 M $HC_2H_3O_2$
zinc		
magnesium		
iron		
copper		

Test results with burning splint: _____

_____

Test results with limewater: _____

pH of acid solution: _____

Number of drops of 0.5 M NaOH added: _____

pH of neutral solution: _____

Critical Thinking: Analysis and Conclusions

1. For each metal that reacted with HCl, write a balanced chemical equation. (*Interpreting data*)

_____

_____

_____

2. For each metal that reacted with $HC_2H_3O_2$, write a balanced chemical equation. (*Interpreting data*)

_____

_____

3. List the reactivity of the metals in decreasing order (fastest to slowest). (*Making comparisons*) _____

4. Explain the difference in reaction rates of a given metal with the two different acids. (*Drawing conclusions*) _____

_____

_____

_____

5. Explain the differences in volumes (number of drops) of HCl and NaOH required to produce a neutral solution in Part D. (*Making comparisons*) _____

_____

_____

Critical Thinking: Applications

1. Describe the type of reaction that occurs between certain metals and an acid. (*Applying concepts*) _____

_____

2. What is the effect of acid rain on statues made of marble (calcium carbonate)? (*Making inferences*) _____

_____

3. Based on your data, write a brief paragraph summarizing some properties of acids and bases. (*Using the writing process*) _____

_____

_____

_____

Going Further

1. Research the effects of acid rain on lakes. Find out the impact of increased acidity on living organisms in a lake. Report on how acid rain is neutralized in some lakes by natural processes or human intervention.

2. Design an experiment to test the effects of acidic and basic soils on plant growth.

Comparing Acid Strengths

Text reference: **Chapter 18**

Introduction

You know from everyday experience that there are several ways to make things stronger. One way is just to use more of a material. Glass used for tables is much thicker than the glass in windows, and much stronger. A sheet of steel 0.5 cm thick is not nearly as strong as one that is 3.0 cm thick. Mixing two or more substances together is another way to increase the strength of the resulting material. Metals, such as gold for jewelry or stainless steel, are made stronger by the addition of other materials.

The strength of acids is a different matter, though. Strength depends upon how many hydrogen ions (H^+), or more properly hydronium ions (H_3O^+), are present in a liter of an acid solution. In turn, this ion concentration depends upon the degree of dissociation of the acid molecules when they dissolve in water. Strength is not a measure of the solution concentration. You will see in this investigation that two different acids, hydrochloric and acetic, can have the same solution concentration but different strengths.

In this investigation, you will work with five different concentrations of hydrochloric acid (HCl) and acetic acid (CH_3COOH, sometimes written as HAc, where "Ac" stands for the acetate ion, CH_3COO^-), ranging from 0.1 M through 0.00001 M. The first three concentrations (in decreasing order) will be provided by your teacher. You will prepare the other two solutions by further diluting some of the 0.001 M samples. When all the concentrations have been readied, you will put 1-mL samples of the acids in the wells of a well plate. In Part A, you will observe and compare the reactivity of magnesium metal and magnesium carbonate in the acid samples. In Part B, you will use some common indicators to compare the concentrations of H_3O^+ ions in the solution samples.

Pre-Lab Discussion

Read the entire laboratory investigation and the relevant pages of your textbook. Then answer the questions that follow.

1. How many moles of HCl are in 2.0 mL of 0.001 M HCl?

2. If 2.0 mL of 0.001 M HCl is diluted with 18.0 mL of distilled water, what will be the molarity of the new solution?

Name_____

3. What important feature of HCl allows you to infer that the concentration of H_3O^+ ions of each HCl solution is numerically equal to the value of the concentration expression? _____

_____

_____

_____

4. Although the concentrations of acids in this investigation are very low, what precautions should be taken when working with them?

_____

_____

_____

Problem

How can the strengths of acids be determined?

Materials

chemical splash goggles
laboratory apron
marking pen or pencil
6 beakers, 50-mL
4 micropipets
distilled water
graduated cylinder, 25-mL
samples of the following
   solutions:
      0.1 M HCl
      0.01 M HCl
      0.001 M HCl

0.1 M CH_3COOH
0.01 M CH_3COOH
0.001 M CH_3COOH
glass stirring rod
well plate
scissors
strip of magnesium (Mg)
magnesium carbonate ($MgCO_3$)
orange IV indicator
methyl orange indicator

Safety

Wear your goggles and lab apron at all times during the investigation. Dilute solutions of hydrochloric and acetic acids are irritating to skin and may damage clothing. Methyl orange and orange IV may stain skin and clothing. Wash spills and splashes with plenty of cold water.

   Note the caution alert symbols here and with certain steps of the Procedure. Refer to page *xi* for the specific precautions associated with each symbol.

Procedure

Part A

1. Put on your goggles and lab apron.

2. Clean and rinse each item of glassware with a small amount of distilled water. Pour the rinse water down the drain. With the marking pencil, label three 50-mL beakers *0.001 M, 0.0001 M,* and *0.00001 M* respectively. Label two micropipets for use with the HCl and CH_3COOH.

3. Refer to Figure 53–1 in completing the dilutions through Step 6. Carefully pour distilled water into a 25-mL graduated cylinder until the water level is exactly 18.0 mL. Obtain 6.0 mL of 0.001 *M* hydrochloric acid (HCl) from your teacher and place it in the 50-mL beaker labeled *0.001 M.* Using the micropipet labeled *HCl,* add 0.001 *M* HCl to the distilled water in the graduated cylinder until the level of the mixture is exactly 20.0 mL. Retain the unused 0.001 *M* HCl in the beaker. Pour this new mixture, now at 0.0001 *M* concentration, into the 50-mL beaker labeled *0.0001 M,* stir, and retain. **CAUTION:** *Hydrochloric acid is corrosive. Care should be taken to avoid contact with your skin or clothing. If contact does occur, rinse with plenty of water and notify your teacher.*

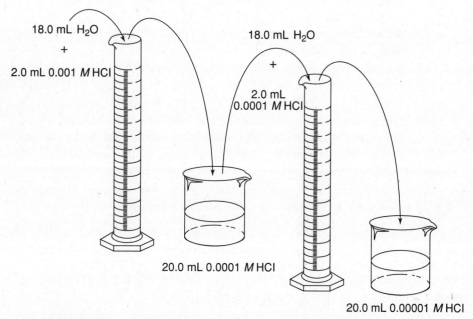

18.0 mL H_2O
+
2.0 mL 0.001 *M* HCl

18.0 mL H_2O
+
2.0 mL
0.0001 *M* HCl

20.0 mL 0.0001 *M* HCl

20.0 mL 0.00001 *M* HCl

Figure 53–1

4. After rinsing the graduated cylinder, stirring rod, and micropipet, add 18.0 mL of distilled water to the graduated cylinder as you did in Step 3. Using the micropipet, add 0.0001 *M* HCl to the distilled water until the level of the mixture is exactly 20.0 mL. Retain the unused 0.0001 *M* HCl in the beaker. Pour this new mixture, now at 0.00001 *M* concentration, into the 50-mL beaker labeled *0.00001 M,* stir, and retain.

5. Obtain 4-mL samples of 0.1 *M* and 0.01 *M* HCl from your teacher and set them aside, arranged along with the beakers containing the other three samples, in decreasing order of concentration.

6. Complete the same procedure and dilution scheme carried out in Steps 2–5 using acetic acid (CH₃COOH). **CAUTION:** *Acetic acid is corrosive. Care should be taken to avoid contact with your skin or clothing. If contact does occur, rinse with plenty of water and notify your teacher.*

7. Using the Data Tables as guides, label the well plate columns with numbers 1–5 and the rows with letters A–D. Place about 1 mL of the 0.1 M HCl in the first wells in rows A and C (wells A1 and C1). Proceed to place 1-mL samples of the remaining HCl concentrations, in decreasing order of concentration, in the other wells in rows A and C. Be certain to rinse the micropipet with distilled water when changing from one concentration to another.

8. Use the same procedure for the acetic acid, placing the designated samples in rows B and D. Be certain to use the acetic acid micropipet and to rinse it with distilled water when changing from one concentration to another.

9. From a larger piece of magnesium ribbon, cut ten pieces approximately 5 mm × 5 mm in size. Place one magnesium metal piece in each of the wells in rows A (with HCl) and B (CH₃COOH). Observe the rate of reaction of the metal in each well. Note if the rate of reaction is faster in one acid than in the other. Note as well if there is an observable pattern for the rate of reaction in the five samples of each of the acids. Observe for at least 2 minutes. Record your observations in Data Table 1.

10. Using pieces of MgCO₃ about the size of a match head, place one sample in each of the wells of rows C and D. Make the same observations as you did in Step 9 and record in Data Table 1.

11. Pour the liquids down the drain and rinse the well plate and sink with running water. Be certain to recover any unreacted metal and dispose of it according to your teacher's directions.

Part B

12. Label the two remaining micropipets for use with the orange IV and methyl orange indicators. With the well plate again clean, fill the wells in rows A–D as you did in Part A. **CAUTION:** *Hydrochloric and acetic acids are corrosive. Care should be taken to avoid contact with your skin or clothing. If contact does occur, rinse with plenty of water and notify your teacher.*

13. With the appropriately labeled micropipet, add a drop of orange IV indicator to each acid sample in rows A and B. Following the same procedure, add methyl orange indicator to the wells in rows C and D.

14. Observe the colors that result in each of the wells and record them in Data Table 2.

15. Pour all the liquids down the drain and rinse the sink with running water. Clean up your work area and wash your hands before leaving the laboratory.

Name_____

Observations

DATA TABLE 1 Reactions of Mg and MgCO₃ with Acid Samples

		1 0.1 M	2 0.01 M	3 0.001 M	4 0.0001 M	5 0.00001 M
A	HCl + Mg					
B	HAc + Mg					
C	HCl + MgCO₃					
D	HAc + MgCO₃					

DATA TABLE 2 Color Changes Using Indicators

		1 0.1 M	2 0.01 M	3 0.001 M	4 0.0001 M	5 0.00001 M
A	HCl + orange IV					
B	HAc + orange IV					
C	HCl + methyl or					
D	HAc + methyl or					

Critical Thinking: Analysis and Conclusions

1. Did the rate of reaction of the magnesium metal appear to be faster in one acid than in the other? Explain your answer. *(Interpreting data)* _____

_____

_____

2. Did the rate of reaction of the magnesium carbonate appear to be faster in one acid than in the other? Explain your answer. *(Interpreting data)* _____

_____

_____

3. Based upon your results in Part A, what can you say about the strength of the acid samples in column 1, rows A–D? In subsequent columns? On what do you base your answer? *(Drawing conclusions)* _____

_____

_____

Name_____

4. In terms of relative concentrations of H_3O^+ ions, describe what the colors of orange IV and methyl orange indicate. *(Making inferences)* _____

_____

5. Based on your data, which of the two acids dissociates more fully in water? *(Drawing conclusions)* _____

_____

6. Do you have evidence indicating whether any one sample of the HCl has a strength about the same as any one sample of CH_3COOH? Explain. _____

_____

_____

Critical Thinking: Applications

1. Based on your observations, which side of the following equations are favored? Explain your reasoning. *(Applying concepts)*

$$HCl(g) \rightleftharpoons H^+(aq) + Cl^-(aq)$$

$$HAc(g) \rightleftharpoons H^+(aq) + Ac^-(aq)$$

_____

_____

_____

_____

2. Muriatic acid, a solution of HCl and water, is used to clean hearths or house sidings. Suppose a store clerk tells you that muriatic acid is perfectly safe to use because it is such a weak acid. Is the clerk correct? Write a paragraph explaining your answer. *(Using the writing process)* _____

_____

_____

_____

_____

Going Further

1. Under your teacher's supervision, conduct a similar investigation to compare the relative strengths of some other common acids, for example, nitric acid, citric acid, and oxalic acid.

Making Table Salt

Introduction

Table salt has been an important commodity throughout history. Its use in preserving foods for long periods of time made salt so valuable that it at times served as the basis of some economic activities and even societal customs. For example, *salarium* (Latin) is the term used to describe the money given to Roman soldiers to purchase salt. The English word *salary* comes from that expression. Seating at a royal table was based upon the relative position of the salt on the table, with people seated "above the salt" having a higher rank than people seated "below the salt."

Most of the table salt (sodium chloride) used today is obtained from underground deposits, either by mining or by pumping water into the deposits and returning the salt solution to ground level for separation. Sea salt is another source of sodium chloride. Sea salt is obtained by evaporating the water from a salt-water solution, leaving behind the precipitated solid. Even today in some parts of the world, sea salt is recovered using the heat energy of the sun and a centuries-old technique. Salt water is placed in bowl-like depressions on the surfaces of large rocks. Over a matter of days the water is evaporated, leaving behind the crystalline salt for collection.

Another way to obtain common table salt involves a process quite different from either mining or the evaporation of existing salt water. Many acid-base reactions yield salts as one of the products. In this investigation, you will react known quantities of hydrochloric acid (HCl) and solid sodium hydroxide (NaOH). The products of this reaction are sodium chloride (NaCl) and water. When the reaction ends, the water is evaporated, leaving table salt as the remaining product. You will be able to calculate the theoretical yield of NaCl and compare it to your actual yield. You also will conduct a flame test for sodium and a precipitate reaction for chlorine to give evidence that the solid product is table salt.

Pre-Lab Discussion

Read the entire laboratory investigation and the relevant pages of your textbook. Then answer the questions that follow.

1. Write the equation for the reaction between solid sodium hydroxide and hydrochloric acid.

   _____

2. How many moles of HCl are in 50.0 mL of a 1.0 *M* HCl solution?

Name _____

3. How many moles of NaOH will completely react with 50.0 mL of 1.0 M HCl?

4. What is the maximum mass of NaOH that will react with 50 mL of 1.0 M HCl?

5. Which of the two substances in this investigation, HCl or NaOH, is the limiting reactant? _____

    _____

6. What special precautions should you take when working with the sodium hydroxide pellets? _____

    _____

Problem

How can table salt be recovered from the reaction between sodium hydroxide and hydrochloric acid?

Materials

chemical splash goggles
laboratory apron
latex gloves
laboratory balance
beaker, 250-mL
marking pen or pencil
hydrochloric acid, 1.0 M
graduated cylinder, 100-mL
micropipet
wash bottle containing distilled
    water
forceps

sodium hydroxide pellets
    (NaOH)
large watch glass
stirring rod
scoopula
lab burner
flame-test loop
small test tube
test-tube rack
micropipet containing silver
    nitrate solution (AgNO$_3$),
    0.1 M

Safety

Wear your goggles and lab apron at all times during the investigation. Sodium hydroxide pellets are very caustic and can burn skin. Silver nitrate is toxic and can stain skin and clothing. Wear latex gloves when handling these chemicals. Tie back loose hair and clothing when working with a flame. Hydrochloric acid is corrosive. It will irritate skin and damage clothing. Avoid spills and splashes. If any of these reagents contact the skin, wash with plenty of cold water and notify your teacher. Hydrochloric acid releases irritating fumes when heated. Heat HCl in the fume hood. Dispose of silver compounds according to your teacher's instructions.

Note the caution alert symbols here and with certain steps of the Procedure. Refer to page *xi* for the specific precautions associated with each symbol.

Procedure

Part A

 1. Put on your goggles and lab apron.

 2. Find the mass of a 250-mL beaker. With a marking pen, mark your beaker with your team number for later identification. Record the mass in the Data Table.

 3. Precisely measure 50.0 mL of 1.00 *M* HCl in a 100-mL graduated cylinder. Use a micropipet to add the final drops of HCl to ensure precision in the measurement of the acid. Carefully pour the acid into the beaker. Rinse the graduated cylinder two times with 2–3 mL of distilled water, adding the rinse water to the acid in the beaker. **CAUTION:** *Hydrochloric acid is corrosive. It will irritate skin and damage clothing. Avoid spills and splashes. Wash any acid that comes in contact with your skin with plenty of cold water.*

4. Put on latex gloves. In your answer to Question 4 of the Pre-Lab Discussion, you found the maximum mass of NaOH that will react with 50.0 mL of 1.0 *M* HCl. Using forceps, place enough sodium hydroxide pellets on the balance that the mass is in excess of this value. Remove pellets one at a time until the mass of the sodium hydroxide pellets is just below the maximum mass that would react. Find the mass of these pellets precisely. Record the mass in the Data Table. **CAUTION:** *Sodium hydroxide pellets are very caustic. Wear gloves. If any sodium hydroxide touches your skin, wash with plenty of cold water and notify your teacher.*

5. Carefully add the NaOH pellets to the HCl in the beaker. Loosely cover the beaker with a large watch glass to prevent any spattering. If the reaction appears to be completed and there is still some solid NaOH unreacted in the bottom of the beaker, gently stir the acid with a stirring rod until all the solid NaOH disappears. Rinse off the stirring rod with distilled water, allowing the rinse water to flow into the beaker. When the reaction is completed, remove the watch glass, noting first to see if there is any liquid on the underside. If liquid has collected, rinse it off with distilled water, letting the rinse water flow into the beaker.

 6. Give the beaker to your teacher for drying overnight. **CAUTION:** *The beaker in the fume hood will release irritating HCl vapors. Do not breathe in the fumes. Clean up your work area and wash your hands before leaving the laobratory.*

Part B

 7. Put on your goggles and lab apron. Obtain your beaker and find its new mass. Record the mass in the Data Table.

8. Using a scoopula, scrape some of the white solid free from the bottom of the beaker for testing. Leave it at the bottom of the beaker.

9. Light a burner and adjust the flame to a medium intensity. **CAUTION:** *Tie back loose hair and clothing when working with a flame.* Press the flame-test loop into the white solid to partially coat the loop. Move the loop to the top of the flame's inner cone and observe the resulting color. Repeat until a definite color has been identified. Record the color in the Data Table.

10. Scoop a pinch or two of the white solid into a small test tube, add distilled water, and stir with a stirring rod until the solid dissolves.

11. Put on latex gloves. Using a micropipet containing 0.1 *M* silver nitrate (AgNO₃) solution, add a small amount to the test tube and place the test tube in a test-tube rack. **CAUTION:** *Silver nitrate is toxic and can stain skin and clothing. Wear latex gloves when handling it.* Observe and record the color of the precipitate in the Data Table.

12. Discard the precipitate from the test tube according to your teacher's instructions. The remaining solid in the beaker can be dissolved in water and poured down the drain. Clean up your work area and wash your hands before leaving the laboratory.

Observations

DATA TABLE

initial mass of beaker (g)	
mass of NaOH (g)	
final mass of beaker and residue (g)	
flame-test color	
precipitate color	

Calculations

1. Calculate the mass of the solid in the beaker.

2. Calculate the theoretical yield of salt based upon the amount of sodium hydroxide used.

3. Calculate the percentage yield of sodium chloride.

Critical Thinking: Analysis and Conclusions

1. What did the result of the flame test indicate about the solid product? *(Interpreting data)* _____

_____

2. When the solid product was dissolved in water and $AgNO_3$ was added to the solution, what did the resulting precipitate indicate? *(Interpreting data)* _____

_____

3. When the reaction was completed (but before the water was evaporated), do you think the remaining solution was acidic, basic, or something else? Explain. *(Making inferences)* _____

_____

_____

4. If you had used exactly 2.00 grams of NaOH and 50.0 mL of 1.00 *M* HCl in the reaction, how would you characterize the nature of the remaining solution? *(Drawing conclusions)* _____

_____

_____

Critical Thinking: Applications

1. Do the flame and silver precipitate tests prove the solid product is NaCl? *(Making judgments)* _____

_____

2. What other tests might be conducted to prove the product is sodium chloride? *(Designing experiments)* _____

_____

_____

3. Do you think the method employed in this investigation could be used to make very large amounts of common table salt? Explain. *(Making judgments)* _____

_____

_____

_____

Going Further

1. Baking soda (NaHCO₃) and baking powder (baking soda + tartaric acid) are salts used in baking to produce fluffy breads, cakes, and muffins. What is the chemical reaction that these two substances undergo? How do they produce the fluffy texture in baked goods? Take a trip to a local bakery to find out how baking soda and powders are used.

2. Research the life and work of Carl Wilhelm Scheele (1742–1786), a Swedish pharmacist and chemist. What was his contribution to the understanding of acids?

Determining the pH of an Unknown

Small Scale Lab 55

Text reference: **Chapter 19**

Introduction

The pH scale uses numbers from 1 to 14 to describe how acidic or basic a solution is. A pH value of 7 is neutral (neither acidic nor basic), a pH value below 7 is acidic, and a pH value above 7 is basic. The lower the pH, the more acidic the solution. The higher the pH, the more basic the solution.

Indicators are often used to measure pH. An indicator is a weak acid (or base) that undergoes dissociation in a known pH range. In this range, the acid (or base) is a different color from its conjugate base (or acid). The three pH indicators used in this investigation are phenolphthalein, a natural indicator, and universal indicator. A natural indicator is one that is made from a material produced by a plant or an animal. A natural indicator can be made from many things, including red cabbage, grapes, and roses. Universal indicator is a mixture of several indicators, chosen so that a range of colors appears over a wide range of pH values.

In this investigation, you will observe the color changes that take place when each indicator is put into eleven solutions that have known pH values ranging from pH 2 to pH 12. You will then use your data as the basis for determining the pH of an unknown solution provided by your teacher.

Pre-Lab Discussion

Read the entire laboratory investigation and the relevant pages of your textbook. Then answer the questions that follow.

1. What is the range of pH values of an acidic solution? _____

2. What is the range of pH values for a basic solution? _____

3. Why does an indicator change colors at different pH values?

   _____

4. What precautions should you take when dealing with acidic and

   basic solutions? _____

   _____

   _____

Problem

How can the pH of an unknown solution be determined using acid-base indicators?

Name _____

Materials

chemical splash goggles
laboratory apron
11 micropipets containing
   solutions numbered
   by pH
well plate

3 micropipets, containing the
   following:
     phenolphthalein
     universal indicator
     natural indicator
micropipet containing unknown
   solution

Safety

Wear your goggles and lab apron at all times during the investigation. Acids are corrosive and bases are caustic. Indicators may stain skin and clothing. Handle all chemicals with care. Avoid spills and contact with your skin. Wash spills and splashes with plenty of cold water. Note the caution alert symbols here and with certain steps of the Procedure. Refer to page *xi* for the specific precautions associated with each symbol.

Procedure

1. Put on your goggles and lab apron. Add five drops of solution 2 to the first three wells of column 2 of your well plate (wells A2, B2, and C2). For columns 3 to 12 of your well plate, repeat using solutions 3 to 12. See Figure 55–1. **CAUTION:** *Acids are corrosive and bases are caustic. Avoid spills and contact with your skin. Wash spills and splashes with plenty of cold water.*

Placement of Solutions 5 through 10

	1	2	3	4		11	12
A		Solution 2	Solution 3	Solution 4		Solution 11	Solution 12
B		Solution 2	Solution 3	Solution 4		Solution 11	Solution 12
C		Solution 2	Solution 3	Solution 4		Solution 11	Solution 12

Figure 55–1

2. Add three drops of phenolphthalein indicator to wells A1 through A12. (Although well A1 is empty, a solution will be added to it in a later step.) Record in the Data Table any color changes you observe. If no color is seen, record *colorless* in the Data Table.

3. Add three drops of the natural indicator to wells B1 through B12. Record in the Data Table any color changes you observe.

4. Add three drops of universal indicator into well C1 through C12. Record in the Data Table any color changes you observe.

5. Obtain from your teacher a solution of unknown pH. Record the solution's identification number in the Data Table. Add five drops of the unknown to the first three wells in column 1 (wells A1, B1, and C1).

6. Compare the color of your unknown in well A1 to the colors in the other wells in row A. Similarly, compare the color of wells B1 and C1 with their respective rows. Record your observations in the Data Table.

 7. Wash all solutions in the well plate down the drain. Clean and dry the well plate. Clean up your work area and wash your hands before leaving the laboratory.

Observations
DATA TABLE

	Indicator	pH of Solution					
		2	3	4	5	6	7
A	phenol-phthalein						
B	natural						
C	universal						

	Indicator	pH of Solution					
		8	9	10	11	12	Un-known
A	phenol-phthalein						
B	natural						
C	universal						

Critical Thinking: Analysis and Conclusions

1. What is the color of phenolphthalein in solutions with pH values ranging from 2 to 6? (*Interpreting data*) _____

_____

Name_____

2. What is the color of phenolphthalein in solutions with pH values ranging from 8 to 12? *(Interpreting data)* _____

_____

3. Which indicator had the greatest number of colors? *(Making comparisons)* _____

_____

4. Which indicator used in the investigation could most precisely identify the pH of your unknown solution? Explain. *(Drawing conclusions)* _____

_____

_____

Critical Thinking: Applications

1. Give an explanation for why universal indicator has a number of different colors over the pH range used in this investigation, whereas most indicators have only two colors. *(Drawing conclusions)* _____

_____

_____

2. Soils have different acidities, affecting the growth of many plants. Some plants do well in a more acidic soil, whereas others do better in a basic soil. Describe a method for testing the acidity of the soil near your home or school. *(Designing experiments)* _____

_____

_____

_____

_____

Going Further

1. An acid-base indicator can be prepared from red cabbage, which turns a number of different colors when added to solutions with different acidities. Research how to prepare cabbage indicator and try making some under your teacher's supervision. Then use the cabbage indicator to test some familiar products such as vinegar and household ammonia. **CAUTION:** *Be careful when handling a knife or a blender and heating anything over a flame. Do not breathe household ammonia. Wear goggles and a lab apron while doing this procedure.*

An Indicator for Acid Rain

Text reference: Chapter 19

Introduction

The effects of acid rain on plants and animals in some forests, lakes, and streams are increasingly troublesome. The damage is most noticeable in areas downwind from heavy automobile traffic and industries that burn high-sulfur coal. Citizens concerned about relieving the problem need to know which polluting acids are causing the damage and how they are finding their way into the environment.

One of the pollutants, nitric acid, is formed from nitrogen monoxide, a gas produced by many industrial processes and by the internal combustion engines of cars, trucks, and buses. The nitrogen monoxide gas released from exhaust pipes reacts very quickly with oxygen to produce nitrogen dioxide gas (NO_2).

$$2NO(g) + O_2(g) \rightarrow 2NO_2(g)$$

Nitrogen dioxide gas reacts readily with water to form both nitric acid (HNO_3) and more nitrogen monoxide (NO).

$$3NO_2(g) + H_2O(l) \rightarrow 2HNO_3(aq) + NO(g)$$

Then nitrogen monoxide gas reacts again with O_2 to produce more nitrogen dioxide gas via the first equation, and the cycle is repeated. Nitric acid is a strong acid that can lower the pH of rain or snow to values well below 4.

Carbon dioxide is another gas that is present in the atmosphere. It also produces an acid when dissolved in water. Carbon dioxide is not considered to be an acid rain pollutant since it forms carbonic acid, which is a weak acid. It dissociates very little in water.

$$CO_2(g) + H_2O(l) \rightleftharpoons H_2CO_3(aq)$$

$$H_2CO_3(aq) \rightleftharpoons H^+(aq) + HCO_3^-(aq)$$

In the environment, carbon dioxide alone does not reduce the pH of rainwater below 5, so it does not cause problems for plant and animal life.

The polluting acids that do cause major damage in the environment, such as nitric, sulfurous, and sulfuric acids, are capable of lowering the pH of the water in clouds to values well below 3.9. This highly acidic rain creates problems over large areas of land and water. On land, plants become less able to extract important minerals such as calcium and magnesium from the soil. They become more susceptible to fungal infections. In water systems, animals and plants cannot develop properly when the pH of the water in lakes and rivers falls too low.

The purpose of this investigation is to find an indicator that will distinguish between the pH effects of the weak acid product of carbon dioxide and the strong acid product of nitrogen oxides. You will study the formation of nitric acid under circumstances similar to its occurrence

Name_____

in nature. You will also compare the sensitivity of three indicators to changes in pH and use your findings to identify the best indicator of acid rain formed from nitrogen oxides.

Pre-Lab Discussion

Read the entire laboratory investigation and the relevant pages of your textbook. Then answer the questions that follow.

1. What is a major source of nitric acid pollution? _____

   _____

2. Why should great care be taken to rinse the petri dish three times with distilled water before attempting each part of the procedure?

   _____

   _____

3. Describe the process by which you will neutralize the polluting gas

   and the source that generates it. _____

   _____

4. Write and balance the net equation for the neutralization reaction that occurs between nitric acid and sodium hydrogen carbonate in

   Step 11. _____

5. Explain why carbon dioxide gas is not normally considered a pollut-

   ant that causes acid rain. _____

   _____

6. How does the condensed liquid you collect on the under surface of

   the petri dish lid simulate the cloud of acid rain? _____

   _____

   _____

Problem

Why is bromcresol green an excellent indicator for detecting the environmentally harmful effects of nitrogen oxides?

Materials

chemical splash goggles
laboratory apron
petri dish
white paper
7 micropipets, filled with the
   following reagents:
      bromcresol green indicator
      bromthymol blue indicator
      universal indicator
      potassium nitrite (KNO_2),
         0.5 *M*
      sulfuric acid (H_2SO_4), 2.0 *M*

sodium hydrogen carbonate
   ($NaHCO_3$), 0.001 *M*
ammonium hydroxide
   (NH_4OH), 2.0 *M*
drinking straw
wash bottle with distilled water
ice chips
petri dish with sealed access
   port
paper towels
black construction paper

Safety

Wear your goggles and lab apron at all times during the investigation. Nitric acid and sulfuric acid are corrosive. Avoid direct contact with them. Wash spills and splashes with plenty of cold water. The NO_2 gas generated in this experiment is irritating to eyes and nasal passages. In Part B, open the petri dish only as directed.

Ammonium hydroxide (NH_4OH) and its fumes are irritating to eyes and nasal passages. Do not inhale the vapors directly. Wash any skin or clothing that comes into contact with NH_4OH solution with plenty of cold water. Note the caution alert symbols here and with certain steps of the Procedure. Refer to page *xi* for the specific precautions associated with each symbol.

Procedure

Part A: Exposure of Indicators to Carbon Dioxide

1. Put on your goggles and lab apron. Rinse both halves of the petri dish three times with distilled water. Dry the dish. Place the bottom half of the petri dish on the white paper background.

2. Place one drop each of bromcresol green, bromthymol blue, and universal indicator in the dish as illustrated in Figure 56–1.

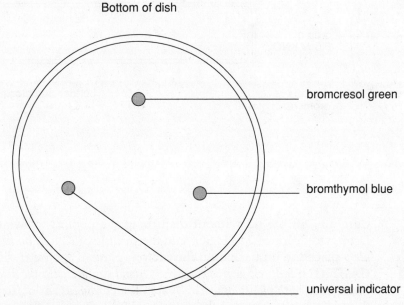

Figure 56–1

3. Expose each of the drops of indicator to carbon dioxide gas (CO_2) by blowing *gently* on the drops for about 1 minute through a clean straw. Observe any color changes that occur within the drops of each indicator during this time. Record these color changes in Data Table 1.

4. Discard the straw in the trash. Without using any detergent, wash the contents of the petri dish into the sink. Rinse the dish three times with distilled water, and dry it.

Part B: Producing Acid Rain

5. Place the bottom half of the petri dish on the white paper background. Use the micropipet to place rows of droplets of bromcresol green in the dish as illustrated in Figure 56–2.

6. Place one drop of 0.5 M KNO_2 in the middle of the dish as illustrated in Figure 56–2. Record the color in Data Table 2.

7. Cover the bottom plate of the petri dish with its lid, and move it to the black paper. Place a piece of ice about 1 cm in diameter in the middle of the top of the lid. Using distilled water from the micropipet, enlarge the puddle of melting ice to about 2 cm in diameter. Droplets of condensed water vapor should appear on the underside of the lid.

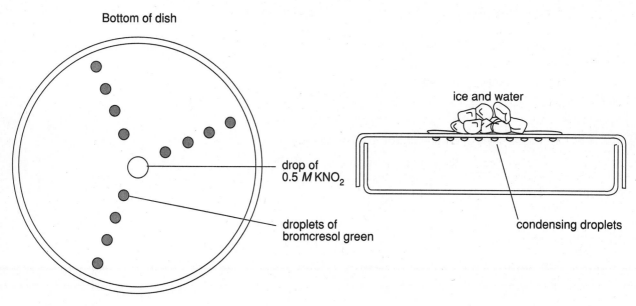

Bottom of dish

drop of
0.5 M KNO_2

droplets of
bromcresol green

ice and water

condensing droplets

Figure 56–2

8. Carefully lift the lid without disturbing the pool of ice water. Drop two drops of 2 M H_2SO_4 into the puddle of KNO_2. *Immediately* place the lid back onto the bottom plate of the petri dish. **CAUTION:** *Sulfuric acid is corrosive. Avoid contact with the acids. Wash spills with plenty of water.* Watch the changes that occur in the indicator and record them in Data Table 2.

9. Wait 2–4 minutes. Carefully remove the lid and *immediately* replace it with the lid having the sealed access port. Set the dish with the new lid aside for now and work with the old lid. Wipe the ice water off the top side of the lid with a paper towel and place the lid upside-down on the black paper.

10. Collect the droplets in the following manner: First, add two drops of distilled water to the center of the lid. Next, collect all

of the fine droplets by tilting and rolling the petri dish lid. Carefully slide the lid back to the white background and add one drop of bromcresol green indicator solution to the collected puddle. Record the resulting color in Data Table 2.

11. Titrate the puddle with drops of 0.001 M $NaHCO_3$. Hold the micropipet vertically as you deliver and count the drops. Gently move the dish to stir the contents. Record in Data Table 2 the number of drops of base (0.001 M $NaHCO_3$) needed to turn bromcresol green to a blue color.

12. Return to the petri dish that has the sealed access port. Raise the tape from the access port and introduce two drops of 2.0 M ammonium hydroxide solution through the port. Immediately replace the tape over the port. Wait about 5 minutes.

13. Wash the contents from the bottom plate of the petri dish into the sink. Rinse the bottom plate again with distilled water and dry it. Clean up your work area and wash your hands before leaving the laboratory.

Observations

DATA TABLE 1   Indicators and CO_2 Gas

Indicator	Observations
bromcresol green	
bromthymol blue	
universal indicator	

DATA TABLE 2

Procedure	Observations
KNO_2 and bromcresol green	
NO_2 and bromcresol green	
water droplets and bromcresol green	
drops 0.001 M $NaHCO_3$	

Calculations

1. Using the equation you wrote in Question 4 of the Pre-Lab Discussion, determine the number of moles of sodium hydrogen carbonate used in the titration with nitric acid. Assume that the volume of one drop from a micropipet held vertically is 4×10^{-5} L.

Name_____

2. How many moles of nitric acid were in the acid droplets? Assume that the sodium hydrogen carbonate exactly titrated the moles of nitric acid present in the droplets.

_____

3. Assume that the volume of your cloudlike droplets was 2×10^{-6} L. What was the molarity of the nitric acid in the droplets?

4. Assume that the acidic droplets you titrated in Part B contained only nitric acid. Use the concentration of nitric acid you just calculated to determine the pH.

Critical Thinking: Analysis and Conclusions

1. The pH range of each indicator is given below:

Bromthymol Blue

$\leftarrow$ blue $\leftarrow$ green $\rightarrow$ yellow $\rightarrow$
(7.6)   (6.0)

Bromcresol Green

$\leftarrow$ blue $\leftarrow$ green $\rightarrow$ yellow $\rightarrow$
(5.5)   (3.8)

Universal Indicator

$\leftarrow$violet$\rightarrow$ $\leftarrow$blue$\rightarrow$ $\leftarrow$blue green$\rightarrow$ $\leftarrow$green$\rightarrow$ $\leftarrow$yellow$\rightarrow$ $\leftarrow$orange$\rightarrow$ $\leftarrow$red$\rightarrow$
(10)   (9)   (8)   (7)   (6)   (5)   (4)

Using these ranges and the color changes observed for each indicator in Part A, state what the indicator tells you about the pH attained by exposing the solutions to carbon dioxide. (*Interpreting data*)

a. bromthymol blue _____

b. bromcresol green _____

c. universal indicator _____

2. Using the given pH ranges of the indicators and the pH you found in Calculation 5, state the color you think you would get with the nitric acid you made and the following indicators. (*Making predictions*)

a. bromthymol blue _____

b. bromcresol green _____

c. universal indicator _____

3. Why did you titrate the bromcresol green–water solution in Part B with your base until the solution turned blue? (*Applying concepts*)

_____

_____

4. Why is bromcresol green a good indicator for testing acid rain? *(Drawing conclusions)* _____

_____

_____

Critical Thinking: Applications

1. Some of the mountainsides near the major highways in Germany and the United States exhibit dead or dying forests. Do the results of your titration demonstrate how NO_2 from car exhaust may be a contributing factor to this damage? Explain. *(Developing hypotheses)*

_____

_____

_____

2. Compare your titration results with those of other groups of students. Discuss which variables may affect the acid concentration. Would these same variables affect the concentration of the polluting acids in clouds in nature? *(Making comparisons)* _____

_____

_____

3. Farmers often spread limestone on soil to "sweeten" the soil. The primary mineral of limestone is calcium carbonate ($CaCO_3$). Write an equation that describes the reaction of nitric acid with calcium carbonate. Then explain why soils and aquatic systems that contain limestone are protected somewhat from acid rain. *(Applying concepts)* _____

_____

_____

4. Marble is a metamorphosed form of limestone. Powdered limestone is an important ingredient in concrete. State at least one economic reason and one aesthetic reason for you to become involved in the process of preventing acid rain. *(Evaluating)* _____

_____

_____

_____

Going Further

1. Catalytic converters are placed on automobiles to prevent the release of specific gases. Scrubbers are often placed on coal-burning stacks. Research the chemistry of the catalytic converter and scrubbers and report your findings to the class.

2. The types of smog in London and Los Angeles present lethal problems. Research these two smog types to determine their sources and their relationship to the substances that cause acid rain. Report your results to the class.

3. Design a procedure that employs the petri dish and bromcresol green to investigate the effect of acid rain on limestone, marble, and concrete. Under the supervision of your teacher, carry out the procedure and report your findings to the class.

Titration with Oxalic Acid   Lab 57

Text reference: **Chapter 19**

Introduction

Titration is a versatile analytical procedure that can be used for a wide variety of chemical analyses. For example, when your town's water supply is tested for purity, or pond water is tested for dissolved oxygen and contaminants, chances are a titration is carried out. Some tests essential for a medical diagnosis require a titration of various body fluids.

A titration makes use of a known reaction between two chemicals. A solution of unknown concentration is reacted with a precisely measured amount of another chemical. An appropriate indicator must be used to determine when chemically equivalent amounts of each chemical are combined, that is, when no excess of either reactant is present. This is known as the equivalence point. To measure solution volumes accurately, finely calibrated pipets and burets are used. Titrations are commonly used to determine the strength of acids or bases.

Acid-base titrations follow a relatively standard procedure for analysis of acid or base strength. The concentration of either an acid or a base solution can be determined. A measured amount of acid neutralized by reaction with a base solution titrated from a buret. Consider the following example:

$$HCl + NaOH \rightarrow NaCl + H_2O$$
(known) (unknown)

The example shows that the reaction is a double replacement in which the products are a corresponding salt and water. For reactions of strong acids and bases, the equivalence point pH is 7, but for weak acids it is somewhat higher. If a graph is made of pH vs. volume of base added (see Figure 57–1), the equivalence point is always halfway along the S curve as labeled in the illustration. Note that there is a large pH change around the equivalence point with very small additions of base.

In this investigation, you will determine the concentration of two basic solutions by titration with oxalic acid, $H_2C_2O_4$, a moderately weak acid with an equivalence point pH of approximately 8. Weak acids are used to titrate bases because the equivalence point is reached more slowly, so the results are more accurate. Phenolphthalein will be used to find the endpoint because it is colorless below pH 8, but turns pink just above pH 8.

Name_____

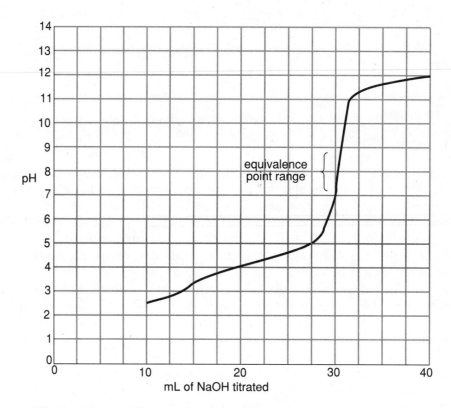

Figure 57–1 *pH curve for titration of oxalic acid*

Pre-Lab Discussion

Read the entire laboratory investigation and the relevant pages of your textbook. Then answer the questions that follow.

1. Why is it difficult to see whether you have added the pH indicator phenolphthalein to the flask of acid solution? _____

_____

2. Write and balance the double replacement reaction equations for this investigation. In each case, how many moles of base are needed to neutralize one mole of acid?
     oxalic acid and sodium hydroxide:

     oxalic acid and ammonium hydroxide:

3. Why must you fill the buret only when its top is below eye level?

_____

_____

4. Look up the term *equivalent*. Give its root derivation, and tell how this root helps to explain the meaning of equivalence point.

_____

_____

5. Why is it better to use a weak rather than a strong acid when you titrate a base? _____

_____

Problem

How can you use the titration process to determine the strength of bases?

Materials

chemical splash goggles
laboratory apron
erlenmeyer flask, 250-mL
laboratory balance
oxalic acid dihydrate
   ($H_2C_2O_4 \cdot 2H_2O$)
distilled water
phenolphthalein
wash bottle

buret
buret clamp
ring stand
sodium hydroxide solution
   (NaOH), pH unknown
2 beakers, 100-mL
white paper
household ammonia (NH_4OH),
   pH unknown

Safety

Wear your goggles and lab apron at all times during the investigation. Place the top of the buret below eye level when filling it to avoid splashing the solutions into the face. Place the buret and buret stand on the floor if necessary. Acids are corrosive and bases are caustic. Wipe up spills and drips immediately with wet towels, and then dry. Wash affected skin areas with cold water after any contact and notify your teacher. Burets are cumbersome and break easily—handle them with care.

   Note the caution alert symbols here and with certain steps of the Procedure. Refer to page *xi* for the specific precautions associated with each symbol.

Procedure

Part A: Preparation

1. Put on your goggles and lab apron. While one lab partner prepares the oxalic acid (Steps 2 and 3), the other will prepare the buret for titration (Steps 4–8).

2. Determine the mass of a 250-mL flask to 0.01 g, then add 1.0–1.5 g oxalic acid dihydrate to the flask, and determine the mass again. **CAUTION:** *Acids are corrosive. Avoid contact with skin, eyes, and clothing. Wash spills with plenty of cold water.* Record these masses in Data Table 1.

Name_____

3. Dissolve the acid in the flask with approximately 100 mL of distilled water. Add two or three drops of phenolphthalein indicator solution to the flask.

 4. Make sure that the buret is clean. If it is not, wash the buret with detergent and a buret brush. Clean the tip by draining some detergent solution through it. **CAUTION:** *Burets are fragile. Use great care in handling them.*

5. Rinse the buret thoroughly with tap water, then rinse once with distilled water, draining final rinses through the tip. Clamp the clean buret to the support stand.

6. Obtain 50–60 mL of sodium hydroxide (NaOH) solution, unknown 1, in a 100-mL beaker. Position the buret so that the top is below your eye level and place an empty beaker under the buret tip to catch drips. **CAUTION:** *Sodium hydroxide is caustic. Keep the top of the buret below eye level when pouring sodium hydroxide. Avoid contact with skin, eyes, and clothing. Wash spills and splashes with plenty of cold water.*

7. Pour approximately 5 mL of base into the buret. Drain this through the tip to remove water and coat the inside of the buret with base. See Figure 57–2.

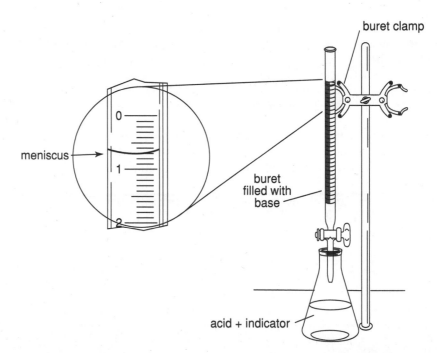

Figure 57–2

8. Now fill the buret to slightly above the zero line. Drain some base through the tip to clear the buret tip of air. Stop between 0.0 and 2.0 mL. Remove the hanging drop at the tip by touching the tip to the inside of the waste beaker. Read the initial volume in the buret and record it in Data Table 1.

Part B: Titration

9. Place the flask with acid and phenolphthalein under the buret. The buret tip should be down about 1 cm inside the mouth of the flask to avoid any outside loss of base. Place a sheet of white paper under the flask to highlight the pink indicator color.

10. Drip the base into the flask while swirling the flask. You can add base quickly at first, but as the pink color starts to last longer, slow the drip rate. When the whole flask flashes pink before turning clear again, add only one or two drops at a time and swirl until the flask is clear before adding more. Occasionally rinse down splashes on the inside of the flask using a little distilled water from a wash bottle.

11. When the faintest pink color persists, stop and record the final volume in the buret.

12. Flush all chemicals down the drain with plenty of water. Wash all beakers and the flask, and clean the buret as described in Step 4.

13. To determine the molarity of ammonia, repeat Steps 2, 3, and Steps 7–12, using clear household ammonia, NH_4OH, in the buret. Record your observations in Data Table 2. **CAUTION:** *Household ammonia is caustic and the fumes are irritating to eyes and lungs. Avoid breathing in vapors.*

 14. Clean up your work area and wash your hands before leaving the laboratory.

Observations
DATA TABLE 1 $NaOH + H_2C_2O_4$

Mass (g)		Volume of NaOH (mL)	
flask		initial	
flask and oxalic acid		final	
oxalic acid		titrated	

DATA TABLE 2 $NH_4OH + H_2C_2O_4$

Mass (g)		Volume of NH_4OH (mL)	
flask		initial	
flask and oxalic acid		final	
oxalic acid		titrated	

Calculations

1. Determine the molarity of the unknown sodium hydroxide solution as follows.

   a. Calculate the number of moles of oxalic acid used for NaOH, using the molar mass of $H_2C_2O_4 \cdot 2H_2O$.

   b. Use your answer to Question 2 of the Pre-Lab Discussion to determine the number of moles of base needed to neutralize the calculated number of moles of oxalic acid.

   c. Calculate the molar concentration of base used.

2. Determine the molarity of ammonium hydroxide, using the same method you used for sodium hydroxide.

Critical Thinking: Analysis and Conclusions

1. Does the amount of water in which the oxalic acid is dissolved affect the outcome of the investigation? Why or why not? *(Applying concepts)* _____

   _____

   _____

2. Titration is capable of yielding highly reproducible results, equivalent to ±1 drop of titrant. Explain how each of the following parts of the procedure contributes to this precision. *(Drawing conclusions)*

   a. Removing drops of titrant hanging from the tip. _____

   _____

   _____

   b. Washing down the inside of the reaction flask with water.

   _____

   _____

   c. Rinsing the buret with the base to be used. _____

   _____

Critical Thinking: Applications

1. Use the pH curve for titration diagramed in the Introduction to determine the effect on pH from the addition of one or two drops of base when pH = 3; when pH = 6. *(Interpreting diagrams)* _____

    _____

    _____

2. Carbonate ions, CO_3^{2-}, are contained in limestone (the major component of which is calcium carbonate, $CaCO_3$), which is used to neutralize acids in soil. Remedies sold to neutralize stomach acid contain carbonate. The equilibrium reaction that carbonate ions undergo with water is called hydrolysis. Write the reaction for this equation, and explain how carbonate neutralizes acids. *(Applying concepts)*

    _____

    _____

Going Further

1. Under the supervision of your teacher, carry out a titration with a pH meter. After each milliliter of titrant is added, record the pH. Graph pH vs. volume of titrant, or enter the values into a computer spreadsheet and use a graphing option to make the graph. If the pH probe is coupled to a computer with an automatic recording option, set a slow, steady drip rate for the buret and record the pH every few seconds. Plot the pH vs. time. From the graph, find the equivalence point pH.
2. Oxalic acid is a natural organic acid present in high concentrations in some plants such as rhubarb. It is used in commercial cleansers that remove rust stains. Many biological processes depend on organic acids that also have commercial value. Research other sources and uses of oxalic acid and other naturally occurring acids.

Rust Marches On

Introduction

One of the most common chemical reactions involving metals is corrosion or, more precisely, spontaneous oxidation. Iron in particular oxidizes very easily, forming a compound commonly called rust. Most people are familiar with how easily rust forms despite the best efforts to prevent it. Cars, bicycles, bridges, nails—all may quickly succumb to spontaneous oxidation reactions.

Rust is actually hydrated iron(III) oxide, $Fe_2O_3 \cdot xH_2O$. When rust forms, a voltaic cell is created on the surface of the material. Iron is oxidized to its 2+ state at the anode, while oxygen is reduced in the presence of water at the cathode. Iron(II) hydroxide forms as an intermediate precipitate. Further oxidation of the iron leads to the familiar red-brown solid known as rust.

In this investigation you will look at the corrosion process, or rusting, from an electrochemical perspective. You will build an electrochemical cell on a steel plate and cause the oxidation of iron, using an indicator to determine the oxidation and reduction half reactions.

Pre-Lab Discussion

Read the entire laboratory investigation and the relevant pages of your textbook. Then answer the questions that follow.

1. What is the oxidation state of iron in $Fe_2O_3 \cdot xH_2O$? What is the significance of the "$\cdot xH_2O$"? _____

    _____

2. In which oxidation state is the iron in Step 1 of the Procedure? How will the presence of oxidized iron be detected? _____

    _____

3. A corroding metal is sometimes called an "unwanted voltaic cell." Briefly explain this statement. _____

    _____

4. What conditions speed up the formation of rust, for example in an automobile? _____

    _____

Name_____

5. Compare E° for the oxidation of iron with two other common metals. Choose one that is more easily oxidized than iron, and one that is less easily oxidized. Write the equation for each half reaction.

_____

_____

_____

Problem

What electrochemical processes are involved in rusting?

Materials

chemical splash goggles
laboratory apron
well plate
piece of white paper
3 micropipets, containing the following solutions:

iron(II) sulfate (FeSO$_4$),
   0.1 M
ferroxyl indicator solution
sodium hydroxide (NaOH),
   0.1 M
steel plate
steel wool

Safety

Wear your goggles and lab apron at all times during the investigation.

Some of the solutions used may be irritating to the skin. If any of them come into contact with skin, wash the area thoroughly with cold water and tell your teacher. Note the caution alert symbols here and with certain steps of the Procedure. Refer to page *xi* for the specific precautions associated with each symbol.

Procedure

1. Put on your goggles and lab apron. With the well plate on a white piece of paper, place two or three drops of iron(II) sulfate, FeSO$_4$, solution in one well of the well plate. Add two or three drops of the ferroxyl indicator solution. Observe the color changes. Record your observations in the Data Table.

2. In a second well, place two or three drops of sodium hydroxide, NaOH, solution. Add two or three drops of ferroxyl indicator solution. Observe and record the color changes.

3. Polish the steel plate with steel wool if necessary. Wipe it clean. Carefully place about 2 mL of ferroxyl indicator solution on the surface of the steel plate. Observe for 5–10 minutes and record your observations.

4. Use a wash bottle to rinse the solutions in the well plate and on the steel plate into the container provided by your teacher. Wash and dry the steel plate. Clean up your work area and wash your hands before leaving the laboratory.

Name _____

Observations

DATA TABLE

Reaction	Observations
$FeSO_4$ + ferroxyl indicator	
NaOH + ferroxyl indicator	
steel plate + ferroxyl indicator	

Critical Thinking: Analysis and Conclusions

1. What ions are indicated by the color changes when ferroxyl indicator is added to the solutions in Steps 1 and 2? *(Interpreting data)* _____

_____

2. Based on your data, which part of the ferroxyl indicator drop on the steel plate is the anode? Explain your answer. Write the balanced chemical equation for the half reaction that is occurring there.

    (Drawing conclusions) _____

    _____

    _____

3. Based on your data, which part of the ferroxyl indicator drop on the steel plate is the cathode? Explain your answer. Write the balanced chemical equation for the half reaction that is occurring there.

    (Drawing conclusions) _____

    _____

    _____

    _____

4. Write the balanced overall equation for the electrochemical reaction in Step 3. *(Drawing conclusions)* _____

5. How are electrons transferred from the anode to the cathode in this process? _____

    _____

Name_____

6. In the space below, make a diagram of the ferroxyl indicator solution on the steel plate. Show where the colors appear and label the anode, cathode, and path of electrons. *(Applying concepts)*

Critical Thinking: Applications

1. Speculate on a reasonable mechanism for the formation of rust. *(Developing hypotheses)* _____

_____

_____

2. Describe two practical ways of protecting iron from corrosion. For each, explain how iron is protected in electrochemical terms. Give an everyday example of each. *(Using the writing process)* _____

_____

_____

_____

_____

_____

_____

_____

Going Further

1. Under your teacher's supervision, design and conduct an experiment to investigate factors that affect the rate of oxidation of iron nails. You may want to consider the effects of metal strain, electrolytes, or the presence of other metals.
2. Find out how galvanization protects iron and steel from rusting. Under your teacher's supervision, simulate galvanized iron by wrapping an iron nail with an appropriate metal. Report on your findings.

Electrolysis of Water

Text reference: **Chapter 21**

Introduction

Most people studying science know that the chemical formula of water is H_2O, and that the letters *H* and *O* represent hydrogen and oxygen, the elements that comprise water. People know this because they were taught it, not because it is obvious from looking at water. For most of history, philosophers considered this clear liquid, which is an essential part of life, to be an element. In the mid-1780s, Antoine Lavoisier realized that water did not fit his new definition of elements, since it could be produced from burning hydrogen and oxygen, and it could be decomposed over high heat. In 1800, water was split into hydrogen gas and oxygen gas using electricity.

In this investigation you will use electrolysis to investigate the chemical makeup of water and the nature of the electrochemical half reactions that occur at each electrode, resulting in the decomposition of water. An electrolyte, sodium sulfate (Na_2SO_4), is used in solution to facilitate electrical conductivity because it does not itself undergo electrolysis under the given conditions.

Pre-Lab Discussion

Read the entire laboratory investigation and the relevant pages of your textbook. Then answer the questions that follow.

1. Which electrode supplies electrons to positively charged ions? ____

   _____

2. At which electrode does oxidation (loss of electrons) occur? Is this electrode positively or negatively charged? _____

   _____

3. Why does the electrolysis process stop if the electrodes come in contact with each other, or short circuit? _____

   _____

   _____

4. Why should you avoid touching the metal electrodes to each other or to your fingers while they are connected to the power source?

   _____

   _____

5. When should you terminate the electrolysis reaction? _____

   _____

Small Scale Lab 61

Problem

What are the electrolysis products and half reactions for the decomposition of water?

Materials

chemical splash goggles
laboratory apron
petri dish bottom or cover
distilled water
sodium sulfate (Na$_2$SO$_4$)
2 platinum or stainless-steel
    insulated electrodes
pH indicator solution

micropipet
2 small test tubes
microscope-slide coverslip
2 notched sponge blocks
metric ruler
9V battery with snap-on leads,
    or DC power supply with
    leads

Safety

Wear your goggles and lab apron at all times during the investigation. To avoid possible shock or burns, do not touch bare wires from the power source or short the wire leads by touching them together. If you spill sodium sulfate or pH indicator on your skin or clothing, wash it off immediately with plenty of water and tell your teacher.

Note the caution alert symbols here and with certain steps of the Procedure. Refer to page *xi* for the specific precautions associated with each symbol.

Procedure

1. Put on your goggles and lab apron. Fill a petri dish or other shallow container nearly full of distilled water. Sprinkle the water with several grains of sodium sulfate (Na$_2$SO$_4$) and stir with one of the electrode tips to dissolve. Add a few drops of pH indicator.

2. Use a micropipet to fill two small test tubes with the solution from the dish. Overfill them slightly.

3. Place a microscope-slide cover slip over the mouth of one of the test tubes to trap the solution. Invert the test tube in the dish of electrolyte solution. Incline the filled test tube with its mouth still submerged in the dish of electrolyte solution. Rest the test tube on a notch in a block of moistened sponge placed outside the dish, as shown in Figure 61–1. Repeat the process for the second test tube.

4. Slide an electrode tip into the submerged mouth of each test tube. Rest the tops of the electrodes on notches in a second sponge block. Be careful as you move each electrode into position that you do not accidentally lift the test tube mouth above the surface. If you do, you will have to refill the test tube.

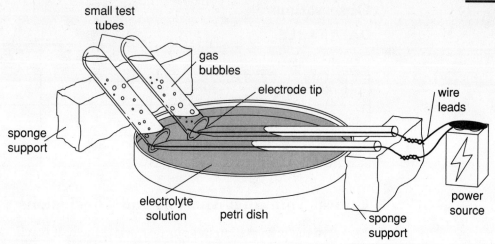

small test
tubes

gas
bubbles

electrode tip

wire
leads

sponge
support

electrolyte
solution   petri dish

sponge
support

power
source

Figure 61–1

5. Connect a 9-volt battery lead, or DC power supply lead, to each electrode. Note which electrode is negative and which is positive. **CAUTION:** *Be careful not to touch the power source leads together, as this may cause the leads to become hot and may damage the battery or power supply.*

6. Soon after connection, you should see gas bubbles rising into the test tubes from each electrode. A little later, look for color changes, indicating a change in pH. Record in the Data Table the color changes at the anode and cathode, and the pH range as indicated in the following table.

TABLE 61–1   pH Ranges of Indicators

	pH < 7	pH = 7	pH > 7
phenol red	yellow	orange	red
bromthymol blue	yellow	green	blue

7. When one test tube is at least half full of gas, disconnect the electrodes, being careful not to short the leads by touching them. Remove the electrodes carefully, keeping the test-tube mouths below the surface of the solution. Holding each tube vertically in the dish, and, being careful not to lift the test-tube mouth above the surface, measure the height of gas in each tube in millimeters. Record in the Data Table the height of gas in each tube relative to the electrode at which it was produced.

8. Discard the electrolyte solution down the drain. Rinse the outside of the electrode casings and tips, the test tubes, and the dish with plenty of water. Clean up your work area and wash your hands before leaving the laboratory.

Name _____

Observations

DATA TABLE

	Anode	Cathode
pH indicator color		
indicated pH range		
height of gas generated (mm)		

Critical Thinking: Analysis and Conclusions

1. From the information in your text, write the half reactions that occur in this investigation. *(Interpreting data)* _____

   _____

2. Based on pH-indicator observations, at which electrode are there excess H^+ ions? Which electrode is H^+-deficient (OH^- in excess)? *(Interpreting data)* _____

   _____

3. Based on your answers to Questions 1 and 2, identify the electrode at which each reaction is occurring. *(Making inferences)* _____

   _____

   _____

4. Add together the two equations for the half reactions from your answer to Question 1 to obtain the overall reaction. Then write the net equation for the reaction. Explain how you reduced the terms in the net equation. *(Making inferences)*
   overall reaction:

   _____

   net equation: _____

   _____

   _____

   _____

5. Calculate the ratio of hydrogen gas to oxygen gas produced in the reaction. *(Interpreting data)* _____

6. What evidence do you have from the data that supports the accepted formula of water? *(Interpreting data)* _____

   _____

   _____

© Prentice-Hall, Inc.

Critical Thinking: Applications

1. If sodium chloride (NaCl) is used as an electrolyte instead of Na_2SO_4, hydrogen is produced, but at the other electrode little gas is collected. Instead, the electrolyte smells pungent like bleach. What ion from the electrolyte could account for this, and what is the half reaction that is occurring? *(Making predictions)* _____

   _____

2. How could you prove that the sodium sulfate (Na_2SO_4) electrolyte did not react in your electrolysis cell? *(Designing experiments)* _____

   _____

   _____

   _____

3. If you used concentrated hydrochloric acid as the electrolyte solution, what products would you be likely to get? In what ratio?

   (Making predictions) _____

   _____

Going Further

1. Research and describe electrolysis cells used to isolate and purify difficult-to-process metals such as aluminum, copper, and sodium.
2. Investigate commercial electroplating with metals such as chromium, silver, and gold. What base metals are suitable as cathodes, and what electrolytes are used? Obtain photographs and/or schematic diagrams of the cells.
3. Read about Michael Faraday and list some of his discoveries in the field of electrochemistry.

Small-Scale Voltaic Cells

Small Scale
Lab **62**

Text reference: ***Chapter 21***

Introduction

From pacemakers and automatic garage door openers to portable hand-held televisions, it seems that the world runs on batteries. These batteries share some common characteristics. All of them, for example, are capable of doing work when a device is connected to their positive and negative terminals. They all derive their energy from a spontaneous chemical reaction that can be described in terms of oxidation and reduction half reactions. They can all be described as some sort of voltaic cell. A typical voltaic cell is illustrated in Figure 62–1.

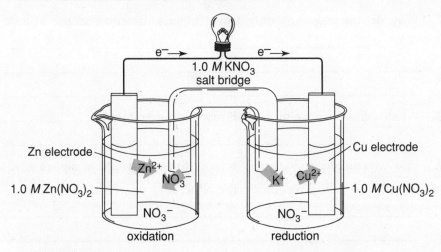

Figure 62–1

The electrons on the zinc atoms possess more chemical potential energy than the electrons on the copper atoms. This difference in potential energy creates the electromotive force, or voltage, of the voltaic cell. The amount of voltage depends on what metals are used. In this case, the voltage is 1.1 volts.

Notice in Figure 62–1 that there is a tube filled with potassium nitrate solution (KNO_3), forming a bridge between the two beakers. This tube is called a salt bridge. The salt bridge maintains the electrical neutrality of the solutions surrounding the electrodes. As the atoms of the zinc electrode lose electrons, they become positively charged ions. These ions enter the solution, causing it to become more positive. It becomes increasingly difficult for electrons to escape from the zinc side of the voltaic cell. At the same time, the atoms of the copper electrode are gaining electrons, causing it to become more negative. The electrode attracts the positive copper ions in the solution, leaving behind negative nitrate ions. This negative charge inhibits the movement of electrons onto the copper

Name⎯⎯⎯⎯⎯⎯⎯⎯⎯⎯⎯⎯⎯⎯⎯⎯⎯⎯⎯

electrode. The salt bridge contains a solution of ions, in this case K^+ and NO_3^- ions. The negative solution surrounding the copper electrode attracts the K^+ ions, and the positive solution surrounding the zinc electrode attracts the NO_3^- ions, thereby neutralizing the electric charge of the solutions.

In this investigation, you will build an unusual apparatus that will allow you to compare the voltage created by a variety of different metallic half-cells.

Pre-Lab Discussion

Read the entire laboratory investigation and the relevant pages of your textbook. Then answer the questions that follow.

1. Write equations that describe the oxidation and reduction half reactions for the voltaic cell shown in Figure 62–1. ⎯⎯⎯⎯⎯⎯⎯

   ⎯⎯⎯⎯⎯⎯⎯⎯⎯⎯⎯⎯⎯⎯⎯⎯⎯⎯⎯⎯⎯⎯⎯⎯⎯

2. Why do the electrons only travel in one direction in the voltaic cell? ⎯⎯⎯⎯⎯⎯⎯⎯⎯⎯⎯⎯⎯⎯⎯⎯⎯⎯⎯⎯⎯

   ⎯⎯⎯⎯⎯⎯⎯⎯⎯⎯⎯⎯⎯⎯⎯⎯⎯⎯⎯⎯⎯⎯⎯⎯⎯

   ⎯⎯⎯⎯⎯⎯⎯⎯⎯⎯⎯⎯⎯⎯⎯⎯⎯⎯⎯⎯⎯⎯⎯⎯⎯

3. What is the purpose of the salt bridge in a voltaic cell? ⎯⎯⎯⎯⎯⎯

   ⎯⎯⎯⎯⎯⎯⎯⎯⎯⎯⎯⎯⎯⎯⎯⎯⎯⎯⎯⎯⎯⎯⎯⎯⎯

4. In which direction do the K^+ ions in the salt bridge in Figure 62–1 move? In which direction do the NO_3^- ions move? ⎯⎯⎯⎯⎯⎯⎯

   ⎯⎯⎯⎯⎯⎯⎯⎯⎯⎯⎯⎯⎯⎯⎯⎯⎯⎯⎯⎯⎯⎯⎯⎯⎯

   ⎯⎯⎯⎯⎯⎯⎯⎯⎯⎯⎯⎯⎯⎯⎯⎯⎯⎯⎯⎯⎯⎯⎯⎯⎯

5. How are standard electrode potentials determined for the half-cells listed in the Standard Reduction Potential table found in the back of this book or in your text? ⎯⎯⎯⎯⎯⎯⎯⎯⎯⎯⎯⎯

   ⎯⎯⎯⎯⎯⎯⎯⎯⎯⎯⎯⎯⎯⎯⎯⎯⎯⎯⎯⎯⎯⎯⎯⎯⎯

6. Why should care be taken when working with potassium nitrate (KNO_3)? ⎯⎯⎯⎯⎯⎯⎯⎯⎯⎯⎯⎯⎯⎯⎯⎯⎯⎯⎯⎯⎯⎯⎯

   ⎯⎯⎯⎯⎯⎯⎯⎯⎯⎯⎯⎯⎯⎯⎯⎯⎯⎯⎯⎯⎯⎯⎯⎯⎯

Problem

Which combination of metallic half-cells will produce a voltaic cell with the greatest potential difference?

Materials

chemical splash goggles
laboratory apron
latex gloves
metal samples, each
    1 cm × 1 cm
      silver
      copper
      zinc
      lead
      magnesium
steel wool
filter paper
scissors
petri dish

6 micropipets, containing the
    following 1.0 M solutions:
      silver nitrate ($AgNO_3$)
      magnesium nitrate
        ($Mg(NO_3)_2$)
      copper(II) nitrate
        ($Cu(NO_3)_2$)
      zinc nitrate ($Zn(NO_3)_2$)
      lead(II) nitrate ($Pb(NO_3)_2$)
      potassium nitrate (KNO_3)
multimeter with leads
paper towel
forceps
tap water
distilled water

Safety

Wear your goggles and lab apron at all times during the investigation. All the solutions are considered toxic. Silver nitrate and copper(II) nitrate are skin and tissue irritants. Silver nitrate causes stains on skin and clothes. Wear gloves when handling this solution. If any of these solutions come into contact with skin or clothing they should be washed off with plenty of water. Dispose of all the solutions according to your teacher's instructions.

Note the caution alert symbols here and with certain steps of the Procedure. Refer to page *xi* for the specific precautions associated with each symbol.

Procedure

 1. Put on your goggles and lab apron. Shine both sides of each piece of metal (the electrodes) with a piece of steel wool.

2. Hold two pieces of filter paper together and cut them so that five paper divisions extend from the center as shown in Figure 62–2 on the following page. The paper should look something like a five-petal flower.

3. Place the shaped filter papers on top of each other in the bottom plate of the petri dish.

  4. Put on latex gloves. Make a standard copper half-cell, as shown in Figure 62–2, by placing two drops of 1.0 M $Cu(NO_3)_2$ solution on one of the paper divisions and placing the shiny piece of copper on the wet spot. Repeat this process with the remaining 1.0 M metallic nitrate solutions and the corresponding metal pieces. **CAUTION:** *The solutions are all considered toxic and irritating to the skin. Wear gloves when handling them. If any of these solutions come into contact with the skin or clothing, wash them off with plenty of water and tell your teacher.*

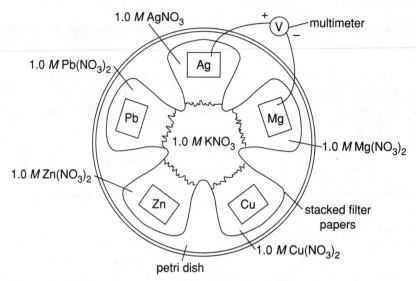

Figure 62–2

5. Make a salt bridge connecting the half-cells by placing two drops of 1.0 M KNO$_3$ solution on the center of the filter paper. The wetness of the salt bridge should run into the wetness caused by the 1.0 M salt solutions around each piece of metal.

6. Set the multimeter to measure DC voltage. If there is a scale setting, select a scale that will allow you to easily read potential differences between zero and two volts.

7. Place the positive probe (usually the red wire lead) on the piece of silver metal. This will be your reference electrode. Place the ground probe (usually the black wire lead) on the piece of magnesium metal. When the dial or digital display stabilizes, record the voltage in Data Table 1. If the voltage is a negative number, reverse the leads.

8. Keeping the positive lead on the silver piece of metal, move the ground lead to each of the remaining pieces of metal. In Data Table 1, record the potential difference that exists between the silver half-cell and each of the remaining half-cells.

9. Move the positive probe to the piece of copper metal. This will now be your reference electrode. Move the ground probe to each of the other pieces of metal. In Data Table 2, record the potential difference that exists between the copper half-cell and each of the other half-cells.

10. Switch off the multimeter.

11. Using forceps, remove the metal pieces (electrodes) from the petri dish and rinse them off with water. Place them on a paper towel to dry.

12. Using forceps, place the wet filter paper in the labeled container provided by your teacher.

 13. Do not dispose of any of the solutions in the micropipets. Simply return them to their appropriately labeled beaker.

14. Rinse the petri dishes with tap and distilled water. Wipe them dry with a paper towel. Clean up your work area and wash your hands before leaving the laboratory.

Observations

DATA TABLE 1   Silver (Ag) Reference Half-Cell

Cell	Voltage (V)	Theoretical Voltage (V)	Percent Error
Ag-Mg			
Ag-Cu			
Ag-Zn			
Ag-Pb			

DATA TABLE 2   Copper (Cu) Reference Half-Cell

Cell	Voltage (V)	Theoretical Voltage (V)	Percent Error
Cu-Mg			
Cu-Ag			
Cu-Zn			
Cu-Pb			

Calculations

1. Calculate the theoretical potential of the cells tested, as shown in the following example for the standard Ag-Cu cell:

   a. Using a table of standard reduction potentials as a reference, determine the reduction potentials (voltages) for both half-cells.

   $$Cu^{2+}(aq) + 2e^- \rightarrow Cu(s) \; (E° = +0.34 \text{ volts})$$

   $$Ag^+(aq) + e^- \rightarrow Ag(s) \; (E° = +0.80 \text{ volts})$$

Name_____

b. Reverse the sign of the potential that is the least positive (most negative) and add the two voltages. Enter the values in the appropriate Data Tables.

+0.80 volts + (−0.34 volts) = +0.46 volts

2. Calculate the percent error for the voltages measured from the cells tested. The accepted value is the theoretical standard value calculated for each cell. Enter the values in the appropriate Data Tables.

Critical Thinking: Analysis and Conclusions

1. How well do the potential differences of the cells constructed in the petri dish compare to the theoretical potential difference of the standard cells? (*Making comparisons*) _____

_____

_____

_____

2. What variables exist within the voltaic cells that may account for the differences between the observed and theoretical values? (*Making inferences*) _____

_____

3. Using the data obtained when silver was the reference electrode, arrange the potential differences of the cells from most positive to least positive. Does the same relative order exist when the theoretical potential differences are arranged from most positive to least positive? *(Making comparisons)* _____

_____

_____

4. Using the data obtained when copper was the reference electrode, arrange the potential differences of the cells from most positive to least positive. Compare this to the arrangement of the potential difference found when silver was the reference electrode. Do both silver and copper have the same order of potential differences? *(Making comparisons)* _____

_____

Critical Thinking: Applications

1. Which of the cells would be the best source of electrical energy in an electrical device? Explain. *(Making judgments)* _____

_____

_____

2. What would be some practical problems in using the metals you chose for Applications Question 1 in a marketable battery? *(Applying concepts)* _____

_____

3. The copper-zinc voltaic cell shown in Figure 63–1 should theoretically have a potential difference of 1.10 volts. What would happen to this voltage if the voltaic cell was used over a period of time? Explain your answer in terms of changes that would take place in the voltaic cell. *(Making predictions)* _____

_____

_____

_____

4. In any voltaic cell, oxidation always occurs at the anode, and reduction always occurs at the cathode.
   a. Which electrode in the copper-zinc voltaic cell is the anode and which is the cathode? *(Classifying)* _____

   _____

   b. Which electrode in the copper-silver voltaic cell is the anode and which is the cathode? *(Classifying)* _____

   _____

Name _____

Going Further

1. Compare the copper-zinc voltaic cell shown in Figure 63–1 to a commercial battery. Make a sketch of the internal structure of the commercial battery, illustrating some of the components common to all voltaic cells. Present your comparison to the class.

2. Research the history of the battery to determine when the earliest batteries were made, how they were constructed, and the purpose for which they were used. Present your findings to the class.

3. Research the construction of the rechargeable battery and report on how the recharging process is carried out.

4. Some name-brand car batteries are advertised to deliver 500 amps of "cranking power" at freezing temperatures. Research some of the name-brand car batteries and construct a report describing what this claim really means.

5. Prepare a report on the toxic waste problem that results from the disposal of used batteries and on some recycling solutions that are already in place.

Zinc Plating of Ornaments

Lab 63
APPLICATION

*Text reference: **Chapter 21***

Introduction

You are probably familiar with gold-, silver-, or chromium-plated items such as jewelry, silverware, and chrome trim on automobiles. However, you may not be familiar with the process that produces them—electroplating.

Electroplating involves the construction of an *electrolytic cell.* In an electrolytic cell a nonspontaneous oxidation-reduction reaction is made to occur by using an external source of electrical energy, such as a battery. The battery adds electrons to the cathode and removes electrons from the anode. As a result, the cathode becomes negatively charged, while the anode becomes positively charged. At the anode the removal of electrons causes the material in the anode to be oxidized and enter the solution as cations. Simultaneously, metallic cations in the solution are attracted to the cathode. When the cations reach the cathode, they gain electrons and are reduced to the metallic state, plating out on the cathode. The concentration of cations in the solution remains constant.

In electroplating, the object to be plated is used as the cathode, and a piece of the metal that will form the plated layer is used as the anode. For example, in order to copper-plate an iron object, you would connect the iron object to the negative terminal of the battery and connect a piece of copper to the positive terminal of the battery. Figure 63–1 shows this electrolytic cell.

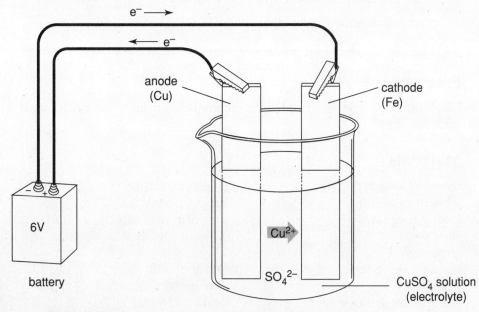

Figure 63–1

Name_____

Electrolytic cells are used to extract pure forms of metals from their ores, for example, aluminum from bauxite and sodium from halite. Impure metals such as gold and silver can be purified by electrolysis. Electrolysis can also be used to extract nonmetals such as hydrogen and oxygen from water, and chlorine from halite.

In this investigation, you will make a zinc-plated ornament and become familiar with the electroplating process. You will describe the process in terms of oxidation-reduction reactions and draw a diagram of the electrolytic cell used.

Pre-Lab Discussion

Read the entire laboratory investigation and the relevant pages of your textbook. Then answer the questions that follow.

1. Write the net ionic equations for the half reactions that are taking place at the anode and the cathode in the example given in the Introduction.

   _____

   _____

2. In an electrolytic cell, does oxidation take place at the anode or the cathode? Where does reduction take place? _____

   _____

3. Why is it important that the copper square be as clean as possible before it is plated? _____

   _____

   _____

4. What are the hazards of working with acrylic paint? What safety precautions should you take? _____

   _____

Problem

How can you use electroplating techniques to make a zinc-plated ornament?

Materials

chemical splash goggles
laboratory apron
2 copper squares
steel wool
paper towel
wide masking tape
pencil
razor blade or razor knife
cotton swab

isopropyl alcohol
bare copper wire, 10-cm
zinc nitrate ($Zn(NO_3)_2$), 1.0 *M*
two wire leads with alligator
    clips
lantern battery
zinc metal strip
beaker, 250-mL

© Prentice-Hall, Inc.

Safety 🥽 👕 🔥 🕯️ ☠️ 🗑️ 🚿

Wear your goggles and lab apron at all times during the investigation.

The copper square and the razor blade or razor knife have sharp edges. Handle them carefully to avoid cuts. Isopropyl alcohol is flammable. Be sure there are no open flames in the laboratory. Zinc nitrate is toxic. Avoid ingestion. The acrylic spray paint is toxic. Do not inhale it. Use it under the fume hood only.

Note the caution alert symbols here and with certain steps of the Procedure. Refer to page *xi* for the specific precautions associated with each symbol.

Procedure

1. Put on your goggles and lab apron.

2. Use a piece of steel wool to polish both sides of the copper square. Rinse it with water and dry it.

3. Cover both sides of the copper square with masking tape. Be sure the tape overlaps the edges of the copper square. Trim off excess tape.

4. Sketch your desired design on one side of the square and cut its outline from the tape with a razor blade or razor knife. Remove the tape from the area you wish to have plated. Be sure the remaining tape is secure. **CAUTION:** *Be careful not to cut yourself with the razor blade or razor knife.*

5. Carefully clean the area with a cotton swab that has been dipped in isopropyl alcohol. Do not touch this area after cleaning. Let it dry. **CAUTION:** *Isopropyl alcohol is flammable. Make sure there are no open flames in the laboratory.*

6. Push a 10-cm piece of copper wire through the hole in the square and make a hook. Be sure the wire makes contact with the bare copper metal.

7. Go to one of the areas for electroplating that your teacher has designated. Using the wire leads with alligator clips, connect one wire between the negative terminal of the battery and the copper wire attached to your ornament. Connect the second wire between the positive terminal and the zinc strip. Insert the zinc strip on one side of the beaker containing the zinc nitrate, $Zn(NO_3)_2$, solution. Carefully insert your ornament into the zinc nitrate, on the side opposite from the zinc strip. Do not allow the two metals to come in contact. See Figure 63–2. Observe the electroplating of the zinc onto the surface of the copper square, and write a description of what you see. Be sure to include your observations of the zinc strip as well. Allow the reaction to continue for 1–2 minutes. **CAUTION:** *Zinc nitrate is poisonous. Do not ingest it.*

Name _____

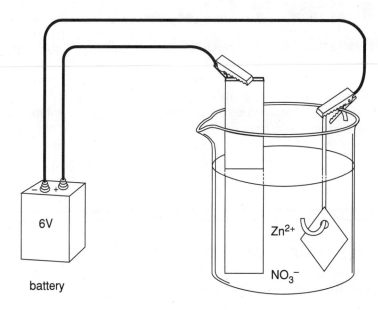

Figure 63–2

8. Remove the ornament from the electroplating solution. Disconnect the wires and wash the ornament in water. Do not rub the area where zinc has been plated. Carefully remove the tape from the ornament. If any area not plated needs more polishing you can do so with steel wool. Be careful not to rub the zinc plate. Carefully pat the ornament dry with a paper towel.

9. Hang your ornament inside a designated area in the fume hood that has been protected with newspapers. Spray both sides with clear acrylic paint and let it dry. **CAUTION:** *Acrylic paint fumes are toxic. Do not breathe the fumes.*

10. Dispose of the solutions as directed by your teacher. Clean up your work area and wash your hands before leaving the laboratory.

Observations

_____

_____

_____

Critical Thinking: Analysis and Conclusions

1. Write the net ionic equations that show what is taking place at the anode and at the cathode during this investigation. *(Interpreting data)*

_____

_____

2. Add labels to Figure 63–2, indicating the cathode, the anode, the Zn(NO$_3$)$_2$ solution, the direction of flow of electrons through the wire, and the direction of flow of ions in the solution. *(Making inferences)*

3. What do you think happens to the mass of the cathode over time as electroplating takes place? The mass of the anode? *(Making inferences)* _____

_____

_____

Critical Thinking: Applications

1. What would have happened in the investigation if the connections from the battery were reversed? Include reactions at the anode and the cathode. What do you think the cathode would look like if the system were allowed to run for several minutes? Explain. *(Making predictions)* _____

_____

_____

_____

_____

_____

2. What would happen if the zinc strip or the zinc nitrate used in this investigation contained metallic impurities? What would determine whether the impurities would interfere or not? *(Developing hypotheses)* _____

_____

_____

3. A piece of copper metal is placed in a solution of zinc nitrate and a piece of zinc metal is placed in a solution of copper(II) nitrate. What would happen to each, if anything? Explain. *(Applying concepts)*

_____

_____

_____

_____

Name _____

4. If you wanted to plate a piece of iron with chromium, to which terminal of the battery would you attach the iron? The chromium?

   (Applying concepts) _____

   _____

   _____

   _____

   _____

Going Further

1. At one time, aluminum was very rare and quite expensive. The electrolysis of bauxite, aluminum ore, provided an inexpensive means of producing aluminum. Research the means by which aluminum was extracted from ore prior to electrolysis and the electrolysis method.

2. Research the processes employed to make gold-plated jewelry and chrome-plated automobile parts.

Reaction Kinetics

Small Scale
Lab **64**

Text reference: **Chapter 22**

Introduction

How fast do products form from reactants in a chemical reaction? The rate of a reaction depends on a number of variables: the nature of the reactants, the temperature, the concentration of the reactants, and the presence of catalysts.

In this investigation, you will determine the effect of the concentration of a reactant on the rate of a reaction that follows the sequence of chemical changes described by the following equations:

$$IO_3^-(aq) + 3HSO_3^-(aq) \rightarrow 3HSO_4^-(aq) + I^-(aq)$$

$$6H^+(aq) + IO_3^-(aq) + 5I^-(aq) \rightarrow 3I_2(aq) + 3H_2O(l)$$

$$I_2(aq) + starch(aq) \rightarrow I_2 \bullet [starch](aq)$$

In this reaction, iodate ion, IO_3^-, reacts with hydrogen sulfite ion, $HSO_3^-(aq)$, in acid solution to give iodide ion, $I^-(aq)$. The iodide ion then reacts with iodate ion to give molecular iodine, $I_2(aq)$. Molecular iodine reacts instantly with starch in solution to form a complex that is blue-black in color. The colored product allows you to determine the time required to reach this point in the reaction. Because this reaction is predictable and easily observed, it is often called the "iodine-clock reaction."

Pre-Lab Discussion

Read the entire laboratory investigation and the relevant pages of your textbook. Then answer the questions that follow.

1. What are the dependent and independent variables in this investigation? What variables, if any, are held constant? _____

   _____

   _____

   _____

2. What is the intermediate product in this reaction? _____

   _____

3. How would it affect your results if $I_2(aq)$ reacted with starch at a slower rate than the reactions that produce $I_2(aq)$? _____

   _____

   _____

Name _____

4. What is the purpose of the mixing pipet? _____

_____

5. What are the hazards associated with using NaHSO₃ solution, and what precautions should you take? _____

_____

_____

Purpose

How does changing the concentration of a reactant affect the rate of chemical reaction?

Materials

chemical splash goggles
laboratory apron
marking pen
well plate
sheet of white paper
micropipet, adapted for mixing
4 micropipets, containing the following solutions:

potassium iodate (KIO₃),
   0.02 M
distilled water
sodium hydrogen sulfite
   (NaHSO₃), 0.02 M
starch solution
distilled water
stopwatch or clock with a
   second hand

Safety

Wear your goggles and lab apron at all times during the investigation. Handle the sodium hydrogen sulfite in acid solution with care; it is corrosive. Avoid spills and contact with your skin. If you spill any, wash it off with large amounts of water and tell your teacher.

    Note the caution alert symbols here and with certain steps of the Procedure. Refer to page *xi* for the specific precautions.

Procedure

1. Put on your goggles and lab apron. Using the marking pen, label the wells from left to right along the top of the well plate *1, 2, 3, 4, 5, 6*. Down the left side, label the rows of wells *A, B, C, D*. Place the well plate on a sheet of white paper.

2. Use the pipet labeled *IO₃⁻* to add two drops of KIO₃ solution to well A1, four drops to well A2, six drops to well A3, eight drops to well A4, ten drops to well A5, and twelve drops to well A6. See Figure 64–1. Make sure to hold the pipet vertically to achieve a consistent drop size.

3. Use the pipet labeled *H₂O* to add ten drops of distilled water to well A1, eight drops to well A2, six drops to well A3, four drops to well A4, and two drops to well A5. No water should be added to well A6. See Figure 64–1.

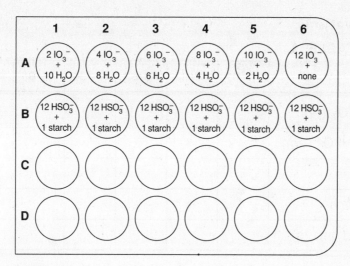

Figure 64–1

 4. Use the pipet labeled HSO_3^- to add twelve drops of hydrogen sulfite solution to wells B1, B2, B3, B4, B5, and B6. Then use the pipet labeled *Starch* to add one drop of starch solution to each of the filled wells in row B. **CAUTION:** *Handle the sodium hydrogen sulfite in acid solution with extreme care. Do not allow any of the solutions to contact your skin. If you spill any of them, wash off immediately with plenty of water and notify your teacher.*

5. Use the pipet labeled *Mix* to draw up all of the hydrogen sulfite solution in well B1. Then, as rapidly and carefully as possible, transfer the contents of the pipet to well A1. The moment the two solutions come into contact, record the start time in the Data Table. Stir the solutions by gently swirling the well plate on the paper. Once you have mixed the solutions thoroughly, it is not necessary to continue moving the plate. Record the finish time in seconds when a dark blue color appears. Then clean the *Mix* pipet by flushing it three times with distilled water.

6. Repeat Step 5 by mixing solutions A2 and B2, A3 and B3, A4 and B4, A5 and B5, and A6 and B6. Record the start and finish times in the Data Table. Also record the number of drops of $HSO_3^-(aq)$ and $IO_3^-(aq)$ in the combined solutions.

7. Calculate the elapsed reaction time for each mixture by subtracting the start time from the finish time. Enter the results in the Data Table.

8. If time permits, repeat Steps 2–7 in a second trial.

 9. Wash the chemicals down the sink with plenty of water. Clean up your work area and wash your hands before leaving the laboratory.

Name_____

Observations
DATA TABLE

	A1/B1	A2/B2	A3/B3	A4/B4	A5/B5	A6/B6
drops $IO_3^-(aq)$						
drops $HSO_3^-(aq)$						
start time						
finish time						
elapsed time (s)						

Critical Thinking: Analysis and Conclusions

1. Make a graph of the elapsed time versus the quantity of iodate ion on the blank graph shown in Figure 64–2. *(Interpreting data)*

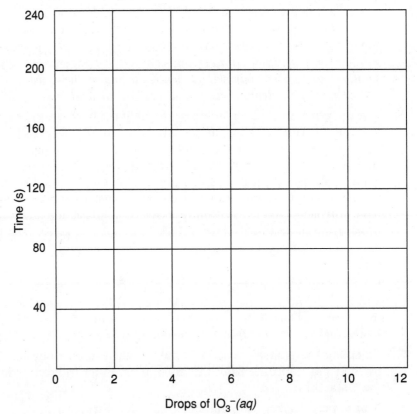

Figure 64–2

2. How does an increase in reactant concentration affect reaction time? *(Drawing conclusions)* _____

_____

3. How does an increase in reactant concentration affect the rate of the reaction? *(Making inferences)* _____

_____

4. How is the reaction rate related to reaction time? *(Making inferences)* _____

_____

Critical Thinking: Applications

1. Suppose you held the iodate ion concentration constant while varying the concentration of hydrogen sulfite ion. How would you expect the reaction rate to depend on the concentration of hydrogen sulfite ion? *(Making predictions)* _____

_____

2. What effect do you think changing the temperature would have on your results? *(Making predictions)* _____

_____

3. Design an experiment to find an answer to the prediction you made in Question 2. *(Designing experiments)* _____

_____

Going Further

1. When household bleach is mixed with a solution of Fe^{3+} ions, O_2 gas is produced. Design an experiment in which the concentration of bleach is varied and the volume of O_2 gas produced each minute is monitored. Under your teacher's supervision, conduct the experiment and report on your results.

Concentration and Reaction Order

Text reference: **Chapter 22**

Introduction

Many chemists have been employed to exploit and control explosive chemical reactions for use in construction and military applications. Since explosive reactions must be exothermic as well as rapid, these chemists need to study factors affecting the rate of exothermic reactions. Temperature, concentration of reactants, gas pressure, surface area of reactants, and presence of a catalyst all affect the rate of a chemical reaction.

In this investigation, you will study how the concentration and temperature of the reactants affect the rate of the following reaction:

$$S_2O_3^{2-}(aq) + 2H^+(aq) \rightarrow S(s) + SO_2(aq) + H_2O(l)$$

The reaction is accompanied by a small net change in energy, so the temperature will remain nearly constant unless changed by an outside influence. The reaction occurs in solution and produces a suspended precipitate of sulfur. The rate can be determined by measuring the time needed to produce enough sulfur to make the solution opaque.

Pre-Lab Discussion

Read the entire laboratory investigation and the relevant pages of your textbook. Then answer the questions that follow.

1. How do you know that the reaction to be studied cannot cause an

    explosion? _____

    _____

2. If ten drops of 0.3 M HCl are mixed with ten drops of 0.3 M $Na_2S_2O_3$, what will be the concentration of each chemical in the mixture?

    _____

3. If the concentration of a reactant is decreased, how would you expect the rate of reaction to be affected? Are the concentration and reaction

    rate directly or inversely proportional? _____

    _____

4. If, when mixing the chemicals to start the reaction, you dripped acid on your hands because you were not being careful, you would have to stop to wash. What negative impact on your data gathering would

    this interruption cause? _____

    _____

Name_____

Problem

How is the reaction rate for the acidic decomposition of thiosulfate ion affected by the concentration and temperature of the reactants?

Materials

chemical splash goggles
laboratory apron
2 sets of 3 micropipets,
    containing the following
    solutions:
        hydrochloric acid (HCl),
            0.3 *M*
        sodium thiosulfate
            (Na$_2$S$_2$O$_3$), 0.3 *M*
        distilled water
graduated cylinder, 10-mL

pencil
paper
well plate
marking pen
mixing micropipet
stopwatch or clock with a
    second hand
paper towels
scissors
tape

Safety

Wear your goggles and lab apron at all times during the investigation. Hydrochloric acid is corrosive. Avoid any direct contact with it. Wash spills and splashes with cold water. Note the caution alert symbols here and with certain steps of the Procedure. Refer to page *xi* for the specific precautions associated with each symbol.

Procedure

Part A

1. Put on your goggles and lab apron. Obtain one plastic micropipet containing 0.3 *M* HCl, another containing 0.3 *M* Na$_2$S$_2$O$_3$, and a third containing distilled water. **CAUTION:** *Hydrochloric acid is corrosive. Avoid any direct contact with it. Wash spills and splashes with cold water.*

2. Fill a 10-mL graduated cylinder with water to exactly 5.0 mL. Holding the micropipet containing HCl vertical to deliver a uniform drop size, count the number of drops of liquid needed to increase the volume to 6.0 mL, then 7.0 mL, then 8.0 mL. Be sure the drops do not hit the side of the graduated cylinder. Record in Data Table 1. Repeat with Na$_2$S$_2$O$_3$ and water.

3. Calculate the averages of the three sets of numbers recorded in Step 2, as shown in Calculation Step 1. Record in Data Table 1. Use this value in the Procedure to dispense exact volumes.

Part B

4. Mark an *x* on a sheet of paper. When placed under the well plate, the *x* should be clearly visible. If it is not already labeled, use a marking pen to label the well plate rows A–D and the columns 1–6. Using the number of drops calculated in Step 3, put exactly 1.0 mL of 0.3 *M* Na$_2$S$_2$O$_3$ solution into each of the six wells in Row A on the well plate.

5. In Row B, put 0.3 *M* HCl as follows. (As in Step 4, count the number of drops to obtain the exact volume required.)

   well B1: 1.0 mL; well B2: 0.8 mL; well B3: 0.7 mL
   well B4: 0.6 mL; well B5: 0.5 mL; well B6: 0.4 mL

6. Place additional drops of distilled water in each well in order to make the total volume of HCl plus water equal to 1.0 mL. For example, well B2 would require 0.2 mL additional water to make the total volume of HCl plus water equal to 1.0 mL. Note that well B1 does not require any additional water.

7. Prepare to time the reaction. Place well B1 over the *x* on the paper. Using the mixing micropipet to withdraw all of the solution from well A1, add it all at once but without splashing to well B1, and start timing when the solutions first come into contact. Look through the mixture at the *x* on the paper. In Data Table 2, record the time elapsed, in seconds, to the point when the *x* becomes completely obscured. Also record the volume of HCl.

8. Place each of the remaining acid wells over the *x* and repeat Step 7 for each.

9. Rinse the mixing micropipet with distilled water. Dispose of the well plate contents as directed by your teacher. Clean and dry the well plate.

Part C

10. Using the number of drops calculated in Step 3, put exactly 1.0 mL of 0.3 *M* HCl into each of the six wells in Row A on the well plate.

11. In Row B, put 0.3 *M* Na$_2$S$_2$O$_3$ as follows. (As in Step 4, count the number of drops to obtain the exact volume required.)

    well B1: 1.0 mL; well B2: 0.8 mL; well B3: 0.7 mL
    well B4: 0.6 mL; well B5: 0.5 mL; well B6: 0.4 mL

12. As in Step 6, place additional drops of distilled water in each well in order to make the total volume of Na$_2$S$_2$O$_3$ plus water equal to 1.0 mL. Note that well B1 does not require any additional water.

13. Prepare to time the reaction. Place well B1 over the *x* on the paper. Using the mixing micropipet to withdraw all of the acid from well A1, add it all at once but without splashing to well B1, and start timing when the solutions first come into contact. Look through the mixture at the *x* on the paper. In Data Table 3, record the time elapsed, in seconds, to the point when the *x* becomes completely obscured. Also record the volume of Na$_2$S$_2$O$_3$.

14. Place each of the remaining acid wells in turn over the *x* and repeat Step 13 for each.

15. Dispose of the well plate contents as directed by your teacher. Clean and dry the well plate.

Name_____

Part D

 16. Cut out the *x* from the white sheet of paper and tape it under one of the wells with the *x* facing up. Put 1.0 mL of 0.3 *M* HCl into that well and 1.0 mL of 0.3 *M* $Na_2S_2O_3$ into another well.

17. Float the well tray on a water bath provided by your teacher. The water should be approximately 10°C warmer than room temperature.

 18. After waiting five minutes, prepare to time the reaction. Withdraw all of the 0.3 *M* $Na_2S_2O_3$ from its well and add it to the HCl in the other well. Look through the mixture at the *x* on the paper. In Data Table 4, record the time elapsed, in seconds, to the point when the *x* becomes completely obscured.

19. Record the room temperature and the temperature of the water bath. Put these values in Data Table 4.

20. As time permits, repeat Steps 16–19, using water baths at varying temperatures.

 21. Dispose of the well plate contents as directed by your teacher. Clean up your work area and wash your hands before leaving the laboratory.

Observations

DATA TABLE 1   Drops to Make 1.0 mL

Liquid	5.0–6.0 mL	6.0–7.0 mL	7.0–8.0 mL	Average
HCl				
$Na_2S_2O_3$				
distilled water				

DATA TABLE 2   Rate with Varying HCl Concentration

Well	Reaction Time (s)	Reaction Rate (1/s)	Volume of HCl (mL)	Initial [HCl] (mol/L)	Final [HCl] (mol/L)
B1					
B2					
B3					
B4					
B5					
B6					

DATA TABLE 3   Rate with Varying Na$_2$S$_2$O$_3$ Concentration

Well	Reaction Time (s)	Reaction Rate (1/s)	Volume of Na$_2$S$_2$O$_3$ (mL)	Initial [Na$_2$S$_2$O$_3$] (mol/L)	Final [Na$_2$S$_2$O$_3$] (mol/L)
B1					
B2					
B3					
B4					
B5					
B6					

DATA TABLE 4   Rate with Varying Temperature

Temperature (°C)	Reaction Time (s)	Reaction Rate (1/s)

Calculations

1. Calculate the average number of drops of each liquid needed to obtain 1.0 mL. Enter the values in Data Table 1.

2. Calculate the reaction rate for each reaction. Note that the reaction rate is the inverse of the time. Enter the values in the Data Tables.

3. Calculate the initial concentration of each of the solutions in wells B1–B6 before the reaction. Enter the values in the Data Tables.

4. Calculate the concentration of each solution after it is mixed with the other reactant. The concentration after mixing will be half the original concentration in each well, since the volume is doubled when mixed with the other reactant. Enter the value in the Data Tables in the columns for final concentration.

5. Calculate the average reaction time at room temperature for well B1 from Parts B and C. Enter the value in Data Table 4.

Name _____

Critical Thinking: Analysis and Conclusions

1. Make a graph of reaction rate vs. HCl concentration from the data for Part B, and a graph of reaction rate vs. $Na_2S_2O_3$ concentration from the data for Part C. *(Interpreting data)*

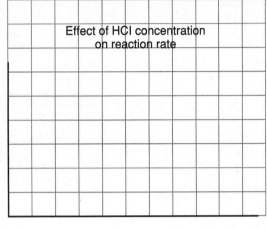

reaction rate (1/sec)

Effect of HCl concentration
on reaction rate

HCl concentration
(mol/L)

reaction rate (1/sec)

Effect of $Na_2S_2O_3$ concentration
on reaction rate

$Na_2S_2O_3$ concentration
(mol/L)

Figure 65–1

2. Decide, in each case, whether the changes in reactant concentration had a significant effect on reaction rate. Determine the reaction rate order for each reactant, using the following definitions:

    zero order—no effect on rate by changes in concentration
    first order—rate directly proportional to concentration
    second order—rate proportional to the square of the concentration
      (e.g., doubled concentration results in a four-fold increase in rate)
    third order—rate proportional to the cube of the concentration.

    (Making inferences) _____

    _____

    _____

3. Most reactions occur in a series of steps. The slowest step controls the rate of the overall reaction. Which of the reactants is involved in the slowest step of the reaction observed in this investigation? Explain. *(Drawing conclusions)* _____

    _____

    _____

4. From your data in Part D, how would you judge the validity of the rule: Changing the temperature of an intermediate-speed reaction by 10°C doubles its rate. *(Making judgments)* _____

    _____

Critical Thinking: Applications

1. TNT (trinitrotoluene), an explosive, occurs naturally as an intermediate product of the decomposition of certain types of organic matter.

    Why does it not explode? *(Developing hypotheses)* _____

    _____

2. Propose ways to increase the rate of oxidation of iron (rusting).

    (Designing experiments) _____

    _____

    _____

3. Hexane, a component of gasoline, releases more energy per mole when it combusts than does nitroglycerine when it explosively decomposes. Explain why hexane is a better fuel and nitroglycerine is

    a better explosive. *(Evaluating)* _____

    _____

    _____

Going Further

1. Do research on the decomposition rates of pesticides or pollutants in the environment. Produce graphs showing how concentrations change over time.
2. Research the life of Alfred Nobel and his work on explosives.
3. Use a computer graphing program to make a graph of the data from Analysis and Conclusions Question 1.

Rates of an Antacid Reaction

Lab 66

APPLICATION

*Text reference: **Chapter 22***

Introduction

Many people are familiar with the "plop, plop, fizz, fizz" that takes place when antacid tablets are dropped into a glass of water. When someone takes an antacid tablet, he or she is probably more interested in gaining relief from an upset stomach than the chemistry that takes place in the glass. However, as the tablet fizzes, it demonstrates a reaction that can be timed and studied.

The ingredients in one brand of fizzing antacid tablets are listed as "aspirin 325 mg;. . . sodium bicarbonate 1916 mg; citric acid 1000 mg." The fizz results when citric acid ($H_3C_6H_5O_7$) reacts with the base, sodium bicarbonate ($NaHCO_3$), to give carbon dioxide, water, and a salt (sodium citrate). The balanced reaction is:

$$H_3C_6H_5O_7\,(aq) + 3NaHCO_3\,(aq) \rightarrow Na_3C_6H_5O_7\,(aq) + 3H_2O(l) + 3CO_2\,(g)$$

All of the ingredients for this reaction are present in the antacid tablet, but nothing happens until it is put into water. The tablet, therefore, provides you with a nice chemical package that you can use to carry out timed kinetics experiments.

Temperature is one of many factors that affect the rate at which a chemical reaction proceeds. Collision theory states that as temperature increases, the particles in a reaction move faster, resulting in a higher frequency of collisions and increased kinetic energy in each collision. Other variables affect reaction rates as well. In this investigation, you will examine the effect of temperature on the rate of reaction of an antacid tablet in water. You will also design your own investigation to determine the effect of another variable on reaction rate, choosing from among those covered in Section 22–3 of your text. After performing this investigation, you will report on how your results fit with your understanding of collision theory and rates of reaction.

Pre-Lab Discussion

Read the entire laboratory investigation and the relevant pages of your textbook. Then answer the questions that follow.

1. Would you describe the antacid tablet–water system as a heterogeneous or homogenous system? Briefly explain your answer. _____

   _____

   _____

2. List as many variables as you can that can affect the rate of a reaction. _____

   _____

Name _____

3. How do you relate each of the variables listed in Question 2 to collision theory? _____

_____

_____

_____

_____

_____

4. How does the length of time it takes for a reaction to occur relate to the rate of the reaction? _____

_____

5. What role (or roles) does water play in the antacid reaction? _____

_____

6. Why should no one ever attempt to swallow a fizzing antacid tablet without first letting it react in water? _____

_____

_____

Problem

Which factors affect the rate of the antacid reaction?

Materials

chemical splash goggles
laboratory apron
tap water, hot and cold
shallow pan or trough
gas-collecting bottles, 500-mL
ice
thermometer
glass square or piece of poster
   board
fizzing antacid tablets
stopwatch or clock with a
   second hand

glass marking pen
graduated cylinder, 100-mL

Additional materials for Part B
mortar and pestle
hydrochloric acid (HCl), 0.1 *M*
sodium hydroxide (NaOH),
   0.1 *M*
saturated solution of carbon dioxide (carbonated water or
   club soda)
graph paper

Safety

Wear your goggles and lab apron at all times during the investigation. The 0.1 *M* hydrochloric acid is corrosive, and 0.1 *M* sodium hydroxide is caustic. If skin or clothing come into contact with these solutions they should be washed with plenty of cold water. Do not ingest the antacid tablet. Ingestion of undissolved antacid tablets causes gas pains and can lead to a herniated stomach. Handle hot water with care to avoid burns. Use hot pads or tongs when handling hot objects. Note the caution alert symbols here and with certain steps of the Procedure. Refer to page *xi* for the specific precautions associated with each symbol.

Procedure

Part A

1. Put on your goggles and lab apron. Place about 3 cm of tap water in the bottom of a pan or trough. Fill the bottle to the brim with ice-cold water. Record the temperature in the Data Table.

2. Place a glass square over the mouth of the bottle and hold it tightly. Invert the bottle, and place it mouth-down into the pan of tap water. Remove your hand and the glass square. Some water may run from the gas-collecting bottle into the pan.

3. Remove a fizzing antacid tablet from its package. Get ready to time the reaction by watching the clock or readying the stopwatch.

4. When the person who is timing gives the signal, tilt the gas-collecting bottle slightly and slip the tablet under the mouth of the bottle. Do not lift the mouth of the bottle above the surface of the water in the pan.

5. Time the reaction until the last bit of tablet stops fizzing. Record the time of reaction in the Data Table.

6. Measure the volume of gas given off as follows: Mark the gas/water line of the bottle with a glass marking pen. Remove the bottle from the pan, let the water run out, invert the bottle, and fill it with water to the mark. Measure the volume of this water using a graduated cylinder. (You may have to fill the cylinder more than once.) Record.

7. Rinse any antacid residue from the bottle. Repeat Steps 1–6 with bottles filled with water adjusted to 10°C, 20°C, 30°C, and 40°C. Adjust tap water to 10°C with ice. Make the temperature of the water 30°C and 40°C by combining hot and cold tap water. Continue to record your observations in the Data Table.

8. Flush leftover solutions down the drain with excess water. If you are not going directly on to Part B, clean up your work area and wash your hands before leaving the laboratory.

Part B: Effects of Other Variables on Reaction Rate

9. Do this section on a separate sheet of paper. Choose a variable from the list you made in Question 2 of the Pre-Lab Discussion. Write this variable on the paper. State a hypothesis that describes how you believe the variable will affect the reaction rate of the antacid in water.

10. Make a list of the materials you wish to use in your procedure. Select them from the Materials list. Seek permission from your teacher if you wish to use additional materials.

Name _____

11. Design a procedure that tests the effect of the variable you have chosen on the rate of the reaction of antacid in water. The procedure must include controls, safety precautions, and any steps necessary for waste disposal.

12. Construct a table for organizing and recording your data.

13. Obtain your teacher's approval, and then carry out the procedure under your teacher's supervision.

14. Clean up your work area and wash your hands before leaving the laboratory.

Observations

DATA TABLE   Effect of Temperature on Reaction Rate

Temperature (°C)	Time (s)	CO_2 (cm³)

Critical Thinking: Analysis and Conclusions

1. Construct separate graphs of the reaction time vs. temperature and of CO_2 volume vs. temperature. *(Interpreting data)*

2. How did the rate of reaction vary with the temperature of the water?

(Drawing conclusions) _____

_____

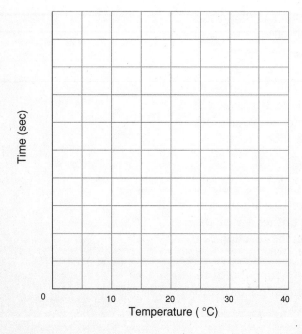

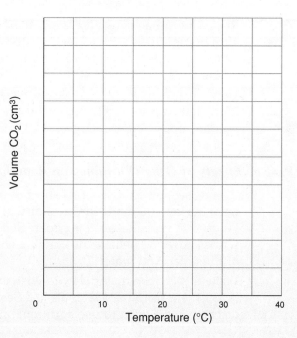

3. Assuming that the same amount of carbon dioxide gas is produced when each tablet reacts, and that the solutions in each gas-collecting bottle are saturated with carbon dioxide, what is the relationship between the solubility of carbon dioxide and temperature? *(Making inferences)* _____

_____

4. State the hypothesis you made for the variable you chose in Part B, and give the rationale you used to make it. *(Developing hypotheses)*

_____

_____

5. State the rationale for each control you used. *(Designing experiments)*

_____

_____

_____

6. On a separate sheet of paper, construct any graphs relevant to your data in Part B and summarize your results. *(Interpreting data)*

7. Did your results support your hypothesis? Explain. *(Drawing conclusions)* _____

_____

_____

8. Compare your results to those of other groups of students who experimented with the same variable. *(Making comparisons)* _____

_____

_____

_____

9. Did any of the other investigations give results that you did not expect? Explain. *(Making judgments)* _____

_____

Critical Thinking: Applications

1. Refer to the equation for the reaction of citric acid and sodium bicarbonate (sodium hydrogen carbonate) given in the Introduction. The initial products of the reaction are sodium citrate and carbonic acid. The carbonic acid (H_2CO_3) immediately decomposes to water and carbon dioxide. Using sodium citrate and carbonic acid as the reaction products, write the rate law for the antacid reaction. *(Applying concepts)*

Name_____

2. Using what you know about Le Chatelier's principle, explain how the equilibrium of the antacid reaction would change with the addition of hydrochloric acid in the stomach. *(Applying concepts)*

 3. If the mass of citric acid is 1000 mg and the mass of sodium bicarbonate (sodium hydrogen carbonate) is 1916 mg, determine which of these substances is the limiting reactant, and which is in excess. *(Applying concepts)*

Going Further

1. Investigate further the chemistry of the antacid reaction. Write to the company that makes the tablets for product information. What is the antacid that forms as the reaction proceeds in the glass? Write a net equation that describes the reaction that occurs when the antacid reacts with the excess acid in your stomach.
2. Survey different brands of antacids in a drugstore to determine the active ingredients they contain. Design a controlled experiment to determine the relative rate at which the recommended dosage of these antacids will neutralize 50 mL of simulated stomach acid (0.1 *M* hydrochloric acid). Under your teacher's supervision, carry out the procedure and report your results to the rest of the class.

Hess's Law

Lab 67

Introduction

Magnesium metal burns with a bright, extremely hot flame to produce magnesium oxide. It would be difficult to measure the heat of reaction, ΔH, since the reaction is rapid and occurs at a high temperature. As you learned in Chapter 12, the value of ΔH for a reaction is the same whether it occurs directly or in a series of steps. This principle, known as Hess's law, allows you to calculate the enthalpy of the magnesium reaction by performing two reactions that are easier to control.

Magnesium oxide, a white powder, reacts (exothermically) with a solution of hydrochloric acid to produce magnesium chloride, liquid water, and heat. Solid magnesium metal reacts with a solution of hydrochloric acid to produce magnesium chloride, hydrogen gas, and (since this reaction is also exothermic) heat. By using the preceding two reactions and knowing the enthalpy for the formation of water (-285.8 kilojoules per mole of water) you will be able to calculate the change in enthalpy for the burning of magnesium in oxygen.

In this investigation, you will measure the heat released by these two reactions. From this information and your knowledge of Hess's law, you will calculate the heat of reaction for magnesium burning in air.

Pre-Lab Discussion

Read the entire laboratory investigation and the relevant pages of your textbook. Then answer the questions that follow.

1. What safety procedures need to be observed when working with each of the following compounds?

   a. magnesium oxide _____

   _____

   b. magnesium chloride _____

   _____

   c. hydrochloric acid _____

2. State Hess's law in your own words. _____

   _____

   _____

Name _____

3. Write the balanced chemical equations for the three reactions described in the Introduction.

_____

_____

_____

4. What is the sign of the change in enthalpy for each of the three reactions used in this investigation? Why? _____

_____

_____

Problem

What is the enthalpy change associated with the reaction of magnesium with oxygen to produce magnesium oxide?

Materials

chemical splash goggles
laboratory apron
magnesium oxide (MgO)
laboratory balance
graduated cylinder, 100-mL
hydrochloric acid (HCl), 1.0 M

2 plastic foam cups
thermometer
cardboard cover for cup
paper towel
piece of magnesium ribbon

Safety

Wear your goggles and lab apron at all times during the investigation. Hydrochloric acid is corrosive and should be handled with care. Wash any splashes or spills immediately with water and notify your teacher. Magnesium oxide dust is toxic if inhaled. Do all steps of the Procedure involving MgO under a fume hood. Magnesium chloride is moderately toxic if ingested. Be sure to keep your fingers and hands away from your mouth. Note the caution alert symbols here and with certain steps of the Procedure. Refer to page *xi* for the specific precautions associated with each symbol.

Procedure

Part A

 1. Put on your goggles and lab apron. Obtain a sample of MgO from your teacher. **CAUTION**: *Magnesium oxide is toxic. Avoid inhalation of the dust. Perform all procedural steps involving MgO in a fume hood.* Measure and record the mass of the MgO to the nearest 0.01 g.

2. Using a graduated cylinder, place 100.0 mL of 1.0 *M* HCl into a plastic foam cup. **CAUTION:** *Hydrochloric acid is corrosive. Use care when handling it. Wash spills and splashes immediately with plenty of water and notify your teacher.* Use a thermometer to measure the temperature of the HCl to the nearest 0.2°C, and record this value. Also record the volume. Place the cup inside another cup.

3. Work under a fume hood. Add the MgO to the HCl. Immediately cover the inner cup with a lid and insert a thermometer into the hole in the lid. Swirl the cup gently to mix the contents.

4. Record the highest temperature reached by the MgO/HCl mixture.

5. Dispose of the magnesium chloride solution in your cup as directed by your teacher. Rinse the cups and dry them with a paper towel.

Part B

6. Obtain a 0.5-cm piece of magnesium ribbon. Measure and record its mass to the nearest 0.01 g.

7. Using a graduated cylinder, place 100.0 mL of 1.0 *M* HCl into a plastic foam cup. **CAUTION:** *Hydrochloric acid is corrosive. Use care when handling it. Wash spills and splashes immediately with plenty of water and notify your teacher.* Measure and record the temperature of the HCl to the nearest 0.2°C. Also record the volume. Place the cup inside another cup.

8. Add the magnesium to the HCl. Immediately cover the inner cup with the lid and insert the thermometer into the hole in the lid. Swirl the cup gently to mix the contents.

9. Record the highest temperature reached by the Mg/HCl mixture.

10. Dispose of the magnesium chloride solution in your cup as directed by your teacher. Clean up your work area and wash your hands before leaving the laboratory.

Observations

Part A

Mass of MgO _____

Volume of HCl _____

Initial temperature of HCl _____

Final temperature of MgO/HCl _____

Part B

Mass of Mg _____

Volume of HCl _____

Initial temperature of HCl _____

Final temperature of Mg/HCl _____

Name _____

⊞ Calculations

Part A

1. Calculate the number of moles of MgO used.

2. Calculate the mass of the HCl solution. Assume the density of the HCl solution is the same as water (1.0 g/mL).

3. Calculate the change in temperature.

4. Calculate the amount of heat released by the reaction. Ignore the heat capacity of the $MgCl_2$, and assume the specific heat of the HCl solution is the same as water (0.00418 kJ/g•°C).

5. Calculate the heat of reaction in kilojoules per mole of MgO.

Part B

6. Calculate the number of moles of Mg used.

7. Calculate the mass of the HCl solution. Assume the density is the same as water (1.0 g/mL).

8. Calculate the change in temperature.

9. Calculate the amount of heat released by the reaction.

10. Calculate the heat of reaction in kilojoules per mole of Mg.

Critical Thinking: Analysis and Conclusions

1. Write the balanced thermochemical equation for the formation of one mole of liquid water from gaseous hydrogen and oxygen.

   (*Applying concepts*) _____

2. Based on your data, write a balanced thermochemical equation for the reaction of one mole of magnesium oxide with hydrochloric acid.

   (*Making inferences*) _____

3. Based on your data, write a balanced thermochemical equation for the reaction of one mole of magnesium with hydrochloric acid.

   (*Making inferences*) _____

4. Combine the three equations from Questions 1–3 so they will add to make a balanced thermochemical equation for the burning of one mole of magnesium in oxygen. You may have to reverse one or more of the equations. (*Making inferences*)

_____

_____

_____

_____

5. Based on your data, calculate the change in enthalpy for the burning of magnesium in oxygen. Use the appropriate sign on your answer.

   (*Drawing conclusions*) _____

6. Calculate the percent error for this investigation given the known heat of reaction is -601.8 kJ/mol Mg. (*Interpreting data*)

Critical Thinking: Applications

1. Given the following information:

$NH_3(g) + HCl(g) \rightarrow NH_4Cl(s)$	$\Delta H = -176.0$ kJ/mol
$N_2(g) + 3H_2(g) \rightarrow 2NH_3(g)$	$\Delta H = -92.2$ kJ/mol
$N_2(g) + 4H_2(g) + Cl_2(g) \rightarrow 2NH_4Cl(s)$	$\Delta H = -628.9$ kJ/mol

   calculate the ΔH for the synthesis of hydrogen chloride gas from hydrogen and chlorine gas. The equation is

   $$H_2(g) + Cl_2(g) \rightarrow 2HCl(g) \quad (Applying\ concepts)$$

   _____

   _____

   _____

   _____

   _____

   _____

2. The Calorie (note the capital C) mentioned in connection with foods is actually a kilocalorie (1000 calories). If 4.18 joules are equal to 1 calorie and a cup of ice cream releases 200 kilocalories, how many cups of ice cream release the same amount of energy as the reaction producing one mole of liquid water from its constituent gases? (*Applying concepts*)

Going Further

1. Investigate the life of Germain Hess, a Swiss chemist who in 1840 proposed the law of heat additivity that came to bear his name. Write a report and present it to the class.

Entropy and Enthalpy Changes

Lab 68

Introduction

Does your bedroom seem to get messy spontaneously? Have you ever noticed how the walls and roof of a deserted building seem to collapse on their own? Can you explain what happens to the arrangement of water molecules as ice melts?

Each of these questions is related to the concept of entropy. Entropy is a measure of the disorder of a system. Spontaneous processes are those that result in a more disordered arrangement of substances, that is, an increase in entropy. Your room gets messy because it has a natural tendency to do so. (Using entropy as an excuse to not clean your room is not recommended!) Old buildings collapse by themselves and water molecules in an ice crystal leave the crystal structure spontaneously because, in both cases, the entropy increases.

In this investigation, you will apply the principle of entropy to three related, spontaneous reactions. You will dissolve solid sodium hydroxide (NaOH) in water, react NaOH solution with hydrochloric acid (HCl), and react solid NaOH with HCl. You will then decide what change in entropy has occurred in each reaction. You will also measure the enthalpy change associated with each reaction.

Pre-Lab Discussion

Read the entire laboratory investigation and the relevant pages of your textbook. Then answer the questions that follow.

1. What is the definition of a spontaneous reaction? _____
   _____

2. How many chemical reactions will be performed in this investigation? Which of them are spontaneous? _____
   _____
   _____
   _____

3. Why must you wear gloves when working with NaOH pellets?
   _____

4. Characterize the following as increasing entropy or decreasing entropy:

   a. gases forming from liquids _____

   b. decreasing the temperature _____

   c. dissolving a solid in water _____

Name_____

5. In what units will the heat of reaction be expressed? _____

_____

Problem

What is the level of entropy and the thermochemical relationship of three chemical reactions?

Materials

chemical splash goggles
laboratory apron
latex gloves
graduated cylinder, 100-mL
distilled water
2 plastic foam cups
weighing paper
laboratory balance
forceps or scoopula

sodium hydroxide pellets
   (NaOH)
thermometer
stirring rod
paper towel
hydrochloric acid (HCl), 1.0 M
sodium hydroxide (NaOH),
   1.0 M
hydrochloric acid (HCl), 0.5 M

Safety

Wear your goggles and lab apron at all times during the investigation. Sodium hydroxide pellets and solutions are caustic. Gloves should be worn when handling the pellets. Hydrochloric acid is corrosive to skin and clothing. If you spill any acid, immediately wash the area with plenty of cold water and notify your teacher. Note the caution alert symbols here and with certain steps of the Procedure. Refer to page *xi* for the specific precautions associated with each symbol.

Procedure

Part A

1. Put on your goggles and lab apron. Use a graduated cylinder to put 100.0 mL of distilled water in a plastic foam cup. Record this volume.

 2. Put on a pair of latex gloves. On a piece of weighing paper, find and record the exact mass of six to seven pellets of solid sodium hydroxide (NaOH). **CAUTION:** *NaOH is caustic. Wear gloves whenever you handle it. Use forceps to handle NaOH pellets.*

3. Place the cup inside another cup. Measure the temperature of the water to the nearest 0.2°C and record this value as the initial temperature (T_i). Pour the NaOH pellets into the cup and begin gently stirring with the stirring rod. Record the highest temperature reached as the final temperature (T_f).

4. Pour the solution down the sink followed by plenty of water. Rinse and dry the cups.

Part B

5. Place one cup inside the other. Using a graduated cylinder, put 50.0 mL of 1.0 *M* HCl into the inner cup. Rinse the graduated cylinder and put 50.0 mL of 1.0 *M* NaOH into it. Record these volumes. **CAUTION:** *NaOH solutions are caustic and HCl solutions are corrosive. Care should be taken when working with them.*

6. Measure the temperature of each solution. Be sure to rinse and dry the thermometer when changing from one solution to another. The temperatures should be within 0.2°C of each other. If not, notify your teacher. Record the HCl value as the initial temperature (T_i).

7. While gently stirring, add the NaOH to the HCl and measure the highest temperature reached. Record this value as the final temperature (T_f).

8. Pour the solution down the sink followed by plenty of water. Rinse and dry the cups.

Part C

9. Place one cup inside the other. Using a graduated cylinder, put 100.0 ml of 0.5 *M* HCl into the inner cup. Record this volume.

10. Repeat Steps 2 and 3 of Part A, using the 0.5 *M* HCl instead of distilled water.

11. Clean up your work area and wash your hands before leaving the laboratory.

Observations

Part A

volume of H_2O

mass of NaOH pellets

initial temperature

final temperature

Part B

volume of HCl solution

volume of NaOH solution

initial temperature

final temperature

Part C

volume of HCl solution

mass of NaOH pellets

initial temperature

final temperature

Name _____

 Calculations

Part A

1. Calculate the mass of the water in the cup. Assume the density of water is 1.0 g/mL.

2. Calculate the temperature change.

3. Calculate the moles of NaOH.

4. Calculate the heat absorbed by the water as the NaOH dissolved. Use 0.00418 kJ/g•°C as the specific heat of water.

5. Calculate the heat released per mole of NaOH. Label this value as ΔH_A.

Part B

1. Calculate the temperature change, the mass of the liquids in the cup, and the moles of NaOH as you did in the calculations for Part A. Assume the density of the HCl and NaOH solutions are the same as water.

2. Calculate the heat absorbed by the liquids as the HCl and NaOH reacted. Assume the specific heat of the solutions is the same as that of water.

3. Calculate the heat released per mole of NaOH. Label this value as ΔH_B.

Part C

1. Calculate the change in temperature, mass of the HCl, and moles of NaOH as before.

2. Calculate the heat absorbed by the liquids as the HCl and NaOH reacted. Assume the liquids have the same specific heat as water.

3. Calculate the heat released per mole of NaOH. Label this value as ΔH_C.

Critical Thinking: Analysis and Conclusions

1. Explain what happens to the entropy in each of the three reactions. *(Making inferences)* _____

_____

_____

_____

_____

2. Write the equations for the reactions in Parts A, B, and C. Include the heat terms as determined in the investigation. How does the sum of A + B compare to the equation for Part C? *(Making comparisons)*

_____

_____

_____

_____

_____

_____

3. Which of these reactions is exothermic? How do you know? *(Interpreting data)* _____

_____

4. Compare the sum of $\Delta H_A + \Delta H_B$ to ΔH_C. Are they different? Explain the source of any error. *(Making comparisons)* _____

_____

5. What process is represented by ΔH_A? By ΔH_B? By ΔH_C? *(Making inferences)* _____

_____

Name_____

Critical Thinking: Applications

1. How would changing the amount of NaOH affect the results of this investigation? *(Making predictions)* _____

   _____

   _____

2. Solid carbon reacts with oxygen gas to form carbon dioxide gas ($\Delta H = -393.5$ kJ/mol C). Carbon monoxide (CO) gas reacts with oxygen gas to form carbon dioxide gas ($\Delta H = -282.8$ kJ/mol CO). What is the enthalpy change for the reaction of solid carbon with oxygen gas to form carbon monoxide gas? *(Applying concepts)*

   _____

   _____

   _____

   _____

   _____

Going Further

1. Go to your physical education department and look at the ingredients on heat packs and cold packs. Devise an experiment that would show the amount of heat evolved or absorbed by the ingredients in the packs. Have your teacher approve your experimental design before you begin. Perform the experiment only under your teacher's supervision.

Thermodynamics of Homemade Ice Cream

Lab 69
APPLICATION

Text reference: **Chapter 23**

Introduction

It's 35°C in the shade and to cool off, you are eating an ice cream cone. As you sit there, you wonder just how ice cream is made. One area of chemistry that helps explains the making of ice cream is thermodynamics. There are three laws of thermodynamics:

1. The total amount of energy in the universe is constant.
2. The entropy of the universe is always increasing.
3. Everything with a temperature above zero kelvins has energy.

You may recognize the first law of thermodynamics as the law of conservation of energy. The second law may be more familiar to you when it is expressed in everyday language: heat always flows from a warmer object to a cooler object. In making ice cream, it is this second law that is of interest.

Another aspect of chemistry involved in producing ice cream deals with the physical properties of solutions, which differ from those of pure solvents. As you learned in Chapter 15, the presence of solute particles in a solution will raise the boiling point or lower the freezing point of the solvent, depending on the number of particles dissolved in a given mass of solvent. The latter characteristic applies to ice cream because the ice cream mixture is mainly a solution of sugar in water, and its freezing point is depressed below 0°C.

Before refrigerators were invented, ice cream was made using ice. In order to solidify by this method, the "hot" ice cream mixture has to lose energy to the "cold" ice. Since ordinary ice is only at 0°C, however, the lowest temperature that the ice cream mixture can reach is 0°C. With the system at thermal equilibrium, the ice cream mixture would still be a liquid.

To freeze the ice cream mixture, it is necessary to use "colder" ice. How do you do that? Again, what you know about colligative properties provides the answer: you make a solution. A salt-ice mixture has a lower freezing point than pure ice, so it acts as "colder" ice. The more salt added to the ice, the lower the freezing point. The ice cream mixture can then lose more energy to the salt-ice mixture and freeze before thermal equilibrium is reached.

In this investigation, you will take advantage of these principles to make homemade ice cream. You will prepare a salt-ice mixture and use it to freeze an ice cream mixture provided by your teacher. Because you should never taste anything in a chemistry laboratory, you will do this investigation in a food science (home economics) lab or nonscience room. Then, yes, you can eat your ice cream!

Name_____

Pre-Lab Discussion

Read the entire laboratory investigation and the relevant pages of your textbook. Then answer the questions that follow.

1. How would you define the second law of thermodynamics? _____

    _____

2. What is thermal equilibrium? _____

    _____

3. What is a colligative property? _____

    _____

4. How does adding salt to ice make ice "colder"? _____

    _____

    _____

5. Why is the salt-ice mixture needed to freeze the ice cream mixture?

    _____

    _____

6. Why must a towel be used when rolling the can? _____

    _____

7. Can the ice cream mixture be rolled too long? Why? _____

    _____

8. What would be the product if pure ice was used instead of the salt-
    ice mixture? Why? _____

    _____

Problem

How can you lower the freezing point of water in order to freeze an ice cream mixture?

Materials

apron   300 g rock salt (NaCl)
clean baby-food jar with lid   thermometer
ice cream mixture   cloth towel
coffee can with lid   2 spoons
2 kg crushed ice

Safety

Wear an apron during this investigation. Do this investigation only in a food science (home economics) lab or a nonscience classroom. Make sure the baby food jar is tightly closed so the salt-ice mixture can't contaminate it. Use a towel when rolling the can to prevent cold burns on your hands. Wipe the baby-food jar off carefully before opening it.

Note the caution alert symbols here and with certain steps of the Procedure. Refer to page *xi* for the specific precautions associated with each symbol.

Procedure

1. Work in the food science (home economics) lab or a nonscience classroom. Put on an apron and wash your hands with soap and water. Describe the ice cream mixture before you begin, and record your observations in the Data Table.

2. Use a spoon to fill a clean baby-food jar three-fourths of the way with the ice cream mixture. Seal the jar tightly with the lid. (If the jar leaks, your ice cream will be salty.)

3. Use another spoon to fill a large can about one-third full with half of the ice and half of the rock salt. Describe the salt-ice mixture. Measure and record its temperature.

4. Put the closed baby-food jar in the can and surround it with the rest of the ice and salt. Put the lid on the can. See Figure 69–1.

5. Wrap the can in a towel to insulate it and to protect your hands. Roll the can back and forth on a table, countertop, or floor for about 15 minutes. Unwrap the can and describe it.

6. Take the lid off the can and describe the salt-ice mixture. Measure and record the temperature of the salt-ice mixture. Remove and rinse the baby-food jar, open the cap, and wipe the rim free of salt.

7. Describe the appearance of the ice cream mixture. Test the product.

8. Wash the jar, can, lids, and spoons. Pour the salt-ice mixture down the drain with plenty of water. Clean up your work area and wash your hands before leaving the room.

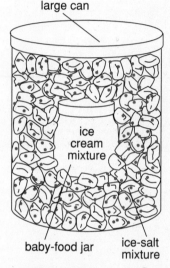

large can

ice cream mixture

baby-food jar   ice-salt mixture

Figure 69–1

Observations

Material	Observation
initial ice cream mixture	
initial salt-ice mixture; temperature	
can after it is rolled	
final salt-ice mixture; temperature	
final ice cream mixture	

Name _____

 Calculations

1. Calculate the theoretical freezing point depression of the ice-salt mixture used in this investigation.

2. Compare your actual freezing point to the one calculated. Determine the percent error.

Critical Thinking: Analysis and Conclusions

1. Discuss the reason for the heat transfer that occurs as the ice melts and the ice cream mixture freezes. *(Drawing conclusions)* _____

   _____

   _____

   _____

   _____

2. How can you account for the percent error in the investigation? *(Interpreting data)* _____

   _____

   _____

   _____

3. How could you speed up the freezing of the ice cream mixture? *(Making inferences)* _____

   _____

   _____

Critical Thinking: Applications

1. Why are ionic compounds such as salt put on sidewalks in winter? *(Applying concepts)* _____

   _____

Making a Cloud Chamber

Small Scale
Lab **70**

Text reference: **Chapter 24**

Introduction

Seeing the invisible radiation emitted from radioactive sources can be quite difficult without the aid of special equipment. Geiger counters can detect radiation and measure how much is being emitted, but they do not reveal the radiation itself or the path that it travels through the air. A cloud chamber is a device that allows you to see the path radiation particles travel after they are emitted from a source.

Alpha and beta radiation are known as *ionizing radiation* because when they interact with other materials, they cause the normally neutral molecules to become ionized. Geiger counters work because of this property of radiation.

In a cloud chamber the air is saturated with a volatile liquid, such as isopropyl alcohol, and cooled. When the radiation travels through this region of cooled saturated air, it ionizes some of the particles. The alcohol vapor is attracted to these ionized particles and the alcohol condenses, forming a cloud. This cloud reveals a visible track of the radiation emitted. The length of the path depends on the initial speed of the radiation, and the density of the cloud depends upon the ability of the radiation to ionize the particles in its path. Figure 70–1 shows what happens on a molecular level inside a cloud chamber.

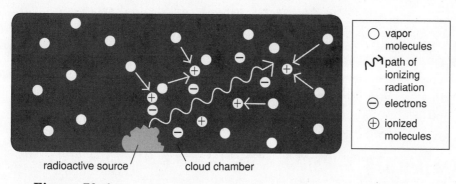

radioactive source   cloud chamber

Figure 70–1

In this investigation you will construct a simple cloud chamber and use it to observe the paths formed by alpha and beta particles. The length and density of the vapor trails will tell you whether you are observing alpha particles or beta particles. Alpha particles move more slowly than beta particles, so they produce shorter trails. Alpha particles also have a greater ability to ionize matter than beta particles, so their trails are more dense.

Name _____

Pre-Lab Discussion

Read the entire laboratory investigation and the relevant pages of your textbook. Then answer the questions that follow.

1. What are alpha particles? Beta particles? _____

   _____

2. What is the mass and electrical charge of an alpha particle? A beta particle? _____

   _____

3. Briefly describe how a vapor trail forms as radiation passes through the cloud chamber. _____

   _____

   _____

4. What is meant by the term *ionizing radiation*? _____

   _____

5. What are the hazards of working with the radioactive substances in this investigation? What precautions should you take? _____

   _____

   _____

   _____

6. What are the hazards of working with dry ice? What precautions should you take? _____

   _____

Problem

How can you use a cloud chamber to observe the trails made by alpha and beta radiation?

Materials

chemical splash goggles
laboratory apron
latex gloves
scissors
piece of black felt
2 plastic petri dish tops or
   bottoms
glue
tape

wash bottle containing
   isopropyl alcohol
paper towel
insulated gloves or tongs for
   handling the dry ice
block of dry ice, 10 cm × 10 cm
radioactive sources
bright light source

Safety

Wear your goggles and lab apron at all times during the investigation. Radioactive sources are harmful if ingested. Wear latex gloves when handling the sources. Dispose of the gloves in the container designated by your instructor. Wash your hands thoroughly with hot water and soap before leaving the laboratory. Dry ice can cause severe tissue damage due to extremely cold temperatures. Use insulated gloves or tongs to handle the dry ice. Isopropyl alcohol is toxic and flammable. Keep the alcohol away from open flames and heat sources. The light source gets very hot. Handle it with caution. Note the caution alert symbols here and with certain steps of the Procedure. Refer to page *xi* for the specific precautions associated with each symbol.

Procedure

 1. Put on your goggles and lab apron.

2. Cut a round piece of black felt so that it will cover the bottom of the petri dish. Place it in the dish. Be sure it lies flat on the bottom.

3. Using Figure 70–2 as a guide, begin assembling the cloud chamber. Cut two strips of black felt. The width of each strip should be the same as the height of the inner walls of the cloud chamber. The length of each strip should be such that the hole on one side of the assembly and about a 2-cm gap on the side opposite the hole are not covered. Secure each strip with glue.

4. Put the top on the assembly so that the cutouts for the hole align, and seal with tape. Do not cover the opening.

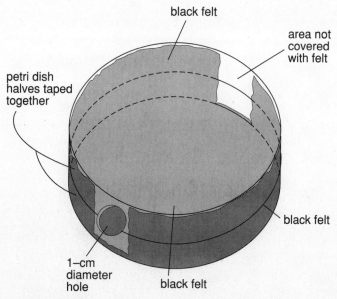

Figure 70–2

Name _____

5. Work in a fume hood. Using the wash bottle with isopropyl alcohol, wet the sides and the bottom of the felt. The sides should be thoroughly moistened. **CAUTION:** *Isopropyl alcohol is toxic and flammable. Avoid its contact with your skin. Wash spills with plenty of water. Keep it away from open flames and heat sources.*

6. Obtain a 10-cm square of dry ice from your instructor. **CAUTION:** *Do not handle the dry ice with your bare hands. Use tongs or insulated gloves.* Set the block of dry ice on a paper towel. Set the cloud chamber on the dry ice. Let it cool for about five minutes.

7. Put on latex gloves. Obtain a radioactive source and insert it through the opening of the cloud chamber. Record the name of the source. **CAUTION:** *Radioactive sources are harmful if ingested. Wear latex gloves when handling the sources.*

8. Turn off the room lights and turn on the light source. Look for cloud trails coming from the radioactive source as alpha or beta particles are emitted. **CAUTION:** *The light source gets very hot. Handle it with caution.*

9. After about five minutes, turn off the light source and let the system cool. Then turn the light back on and observe again.

10. If more than one source is available, replace the first source with a different source and repeat Steps 7–9.

11. Dispose of the latex gloves, dry ice, and radioactive sources as directed by your teacher. Clean up your work area and wash your hands before leaving the laboratory.

Observations

Radioactive source: _____

In the space provided, make a drawing of your cloud chamber showing the location of the source and the vapor trails formed by the radiation.

Critical Thinking: Analysis and Conclusions

1. How many different types of trails are there? *(Interpreting data)*

   _____

   _____

2. Based on the information in the Introduction, identify the vapor trails you saw as having been made by alpha particles or beta particles. If necessary, compare your results with the results of classmates who used different sources. *(Making comparisons)* _____

   _____

   _____

3. On the drawing you made in the Observations, distinguish between the tracks made by alpha particles and those made by beta particles, and label them. *(Interpreting diagrams)*

Critical Thinking: Applications

1. Why do you think the paths of gamma rays cannot be seen in a cloud chamber? *(Applying concepts)* _____

   _____

2. Sometimes a vapor trail can be seen in the cloud chamber even though no radioactive source is in it. What do you think causes the vapor trails? *(Making predictions)* _____

   _____

3. Alpha particles are the least penetrating of all forms of radiation, yet they can cause serious tissue damage. Why? *(Applying concepts)*

   _____

   _____

Going Further

1. Research other methods used to observe the paths made by radiation, including bubble chambers and Geiger counters. Report on your findings.
2. If the light source is bright enough and you have access to a camera you may wish to attempt to photograph the particle trails made.
3. Ionizing radiation is both harmful and useful. Research the effects of ionizing radiation and the application of it to treat cancer. You might be able to visit a hospital and learn firsthand about radiotherapy.

Using a Radon Test Kit

Lab **71**
APPLICATION

Introduction

Radon gas is a product in the radioactive decay series from naturally occurring uranium-238 to stable lead-206. Radon-222 is the only gas in the series and has a half-life of 3.82 days. Radon gas is released into the atmosphere through cracks in granite rock and can accumulate to dangerous levels in the basements of buildings.

Health concerns about radon gas and the study of its effects have been increasing since 1972. Environmental Protection Agency standards for measuring radon and its daughter elements, as well as suggested safe levels of radon, were established in the mid 1980s. These health concerns are not new. As early as the sixteenth century, mine workers in Germany were said to be dying from a disease called mountain sickness, which is now believed to have been caused by radon gas. Exposure to radon has more recently been identified as a cause of lung cancer.

The unit used in the detection of radiation is the pCi/L (picocuries per liter of air). A curie (Ci) is defined as 37 billion disintegrations per second, which is the rate of decay of 1 gram of radium (Ra). The threshold, or upper limit before corrective measures should be taken to reduce radon levels, is 4 pCi/L.

In this investigation you will use a radon detector to determine the radon level in the basement of a building. Three common ways to test for radon are liquid scintillation counters, alpha-track devices, and charcoal-adsorbent detectors. Most home test kits are of the charcoal-adsorbent type and must be left in place for 4–7 days. The kit is then returned to the manufacturer for evaluation. For a reliable test, there must be little or no air movement that would allow the radon to dissipate. The best places to put the test kits are quiet areas of basements. The results of your test will be reported in pCi/L by the manufacturer of the test kit.

Pre-Lab Discussion

Read the entire laboratory investigation and the relevant pages of your textbook. Then answer the questions that follow.

1. What naturally occurring element is the first precursor in the radioactive decay chain that produces radon? _____

2. Why is radon hazardous? _____

3. What is the basic unit used to report radon radiation levels? _____

_____

4. Where are samples usually taken to test radon levels? Why? _____

_____

_____

5. What might you learn about radon test kits if your class is able to use two or more brands of kits in the investigation? _____

_____

_____

Problem

How can you determine the radon level in the basement of a building using a commercial test kit?

Materials

1 or more commercial radon test kits

Safety

Use the test kits only as directed. If the test is done at home, secure the permission of an adult responsible for the premises before proceeding.

Procedure

1. Following the directions on the test kit, place the sample collector in a quiet part of a basement 70–100 cm above ground level. For a reliable test, there must be no air movement. If more than one brand of test kit is used, place all of the kits in the same general vicinity. If additional locations are to be tested, use one or more kits at each site.

2. After the sample has been collected, follow the directions for sending in the kit for testing. The results will be returned to the school. Record the results in the Data Table.

Observations

DATA TABLE

Kit Manufacturer	Test Site	pCi/L

Critical Thinking: Analysis and Conclusions

1. What level of radon gas was shown to be present in the building
    tested? *(Interpreting data)* _____

2. Calculate the average value of radon levels indicated by the kits in
    one location and find the percentage deviations from the average.
    (Interpreting data)

3. Do your results suggest that action should be taken to reduce radon
    levels? _____
    _____

Critical Thinking: Applications

1. Cumulative effects of carcinogens create a serious threat to some
    people. Propose a worst-case scenario for increased lung-cancer risk.
    (Making predictions) _____
    _____
    _____

2. To save energy, many homes have been made more airtight.
    How could this condition increase radon levels in high-risk areas?
    (Developing hypotheses) _____
    _____

3. In some cases, the level of radon has been found to be as high as
    2,700 pCi/L in one house, while a house 100 meters away has levels
    less than 20 pCi/L. How is this possible? *(Developing hypotheses)*
    _____
    _____

4. If radon decayed to polonium with a half-life of several minutes
    rather than 3.82 days, the health danger would be less. Explain.
    (Applying concepts) _____
    _____

Going Further

1. Devise an experiment that could, over several hours, trap daughter elements of radon-222 and test for their presence using a Geiger counter. Under your teacher's supervision, conduct the experiment. Report on your results.

2. Find out how different types of radon detectors (liquid scintillation counters, alpha-track devices, and charcoal-adsorbent detectors) work. Write a brief summary of your findings.

Melting Point of an Organic Compound

Small Scale **Lab 72**

Introduction

The first manufacturing lab for drugs in the United States was established in 1778. Its purpose was to supply medicines to George Washington's troops. Today the Food and Drug Administration (FDA) controls legal drugs sold in the United States. Before a drug may be offered for sale, tests must prove conclusively that it is safe and pure. One method to determine the purity of a compound is the determination of its melting point. If you did Investigation 42 in this manual, you studied the effects of bond type and polarity on the melting point of pure chemicals. You learned that every compound has a characteristic melting point that is a function of its chemical structure. When impurities are present, the compound will show a melting point that is lower and possibly wider in range than that of the pure compound. A compound containing small amounts of impurities may, in fact, melt several degrees below its pure form. If the melting point is more than a few degrees off, the compound may be a different product altogether.

Many drugs, such as aspirin, can be produced in the laboratory. Aspirin is an example of a class of organic compounds called esters. You will learn more about the making of esters in the next chapter. In this investigation, you will determine the melting point of aspirin. You will then compare your results with a reference standard for this chemical product.

Pre-Lab Discussion

Read the entire laboratory investigation and the relevant pages of your textbook. Then answer the questions that follow.

1. Aspirin is an allergen. Look up the meaning of the word *allergen* in a dictionary, and explain why it appears in a caution in the Safety section. _____

   _____

2. A hot oil bath is used in the Procedure. Why doesn't the Procedure call for a hot water bath? _____

   _____

3. Why should you place the thermometer bulb and the melting point tube 3 cm above the bottom of the beaker and not on the bottom?

   _____

   _____

4. Why will cooling the oil bath and the melting point tube allow you to repeat the Procedure and check your answer? _____

_____

Problem

How can you use the melting point to determine the purity of an organic compound?

Materials

chemical splash goggles	thermometer clamp
laboratory apron	ring stand
spatula	vegetable oil
aspirin	beaker, 250-mL
glass square or weighing paper	wire gauze square
melting point tube	lab burner
rubber band	iron ring
thermometer fitted with a one-hole stopper or cutaway cork	matches or striker

Safety

Wear your goggles and lab apron at all times during the investigation. Acetylsalicyclic acid (aspirin) is an allergen. It may cause bleeding after ingestion. Do not taste the aspirin. The oil bath and lab burner are hot. Do not touch the beaker or oil during the heating process. Tie back hair and loose clothing before lighting the burner.

Melting point tubes are fragile. Handle them with care. Note the caution alert symbols here and with certain steps of the Procedure. Refer to page *xi* for the specific precautions associated with each symbol.

Procedure

   1. Put on your goggles and lab apron. Using a spatula, crush some aspirin crystals on a glass square or a piece of weighing paper. Force a small amount of crystals into the melting point tube. Invert the tube and tap it gently until the crystals fall to the bottom. Repeat the process until there is about 1 cm of crystals packed into the bottom end of the tube. **CAUTION:** *Melting point tubes are fragile. Handle them with care.*

2. Obtain a thermometer fitted with a one-hole stopper or cutaway cork. Using a rubber band, attach the melting point tube to the bottom of a thermometer. Make sure that the closed end of the tube is down. The bottom of the tube should be level with the bulb of the thermometer. Clamp the thermometer to a point near the top of a ring stand. See Figure 72–1.

3. Set up a ring stand, ring, wire gauze square, and lab burner. Refer to Figure 42–2 in Investigation 42 in this book as a reminder of the setup of the apparatus. Pour about 100 mL of oil into a 250-mL beaker. Set the beaker on the wire gauze square. Lower the thermometer into the oil. The bulb of the thermometer should be about 3 cm from the bottom of the beaker.

 4. Light the burner with the matches or striker. Heat the oil in the beaker until the temperature reaches about 110°C. Lower the burner flame to reduce the rate of heating. Continue to raise the temperature of the oil very slowly. **CAUTION:** *Tie back any hair or loose clothing that could come into contact with the flame. The heated oil is very hot. Do not touch the beaker or the hot plate with your bare hands.*

5. One partner should watch the crystals in the melting point tube closely while the other partner watches the thermometer. When the crystals melt, read the thermometer at once. Record the temperature in the Data Table.

6. Allow the oil and the melting point tube to cool to at least 120°C. Heat and observe the melting point a second time. If the temperature is not within one degree of your first reading, repeat this step.

 7. Make sure your burner is shut off. Remove the thermometer from the oil bath, and allow it to cool. Put the melting point tube in the container provided by your teacher. Return the oil to a container provided by your teacher. Clean oil from your thermometer. Clean up your work area and wash your hands before leaving the laboratory.

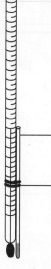

thermometer

melting point tube

rubber band

Figure 72–1

Observations

DATA TABLE   Melting Point of Aspirin

Material	Melting Point (°C)
pure aspirin reference	135
aspirin trial #1	
aspirin trial #2	
average of trials #1 and #2	

Critical Thinking: Analysis and Conclusions

1. Calculate the difference between the melting point of pure aspirin and your sample. Does your compound appear to be aspirin? Why or why not? *(Interpreting data)* _____

_____

_____

Name

2. If your melting point had been several degrees higher than the melting point of pure aspirin, what could you conclude? *(Drawing conclusions)*

3. If your melting point had been 1 degree lower than the melting point of pure aspirin, what could you conclude? *(Drawing conclusions)*

4. If your melting point had been 5 degrees lower than the melting point of pure aspirin, what could you conclude? *(Drawing conclusions)*

Critical Thinking: Applications

1. What have you learned about aspirin in this investigation that can be useful to you? *(Applying concepts)*

2. How would your results be affected if the hot oil bath was heated more rapidly? *(Making predictions)*

Going Further

1. Research the folk history of naturally occuring aspirin compounds. Find out what plants contain salicylic acid or its derivatives and how people of various cultures have used the compound. Prepare a short report for the class.

2. Research the discovery of aspirin in the laboratory and the history of its use. Report on a recent study of aspirin in the scientific literature.

Properties of an Alkyne

Introduction

Hydrocarbons are compounds made up of only carbon and hydrogen. Hydrocarbons made of straight carbon chains are called aliphatic hydrocarbons, and include the alkanes, alkenes, and alkynes. Alkanes are saturated hydrocarbons, while alkenes and alkynes are unsaturated. In all cases, hydrocarbons with just a few carbon atoms are gaseous at room temperature and pressure. As the number of carbon atoms increases, the compounds are mostly liquids, and then solids. The number of unsaturated bonds also helps to determine whether a specific compound is a solid, liquid, or gas.

The main source of aliphatic hydrocarbons is petroleum. They are used as fuels, lubricants, waxes, and road-surfacing material, and in the production of plastics and cosmetics.

The first member of the alkynes is called ethyne, more commonly known as acetylene. Its major use is as a fuel in torches that cut and weld metals. In this investigation, you will prepare acetylene (ethyne) from a reaction of calcium carbide (CaC_2) with water and examine some of its chemical and physical properties.

Pre-Lab Discussion

Read the entire laboratory investigation and the relevant pages of your textbook. Then answer the questions that follow.

1. Give the molecular formula and the structural formula for acetylene (ethyne).

2. Distinguish between the term *saturated* and *unsaturated* hydrocarbons. _____

   _____

   _____

3. Identify three items used by you or your family that are derived from aliphatic hydrocarbons. _____

   _____

4. What do the colors of phenolphthalein indicate? _____

   _____

   _____

5. What safety precautions need to be taken with the candle? _____

_____

6. Why should the reaction in Procedure Step 6 be allowed to run for a short time before collecting the acetylene gas? _____

_____

Problem

How can acetylene be produced, and what are its properties?

Materials

chemical splash goggles
laboratory apron
large test tube
one-hole rubber stopper, #00
thin-stem micropipet
scissors
clear adhesive tape
beaker, 600-mL

water
graduated micropipet
forceps
2 pieces of calcium carbide
matches
candle
phenolphthalein indicator

Safety

Wear your goggles and lab apron at all times during the investigation. Calcium carbide reacts with water to produce acetylene, a flammable gas. Keep the calcium carbide dry and away from any open flames. Tie back loose hair and clothing. Do not leave the burning candle unattended. Do not inhale the acetylene gas or the soot.

Note the caution alert symbols here and with certain steps of the Procedure. Refer to page *xi* for the specific precautions associated with each symbol.

Procedure

1. Put on your goggles and lab apron. Obtain a large test tube, a #00 rubber stopper, and a thin-stem micropipet.

2. Cut the pipet stem as shown in Figure 73–1 (top), so that a small part of the bulb remains with the stem.

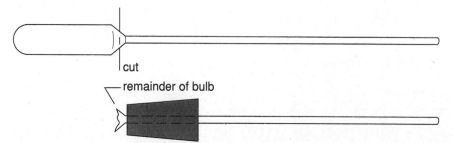

Figure 73–1 *Preparing the pipet stem and stopper*

3. Insert the stem through the bottom (narrow end) of the stopper and pull it through the hole so it fits snugly in the stopper. (See bottom of Figure 73–1.) If the pipet stem does not fit snugly, take it out and wrap a small piece of tape around the end.

4. Cut a graduated pipet (as shown in Figure 73–2) to be used in collecting the acetylene gas.

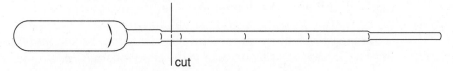

cut

Figure 73–2 *Cutting the collecting pipet*

5. Fill the beaker three-fourths full with water. Use some of this water to completely fill the graduated pipet bulb.

6. Fill the test tube two-thirds full with water. Using the forceps, drop a pea-sized piece of calcium carbide into the test tube and insert the stopper with the pipet stem. Allow the reaction to run for 10–15 seconds.

7. Work with a partner. One person should hold the test tube and bend the pipet stem so that its end is under water in the beaker. (See Figure 73–3.) The other person should place the water-filled graduated pipet bulb over the outlet and collect the acetylene gas being generated. Once the pipet bulb is filled with gas, cover the mouth of the pipet bulb with your finger to keep the collected gas in the pipet bulb.

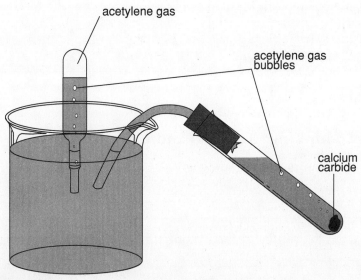

acetylene gas

acetylene gas
bubbles

calcium
carbide

Figure 73–3

8. Light the candle. **CAUTION:** *Tie back loose hair and clothing. Do not leave the burning candle unattended.*

9. Holding the pipet bulb to the side of the candle flame and about 3 cm away, quickly squeeze the collected gas into the flame. Do not allow the pipet bulb to touch the flame. Observe how well the acetylene burns and how much soot is produced. Record your observations in the Data Table. **CAUTION:** *Do not inhale the acetylene gas or the soot.*

10. Repeat Steps 5–9, except this time start with the graduated pipet bulb half full of air. With the forceps, add more calcium carbide if necessary. Once the acetylene gas has displaced the water, cover the mouth of the pipet with your finger and shake to mix the gases. Then test the mixture in the candle flame. Try smaller amounts of acetylene such as one fourth and one eighth of the graduated pipet bulb. Record your observations in the Data Table. Blow out the candle after you have finished the tests.

11. Remove the stopper from the test tube that originally contained the water and calcium carbide and add one drop of phenolphthalein indicator. Record your observations in the Data Table.

12. Put any leftover calcium carbide in the container provided by your teacher. Wash the solution in the test tube down the drain with plenty of water. Clean up your work area and wash your hands before leaving the laboratory.

Observations
DATA TABLE

Test	Observation
pure acetylene	
1:1 air-acetylene mixture	
3:1 air-acetylene mixture	
7:1 air-acetylene mixture	
phenolphthalein	

Critical Thinking: Analysis and Conclusions

1. Describe the physical and chemical properties of acetylene. *(Interpreting data)* _____

_____

2. What do the results of the phenolphthalein indicator test tell you? *(Interpreting data)* _____

_____

3. Write the balanced equation for the production of acetylene from calcium carbide. *(Making inferences)*

_____

4. Is the burning of pure acetylene complete or incomplete combustion? What do you think the soot is? *(Interpreting data)* _____

_____

5. Write the balanced equation for the incomplete combustion of acetylene. *(Making inferences)*

_____

6. Did any of the mixtures burn without producing soot? Is this complete or incomplete combustion? *(Interpreting data)* _____

_____

_____

7. Write the balanced equation for the complete combustion of acetylene. *(Making inferences)*

_____

Critical Thinking: Applications

1. Suggest some reasons why alkynes such as acetylene are not used as motor fuels. *(Applying concepts)* _____

_____

_____

2. When an acetylene torch is lit, the flame is usually orange and a lot of soot is produced. When a valve on the torch is adjusted, the flame becomes blue and less soot is produced. What is the function of the valve? *(Applying concepts)* _____

Going Further

1. Research the commercial methods used to obtain the various aliphatic hydrocarbons from petroleum and the uses of these compounds.
2. Hydrocarbon fuels are a blend of several different substances. The blend depends on the particular application. Fuel used in airplanes is different from fuel that would be used in a lawn mower. Research the composition and applications of various types of hydrocarbon fuels.

Playing with Polymers

Introduction

The world's great bridges are suspended on steel cables that possess the strength and flexibility to support heavy loads of traffic and changing stresses from wind. In the future, these steel cables may be replaced by cables made of spider silk, or some similar material. Spider silk is composed of a repeating pattern of monomers, or smaller molecules, linked together to create very long molecular chains, or polymers. The silk used in some spider webs is reported to be five times stronger than steel, thirty times as flexible as nylon (a synthetic polymer), and to have three times the impact resistance of Kevlar (a synthetic polymer used in bullet-proof vests).

Unfortunately, spiders are more interested in catching flies in their silk than in building bridges. Chemists and engineers, therefore, have the job of discovering how to mass-produce spider silk or similar polymers, either mechanically or by genetic engineering.

Polymers in nature give texture to living tissues. Cellulose and carbohydrates are important plant polymers made from the same monomer, glucose. Chains of amino acids, called proteins, form not only the silk of spiders and silkworms, but also skin, muscle, and hair. Even lobsters and insects are encased in a polymer, chitin.

Under certain conditions, polymer chains can become cross-linked (hydrogen bonded) to other chains and to parts of themselves, as shown in Figure 74–1. Even though the hydrogen bonds are weak by comparison to covalent bonds, more and stronger cross-linking between neighboring polymers results in greater resiliency (resistance to being deformed).

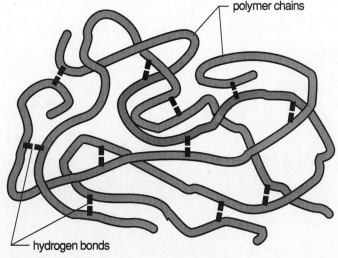

Figure 74–1

Name _____

Cross-linked polymers in a large amount of liquid form a colloidal suspension known as a gel. A gel, which consists of a solid dispersed in a liquid, has a structure that prevents it from flowing. Water molecules may form part of the loose irregular structure. The amount of water present can also affect the properties of the material.

In this investigation you will prepare two natural polymer gels and explore their properties.

Pre-Lab Discussion

Read the entire laboratory investigation and the relevant pages of your textbook. Then answer the questions that follow.

1. Are protein polymers, such as the ones in this investigation, formed

   by addition or condensation? _____

2. Monomer molecules have specific molar masses, many less than 100 g/mol. Explain how these monomers become molecules with variable masses in the tens or even hundreds of thousands of grams

   per mole. _____

   _____

3. Study the Materials list (excluding chemicals) and list the items that

   you believe are made of natural polymers. _____

   _____

4. Why is acetic acid hazardous? What safety precautions must be

   followed? _____

   _____

   _____

Problem

What are the properties of some natural polymer gels?

Materials

chemical splash goggles	ring stand
laboratory apron	iron ring
latex gloves	2 beakers, 100-mL
skim milk	distilled water
2 paper medicine-dose cups	hot plate
acetic acid, 6.0 *M*	sugar-free gelatin mix
2 wooden splints	warm water
2 filter papers	scalpel
funnel	

Safety

Wear your goggles, gloves, and lab apron at all times during the investigation. Polymers are difficult to remove from clothing. Acetic acid is corrosive. Rinse the milk protein gels with water before handling them. If you spill acetic acid on your skin or clothing, wash it off immediately with plenty of water and tell your teacher. The hot plate and beaker will get hot. Be careful not to touch them. Do not touch the blade of the scalpel. Under no circumstances should you taste the milk or gelatin.

Note the caution alert symbols here and with certain steps of the Procedure. Refer to page *xi* for the specific precautions associated with each symbol.

Procedure

Part A

1. Put on your goggles, gloves, and lab apron. Obtain 20 mL of skim milk in a paper medicine-dose cup and add 2 mL of 6.0 *M* acetic acid. Stir with a wooden splint and let stand for a few minutes. Do not drink the milk. **CAUTION:** *Acetic acid is corrosive. If you spill any on your skin or clothing, wash it off immediately with plenty of water and tell your teacher.*

2. Set up the ring stand and iron ring. Fold the filter paper and place it in the funnel. Put the funnel into the iron ring so that it will drain into a beaker. Filter the coagulated milk protein by pouring the acidified milk into the funnel. Pour slowly, so that the liquid does not rise above the edge of the filter paper in the funnel. It will take several minutes for the clear filtrate to drain from the protein complex.

3. While you wait, turn on a hot plate and boil 20 mL of distilled water in a 100-mL beaker. Reduce the heat and add a package of sugar-free gelatin. Stir with a wooden splint. **CAUTION:** *The hot plate and beaker will get very hot. Be careful not to burn yourself.*

4. Gently heat the gelatin in the beaker while stirring in order to completely hydrate the gelatin protein. Turn off the hot plate.

5. Carefully pour the hot gelatin into a medicine-dose cup and let it cool. Do not taste the gelatin.

6. Return to the milk protein. When the liquid stops draining, rinse the filtered protein with 10 mL of distilled water. Let the water drain through the filter.

7. Remove the filter from the funnel, gather the top edge, and gently squeeze the filter to remove additional water. Be careful not to break the filter paper.

8. Open the filter and use your fingers to push the protein complex into a pile in the middle of the filter paper. Gather the edge of the filter paper with the protein enclosed and twist the paper gently, forcing the protein into a ball inside the paper. If the paper rips, replace with a second piece.

9. Observe the gelatin and the milk protein. Record your observations in the Data Table. Leave the polymer gels to dry overnight. Clean up your work area and wash your hands before leaving the laboratory.

Part B

10. Put on your goggles, gloves, and lab apron. Remove the gelatin from the cup by heating the cup in warm water and scraping out the gelatin, or by cutting the cup. Shape the gelatin block into a ball by slicing it with a scalpel and then smoothing it with warm water. **CAUTION:** *Be careful not to cut yourself with the scalpel.*

11. Describe the gelatin ball. Investigate its resiliency and cohesiveness. Try to bounce it, squash it, pull it apart, and so on. How easy is it to deform and/or separate into pieces—processes that require neighboring polymer molecules to slip past each other? Try to deform the polymer slowly, and then rapidly. Record your observations in the Data Table.

12. Remove the milk protein polymer ball and test it as you did the gelatin ball. Record your observations in the Data Table.

13. The polymer gels may be disposed of in the dry waste container. Flush excess liquids down the drain with lots of water. Clean up your work area and wash your hands before leaving the laboratory.

Observations

DATA TABLE

Polymer Gel	Day 1	Day 2
gelatin		
milk protein		

Critical Thinking: Analysis and Conclusions

1. Which polymer gel do you think has more cross-linking? Which one has less? Explain. *(Drawing conclusions)* _____
   _____
   _____

2. What difference did leaving the polymer gel balls out overnight make? *(Making comparisons)* _____

3. What role do you think water plays in keeping the gel flexible?
    (Making inferences) _____

    _____

Critical Thinking: Applications

1. In wood, strong polymer chains of cellulose and lignin are aligned
    in rows and layers and held in place by hydrogen bonds. What
    property of wood results from this structure? *(Applying concepts)*

    _____

    _____

2. The latex polymer used to make natural rubber is a primary compo-
    nent of the sap of rubber trees, dandelions, milkweed, and other
    plants. Suggest how you would attempt to make a polymer gel from

    the liquid sap. *(Designing experiments)* _____

    _____

3. When water is added to flour and kneaded, a dough is formed. More
    kneading makes the dough tougher. Which of the following do you
    think explains what happens when dough is formed? Explain your
    answer. *(Applying concepts)*
    a. A chemical reaction occurs, and a new compound is formed.
    b. Monomer molecules form a polymer molecule.
    c. Cross-linking bonds form between polymer molecules.

    _____

    _____

    _____

Going Further

1. Compile a list of the common names of as many polymers as you
    can find. For each one, include the structural formula of the mono-
    mer(s) from which it is constructed and a list of its uses.

Observing Fermentation

Lab 75
APPLICATION

Text reference: ***Chapter 26***

Introduction

Imagine a group of chemicals that possess a "life force"—the ability to generate life. In the early 1800s, such chemicals were thought to exist, and were called "organic" chemicals. These chemicals seemed to be the essential difference between living (organic) and nonliving (inorganic) things. But by the middle of the 1800s, some organic chemicals had been synthesized without the use of living tissue. Chemists today can make nearly any organic chemical, including pieces of DNA, in the lab, but it is still cheaper and easier to extract many organic chemicals from living organisms.

In this investigation, you will produce ethanol (ethyl alcohol) from sugars by fermentation with yeast. This is the same biochemical process that occurs in bread making and in the brewing process. Today most ethanol is produced by fermentation, just as it was in ancient times. In the last century and a half, though, notions of magical chemicals have been replaced by a better understanding of the organic chemistry involved in fermentation. Still, the series of complex chemical reactions that the yeast performs in order to convert sugar to alcohol are no less remarkable. The overall reaction for glucose fermentation to ethanol is:

$$C_6H_{12}O_6(aq) \xrightarrow{\text{yeast enzymes}} 2CO_2(g) + 2C_2H_5OH(l)$$

Ethanol has a variety of uses. It is used widely as an industrial solvent, as an ingredient in many household products and medications, and as a starting chemical from which a large variety of other chemicals are produced.

In this investigation, you will observe the reaction of a mixture of yeast and molasses. The yeast uses the dissolved sugar as an energy source to grow and reproduce. Ethanol and carbon dioxide are its waste products, and the ethanol eventually kills the yeast before all the sugar is reacted. You will run the reaction at several temperatures and identify the temperature at which the reaction proceeds most efficiently.

Pre-Lab Discussion

Read the entire laboratory investigation and the relevant pages of your textbook. Then answer the questions that follow.

1. What functional group identifies ethanol as an alcohol? _____

_____

2. Predict how raising the temperature will affect the rate of the fermentation reaction. _____

_____

_____

Problem

What is the optimal temperature for yeast to grow and ferment sugar?

Materials

chemical splash goggles
laboratory apron
erlenmeyer flask, 50-mL
molasses and yeast fermentation
  mixture
one-hole stopper fitted with a
  micropipet stem

water tub
hot and cold tap water
thermometer
clock or watch with a second
  hand

Safety

Wear your goggles and lab apron at all times during the investigation. The fermenting mixture is toxic; do not drink it. Do not store the mixture in an airtight container; high pressure may rupture the container. Note the caution alert symbols here and with certain steps of the Procedure. Refer to page *xi* for the specific precautions associated with each symbol.

Procedure

1. Put on your goggles and lab apron. Obtain 30–40 mL of molasses and yeast fermentation mixture in a 50-mL flask. Stopper the flask with a one-hole stopper that has a plastic micropipet stem in the hole. Be sure that the stem is above the surface of the liquid in the flask.

2. Fill a plastic tub with warm tap water. Adjust the temperature to 20–25°C and immerse the flask with the fermentation mixture completely in the water so the whole stem is below the surface. There should be enough fluid in the flask so that it sinks. (Add a marble or two if needed to submerge the flask.) You should observe bubbles of carbon dioxide gas escaping from the flask through the stem.

3. With the flask immersed, allow the fermentation to proceed for about 15 minutes, or until the bubbling rate has become constant. When bubbling appears to be at a constant rate, count the bubbles produced in one minute. Record the bubble rate and the water bath temperature in the Data Table.

4. Repeat Step 3 using the same fermentation mixture, but with water-bath temperatures of about 30–35°C, 40–45°C, 50–55°C, and 60–65°C. Adjust the water temperature by adding hot or cold water to the bath. In each case, immerse the flask and wait a few minutes to allow the fermentation rate (bubble rate) to become constant. Then count the number of bubbles produced in one minute. Record the number of bubbles per minute and the temperature of the water bath in the Data Table.

5. Give your flask to your teacher, who will arrange for the fermentation to continue overnight. It may be necessary to first add a few milliliters of fermentation mixture to the flask to restart the process. Clean up your work area and wash your hands before leaving the laboratory.

 6. The next day, put on your goggles and lab apron. Retrieve your flask and check to see if fermentation has stopped (no bubbles seen). **CAUTION:** *The contents of the flask may be toxic. Do not ingest them.* Open the flask and note the odor. Return the flask with its contents to your teacher who may distill the combined contents to produce ethanol. Clean up your work area and wash your hands before leaving the laboratory.

Observations

DATA TABLE   Fermentation Reaction Rate

Temperature (°C)	Reaction Rate (bubbles/min)

Critical Thinking: Analysis and Conclusions

1. Using Figure 75–1, make a graph of temperature vs. reaction rate (bubbles / min) from your data. *(Interpreting data)*

2. What was the optimal temperature for the reaction? Does your graph support your prediction about reaction rate change given in Question 2 of the Pre-Lab Discussion? *(Interpreting diagrams)* _____

_____

_____

_____

3. What causes the bubbling in the fermentation mixture during fermentation? *(Making inferences)* _____

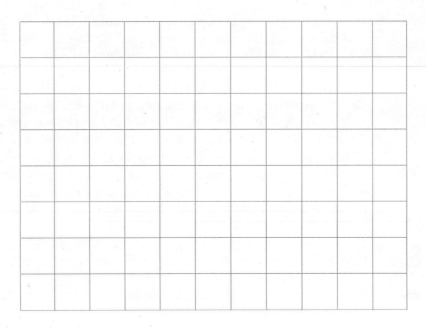

Figure 75–1

4. Suggest a reason that the reaction slowed down as the temperature was increased past the optimal point. *(Developing hypotheses)*

_____

Critical Thinking: Applications

1. Part of the art of bread making involves determining the temperature at which the dough is set to rise, and the amount of sugar and salt in the dough. Explain. *(Evaluating)* _____

_____

2. What happens to the ethanol when the bread is baked? *(Developing hypotheses)* _____

Going Further

1. Make bread with yeast and observe the rising action. Try to relate the rising of the bread and the aroma to your observations in this investigation.
2. Do library research to investigate the effects of ethanol on the human nervous system and on other organisms. In particular, try to find out how ethanol acts chemically to cause intoxication.

Making Slime

Text reference: **Chapter 26**

Introduction

As you learned from doing Investigation 74, polymer chains can be linked together to form substances with a variety of properties. While the polymer chains are held together by strong covalent bonds, they are linked to each other by weak hydrogen bonds. The amount of cross-linking determines how resilient the gels or plastics are, that is, how much they can be deformed. Such substances include materials as soft as gelatin and as strong as Kevlar.

Chemists and engineers have invented and produced many varied polymers. Many are called plastics because they can be shaped or molded, usually with heat. Most are formed from repeating units called monomers that are derived from petroleum. Depending on the monomer molecules used and the technique used to join, or polymerize, them, polymers of vastly different properties may result. From fabrics to surface coatings to the objects of everyday life, synthetic polymers seemingly envelop the modern world.

Polyvinyl alcohol has the formula $[-CH_2-CH(OH)-]_n$. The structures of the vinyl alcohol monomer (which does not exist in isolation) and polyvinyl alcohol are shown in Figure 76-1.

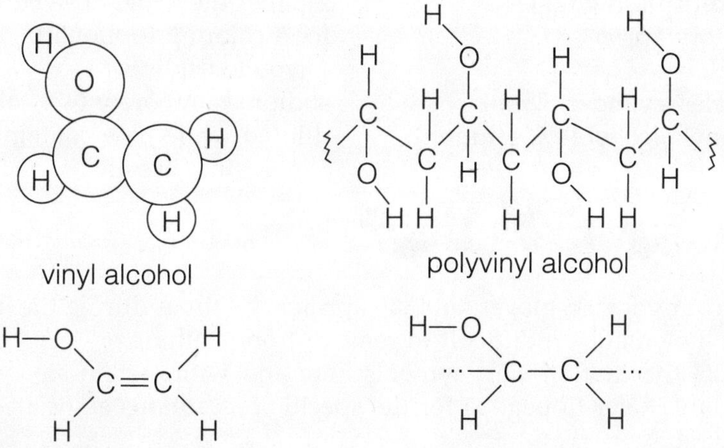

vinyl alcohol

polyvinyl alcohol

Figure 76–1

Sodium tetraborate dissociates in solution to form the borate ion, $B(OH)_4^-$. Borate ions form hydrogen bonds with the hydroxyl groups of polyvinyl alcohol, linking chains of polyvinyl alcohol to each other.

In this investigation you will make two synthetic polymers, one from polyvinyl alcohol and the other from polyvinyl acetate. After producing the polymers, you will observe and compare some of their properties.

Name _____

Pre-Lab Discussion

Read the entire laboratory investigation and the relevant pages of your textbook. Then answer the questions that follow.

1. Are the polymers in this investigation formed by addition or condensation? _____

2. Study the materials list (excluding chemicals) and list the item(s) that you believe are made of synthetic polymers. _____
_____

3. In each of the comparisons below, say which substance you think has the most cross-linking, and explain why.

   a. liquid epoxy glue/hardened epoxy glue _____
   _____

   b. Silly Putty/ a superball _____
   _____

   c. Kevlar/rubber band _____
   _____

Problem

How does cross-linking change the properties of a polymer?

Materials

chemical splash goggles
laboratory apron
latex gloves
graduated cylinder, 25-mL
polyvinyl alcohol (4% solution)

2 paper medicine-dose cups
food coloring (optional)
2 wooden splints
sodium tetraborate (4% solution)
diluted white glue containing
   polyvinyl acetate

Safety

Wear your goggles, gloves, and lab apron at all times during the investigation. Polymers are difficult to remove from clothing.

Note the caution alert symbols here and with certain steps of the Procedure. Refer to page *xi* for the specific precautions associated with each symbol.

Procedure

Part A

1. Put on your goggles, gloves, and lab apron. Measure 25 mL of 4% polyvinyl alcohol solution in the graduated cylinder and pour it into a paper medicine-dose cup. Add food coloring if you wish, and stir with a wooden splint until the color is evenly mixed.

2. Add 2 mL of 4% sodium tetraborate solution to the medicine-dose cup. Stir the two solutions together until the liquid becomes thick and pulls away from the sides of the cup.

3. Remove the polymer gel from the cup. Squeeze excess fluid from the gel as you shape it into a ball.

4. Set the ball aside to dry overnight.

 5. Repeat Steps 1–4, substituting diluted white glue for the polyvinyl alcohol solution. Flush excess liquid down the drain with lots of water. Clean up your work area and wash your hands before leaving the laboratory.

Part B

 6. Put on your goggles, gloves, and lab apron. Test each polymer for resiliency and cohesiveness. Try to bounce it, squash it, pull it apart, and so on. Check the polymer gel shear strength. How easy is it to deform and/or separate into pieces, which requires neighboring polymer molecules to slip past each other? Try to deform the polymer slowly, and then rapidly. Record your observations.

 7. The polymer gels may be disposed of in the dry waste container. Clean up your work area and wash your hands before leaving the laboratory.

Observations

_____
_____
_____
_____
_____

Critical Thinking: Analysis and Conclusions

1. What is the physical effect of cross-linking a polymer? *(Interpreting data)* _____

2. Are the substances produced in this reaction solids or liquids? Explain your answer. *(Drawing conclusions)* _____
_____
_____

3. What happens when you try to deform the polymers? What do you think this tells you about their structures? (*Drawing conclusions*)

_____

_____

_____

_____

Critical Thinking: Applications

1. Modern life depends on the use of polymers, but there is an environmental cost. Write at least a paragraph about how this statement pertains to the question asked at nearly every grocery checkout counter today, "Paper or plastic?" (*Using the writing process*)

_____

_____

_____

_____

2. In some plastics, most of the polymer molecules are aligned in one direction. How does this explain why plastic such as food wrap and tape are easier to tear lengthwise than across? (*Applying concepts*)

_____

_____

3. Plasticizers are substances often added to polymer plastics, such as polyvinyl chloride, to reduce the number of cross-links between polymer chains. How do you think the addition of plasticizers helps explain the properties of easily torn vinyl sheeting (as used for raincoats), flexible vinyl siding, and rigid PVC pipes? (*Applying concepts*) _____

_____

_____

Going Further

1. One of the major uses of alkenes and some alkynes is the production of plastics by the process of polymerization. Research these polymerization processes. Under the supervision of your teacher, try one or more of these processes in class.
2. Using a reference book, find the names and properties of other cross-linked polymers. Research and report on their uses.

Analyzing Commercial Aspirin

Small Scale Lab **77**
APPLICATION

Text reference: **Chapter 26**

Introduction

Aspirin is one of the most commonly used medications in the world. It has been used for almost 100 years to treat pain, inflammation, and fever. The chemical name for aspirin is acetylsalicylic acid, or simply ASA. It can be prepared in the laboratory by the reaction between salicylic acid and acetic acid, as shown in Figure 77–1.

Salicylic acid   Acetic acid   Acetylsalicylic acid

Figure 77–1

You may have detected the vinegarlike smell of acetic acid upon opening an old bottle of aspirin. This odor often is evidence of hydrolysis, or the reaction of aspirin with water from the environment. In this process, some ASA is lost as salicylic acid and acetic acid are formed. The tablets are then partly ASA and partly salicylic acid.

In this investigation, you will determine the quantity of salicylic acid that is present in one or more commercial aspirin products. You will first prepare a set of solutions of increasing known concentrations of salicylic acid. Then you will test the solutions, using iron(III) ion solution as an indicator. The substance formed by the reaction between iron(III) ions and salicylic acid gives the solution a violet color. The intensity of the color is a measure of the concentration of salicylic acid. You will then similarly prepare and test a solution made from an ASA tablet. By comparing the color of the unknown solution to the colors of the known solutions you can determine the concentration of salicylic acid in the ASA tablet.

Pre-Lab Discussion

Read the entire laboratory investigation and the relevant pages of your textbook. Then answer the questions that follow.

1. How is aspirin made? _____

_____

2. What safety precautions should be taken with the iron(III) ion solution? _____

_____

3. What is the purpose of the ten solutions in rows A and B? _____

_____

_____

4. What class of organic compounds does acetic acid belong to?

_____

Problem

How can you determine the quantity of uncombined salicyclic acid in a commercial aspirin product?

Materials

chemical splash goggles
laboratory apron
marking pen
well plate
sheet of white paper
commercial aspirin tablet
mortar and pestle
beaker, 50-mL
25 mL water-ethanol solution

3 micropipets, each containing
  one of the following:
    distilled water
    salicylic acid solution,
     standardized
    iron(III) ion solution
stirring rod
graduated cylinder, 25-mL
empty micropipet

Safety

Wear your goggles and lab apron at all times during the investigation. The iron(III) ion solution contains acid and is corrosive. The water-ethanol solution contains methanol and is toxic if ingested. Handle both solutions with care. Avoid spills and contact with your skin. If you spill either solution, wash it off with plenty of water and tell your teacher.

Note the caution alert symbols here and with certain steps of the Procedure. Refer to page *xi* for the specific precautions associated with each symbol.

Procedure

 1. Put on your goggles and lab apron. Using the marking pen, number the wells of the well plate from left to right along the top: *1, 2, 3, 4, 5.* Down the left side, label the rows of wells: *A, B, C.* Place the well plate on a sheet of white paper. See Figure 77–2.

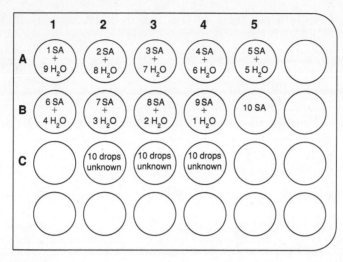

Figure 77–2

2. Use the pipet containing the standard salicylic acid solution to add 1 drop of solution to well A1, 2 drops to well A2, 3 drops to well A3, 4 drops to well A4, and 5 drops to well A5. Moving to row B, add 6 drops of standard salicylic acid to well B1, 7 drops to B2, 8 drops to B3, 9 drops to B4, and 10 drops to B5. Always hold the pipets vertically and count the number of drops carefully.

3. Use the pipet containing water to add 9 drops of water to well A1, 8 drops to A2, 7 drops to A3, 6 drops to A4, and 5 drops to A5. Moving to row B, add 4 drops of water to well B1, 3 drops to B2, 2 drops to B3, and 1 drop to B4.

4. Use the pipet containing iron(III) ion solution to add 1 drop of solution to each well in rows A and B. **CAUTION:** *Handle the iron(III) ion solution with care. It contains acid and is corrosive. If you spill any on your skin or clothes, wash it off with plenty of water and tell your teacher.* Record your observations of the colors that appear.

5. Examine the label of an aspirin container to find the mass of ASA in one tablet as stated by the manufacturer. Record this amount. Remove one tablet from the container and crush it into a fine powder with the mortar and pestle.

6. Use the graduated cylinder to transfer 25 mL of the water-ethanol solution into the beaker. **CAUTION:** *Handle the water-ethanol solution with care; it is toxic if ingested.* Add the powdered aspirin and stir, allowing the starch or other binder in the aspirin to settle to the bottom of the beaker. The acetylsalicylic acid (aspirin) and any salicylic acid should now be dissolved in the water-ethanol solution.

7. Use the empty pipet to transfer 10 drops of the dissolved aspirin solution into well C2. Use the pipet containing iron(III) ion solution to add 1 drop of iron(III) ion solution to this well.

8. Compare the color of the aspirin solution in well C2 to the standard solutions you previously prepared in rows A and B. If necessary, hold the wells up to a strong light source to determine which well provides the best color match to well C2. Record your results.

9. Repeat Steps 7 and 8 using wells C3 and C4. Record your results.

 10. Dispose of all chemicals by flushing them down the drain with plenty of water. Clean up your work area and wash your hands before leaving the laboratory.

Observations

Color of test solutions
  A1–B5

        _____

        _____

Mass of ASA in tablet   _____

Best match to C2   _____

Best match to C3   _____

Best match to C4   _____

Calculations

1. The stock solution of salicylic acid contains 3.0 mg of salicylic acid per mL. Calculate the concentration of salicylic acid for each of the wells in rows A and B. Record these values in the Data Table. (Assume all of the solutions require equal numbers of drops to make 1 mL.)

$$\text{Concentration} = \frac{\text{drops of standard solution}}{\text{total drops in well}} \times 3.0 \text{ mg/mL salicyclic acid}$$

DATA TABLE **Salicylic Acid Concentration (mg/mL)**

	1	2	3	4	5
A					
B					

2. If the molar mass of ASA is 180.2 g/mol, how many moles of ASA were stated by the manufacturer to be present in the tablet you tested?

Critical Thinking: Analysis and Conclusions

1. Referring to the color match obtained in Step 8 of the Procedure and the values calculated above, state the concentration of salicylic acid in mg/mL for the tablet that you tested. *(Interpreting data)* _____

_____

_____

2. Using this concentration, calculate the mass of salicylic acid that was present in the tablet. (Recall that you used 25 mL of solution to dissolve all the soluble materials in the tablet you tested.) *(Drawing conclusions)*

   mass of salicylic acid =

3. If the molar mass of salicylic acid is 138.1 g/mol, how many moles of salicylic acid were in the tablet you tested? *(Interpreting data)*

4. If all the salicylic acid present was formed from the decomposition of ASA, what percentage of the ASA in the tablet you tested had decomposed in storage? *(Interpreting data)*

Critical Thinking: Applications

1. In this investigation, it was proposed that all the salicylic acid observed was the result of the decomposition of ASA from exposure to water vapor in the environment. Suggest another source of salicylic acid that may be related to the manufacturing process.

   (Developing hypotheses) _____

   _____

   _____

2. What additional measurement would you need to obtain in order to determine the percentage of ASA by mass in a commercial aspirin tablet? *(Applying concepts)* _____

   _____

3. If ASA is produced in an equilibrium reaction system, what procedure (other than adding more of one reactant) could be used to increase the percent yield of ASA? *(Designing experiments)* _____

   _____

Name _____

Going Further

1. Construct models of salicylic acid, acetic acid, and ASA using materials supplied by your teacher.
2. A medication that is in competition with aspirin is acetaminophen, a distant chemical relative that contains no salicylates. Find its formula in a reference book. Construct a model of this molecule.
3. Currently many physicians advise against the use of aspirin by certain patients. Do some library research to determine why. As part of your research, define and discuss the contraindications of aspirin.

Making Sauerkraut

Introduction

Fermented cabbage, or sauerkraut, has been produced for at least 2000 years. It has played a role in the cooking of many countries where cabbage is grown. Chinese manuscripts tell of its use to feed laborers working on the Great Wall of China. Since the Middle Ages, it has been part of the table fare in Germany and Austria. The word *sauerkraut* is German for "sour cabbage."

Making sauerkraut involves adding salt and water to shredded cabbage. The salt causes water and glucose in the cabbage cells to migrate into solution through the cell walls. The next step depends on the action of bacteria.

Normal cellular respiration consists of the oxidation—or breaking down in the presence of oxygen—of nutrients to produce energy for the cell. For organisms that live without oxygen, the biochemical pathway to produce energy is through fermentation. Anaerobic bacteria live naturally on the surface of the cabbage. Enzymes from these bacteria act on the glucose to produce lactic acid, which gives the sauerkraut its sour taste. The reaction is:

$$C_6H_{12}O_6 \rightarrow 2CH_3CH(OH)COOH$$

glucose   lactic acid

In this investigation you will prepare sauerkraut and test it for the presence of lactic acid.

Pre-Lab Discussion

Read the entire laboratory investigation and the relevant pages of your textbook. Then answer the questions that follow.

1. Where is sauerkraut commonly produced? _____

   _____

2. What is the basic process for making sauerkraut? _____

   _____

3. What is accomplished by the process of fermentation in this investigation? _____

   _____

4. What does the term *anaerobic* mean? _____

   _____

5. Why is the fermentation process important to the survival of living organisms? _____

_____

6. What test will indicate when the reaction is almost complete?

_____

Problem

How can you use the making of sauerkraut to study fermentation?

Materials

apron
200 g cabbage
kitchen scale
cutting board
shredder or knife
pint jar with lid

bowl
spoon
table salt (NaCl)
wide-range or acid-range pH
    paper

Safety

Wear an apron during this investigation. Wash your hands with soap and water before beginning your work. Do this investigation only in a food science (home economics) lab or a nonscience classroom. Be careful not to cut yourself with the knife or shredder. Make sure that the lid on the jar is loose, otherwise pressure could build up, breaking the jar.

    Note the caution alert symbols here and with certain steps of the Procedure. Refer to page *xi* for the specific precautions associated with each symbol.

Procedure

Part A

1. Work in the food science (home economics) lab or a nonscience classroom. Put on an apron and wash your hands with soap and water.

2. Using the kitchen scale, measure approximately 200 grams of cabbage. On a cutting board, use a shredder or knife to chop the cabbage into pieces about 5 millimeters wide. **CAUTION:** *Be careful not to cut yourself with the knife or shredder.*

3. Pack the cabbage into the pint jar and add about 5 grams of table salt. Carefully fill the jar with water until the cabbage is covered. Tap the sides of the jar to get rid of air bubbles.

4. Use the spoon to remove some of the cabbage water. Test its pH with pH paper. Record your results in the Data Table.

5. Cover the jar loosely so that gases can escape. Put the jar in the bowl (in case it overflows) and set it aside for 2 to 4 weeks. This allows for the natural fermentation of the cabbage. **CAUTION:** *Make sure that the jar lid is loose, otherwise pressure could build up, breaking the jar.*

6. Clean up your work area and wash your hands before leaving the room.

Part B

7. Test the pH of the cabbage water every 5 days until a pH of 4 or lower is obtained. Record your results in the Data Table.

8. If you wish, drain the liquid from your sauerkraut, place it in a saucepan with fresh water, bring to a boil, and serve it with your favorite hot dog.

 9. Wash the jar and spoon. Clean up your work area and wash your hands before leaving the room.

Observations

DATA TABLE

Day	pH
start	
5	
10	
15	
20	
25	

Critical Thinking: Analysis and Conclusions

1. What changes in pH were noted during the course of this investigation? *(Interpreting data)* _____

_____

2. How long did the fermentation process take? *(Interpreting data)* _____

_____

3. By slowly filling the jar and then tapping it, air was kept out of the cabbage-water-salt mixture. Why is this important? *(Making inferences)* _____

_____

4. Your sauerkraut does not contain any artificial preservatives. What do you think keeps it from spoiling? *(Making inferences)* _____

_____

Name _____

Critical Thinking: Applications

1. What other fermentation processes are of economic importance? *(Giving an example)* _____

    _____

    _____

    _____

    _____

    _____

2. Osmotic pressure is important in the transfer of water in and out of the cells in living systems. How does osmosis work in the production of sauerkraut? *(Applying concepts)* _____

    _____

    _____

    _____

Going Further

1. Investigate the production of such foods as half-sour pickles, half-sour green tomatoes, and kimchi. Under the supervision of your teacher, try one or more of these processes.

Organic and Inorganic Catalysts

Lab 79

Introduction

A catalyst is a substance that can increase the rate of a chemical reaction without being consumed in the reaction. Enzymes are substances that function as catalysts in living organisms. They are proteins that regulate almost all of the biochemical reactions in plants, animals, and micro-organisms.

Enzymes were first discovered in the mid-nineteenth century by scientists studying metabolic processes, and the importance of these chemicals to biochemical reactions was quickly realized. Among the first enzymes to be classified were amylase, which converts starch into sugar, and pepsin, one of the digestive juices present in the stomach.

In this investigation, you will compare the effects of several organic catalysts and two inorganic catalysts on the decomposition of hydrogen peroxide. You will also investigate the effect of high temperatures on the catalytic ability of both organic and inorganic catalysts.

Pre-Lab Discussion

Read the entire laboratory investigation and the relevant pages of your textbook. Then answer the questions that follow.

1. What qualitative observations must you make in order to determine the best catalyst for the decomposition of hydrogen peroxide? ____

   _____

   _____

2. Which are the inorganic catalysts you will be testing? _____

   _____

3. Which are the organic catalysts you will be testing? _____

   _____

4. What are some dangers involved in using hydrogen peroxide? What precautions should be taken? _____

   _____

   _____

5. Enzymes are well known for their specificity. Explain one of the accepted models for the observation that enzymes are specific to the substrate. _____

   _____

Lab 79

Problem

How do organic and inorganic catalysts compare in their ability to catalyze the decomposition of hydrogen peroxide?

Materials

chemical splash goggles
laboratory apron
8 test tubes
marking pencil
test-tube rack
hydrogen peroxide (H_2O_2), 6%
microspatula
manganese dioxide (MnO_2)
iron(III) chloride ($FeCl_3$)

small piece of each of the
  following:
  banana
  potato
  fresh pineapple
  apple
  liver or the blood from calf
    liver
beaker, 600-mL
hot plate
test-tube holder

Safety

Wear your goggles and lab apron at all times during the investigation. Use caution when heating objects. Hydrogen peroxide is a strong oxidizing agent and may cause burns to eyes or skin. Avoid contact with your eyes and hands. Iron(III) chloride is irritating to skin. Avoid direct contact with it. If either of these solutions makes contact with your skin, wash with plenty of cold water. Do not eat any of the foods.

Note the caution alert symbols here and with certain steps of the Procedure. Refer to page *xi* for the specific precautions associated with each symbol.

Procedure

1. Put on your goggles and lab apron. Number the test tubes 1–8. Place approximately 5 mL of H_2O_2 in each of the eight test tubes. **CAUTION:** *Hydrogen peroxide is a strong oxidizing agent and may cause burns to eyes or skin. Wash spills or splashes with plenty of water.*

2. Leave test tube 1 as a control by adding nothing to it. Observe the rate at which oxygen gas bubbles are produced. Record your observations in Data Table 1.

3. To test tube 2, use a microspatula to add a small amount of MnO_2 and observe. Record your observations in Data Table 1.

4. To test tube 3, add a similar amount of $FeCl_3$. Observe and record. **CAUTION:** *Iron(III) chloride is irritating to skin. Avoid direct contact with it. If it makes contact with your skin, wash with plenty of cold water.*

5. Add a small piece of banana to test tube 4, a small piece of potato to test tube 5, a small piece of pineapple to test tube 6, and a small piece of apple to test tube 7. Observe and record after each addition.

6. To test tube 8, add a few drops of blood or a small piece of liver. Observe and record.

 7. Dispose of the contents of your test tubes as follows. Empty the contents of test tube 2 into a container provided by your teacher. Pour the liquids in the remaining test tubes down the drain. Place all solid pieces of fruit in the garbage can. Then wash and dry your test tubes.

 8. Set up a boiling water bath on a hot plate, using a 600-mL beaker about one-third full. **CAUTION:** *Do not touch hot objects with your bare hands.*

9. Into empty test tubes 2–8, place the same amount of each catalyst as was used in that test tube during Steps 2–6. **CAUTION:** *Do not add the hydrogen peroxide yet.*

 10. Heat all of the test tubes in the boiling water bath for about 6 minutes. Using the tongs, remove the test tubes from the water bath and allow them to cool in the test-tube rack to about room temperature.

11. Add approximately 5 mL of hydrogen peroxide to each of the eight test tubes and again observe the rate of oxygen gas produced. Record your observations in Data Table 2.

12. Dispose of the contents of your test tubes and wash them as before. Clean up your work area and wash your hands before leaving the laboratory.

Observations

DATA TABLE 1 Catalysis Before Heating

Test Tube	Catalyst	Observations
1		
2		
3		
4		
5		
6		
7		
8		

DATA TABLE 2   Catalysis After Heating

Test Tube	Catalyst	Observations
1		
2		
3		
4		
5		
6		
7		
8		

Critical Thinking: Analysis and Conclusions

1. On the basis of your observations, which catalyst accelerated the decomposition of hydrogen peroxide the most effectively? How could you tell? *(Making comparisons)* _____

    _____

    _____

2. Which of the organic catalysts accelerated the reaction most effectively? *(Making comparisons)* _____

    _____

3. How were the inorganic catalysts affected by heating them to 100°C? *(Interpreting data)* _____

4. How were the organic catalysts (enzymes) affected by heating them to 100°C? *(Interpreting data)* _____

    _____

Critical Thinking: Applications

1. Write a balanced chemical equation for the decomposition of hydrogen peroxide. *(Making inferences)* _____

2. What does it mean to denature a protein? *(Applying concepts)* _____

    _____

    _____

3. Could you use canned pineapple rather than fresh pineapple and obtain the same results for this activity? Why or why not? *(Developing hypotheses)* _____

_____

_____

4. After completing this investigation, suggest a reason that fresh pineapple cannot be used to make fruit gelatin. _____

_____

_____

Going Further

1. Investigate the reason that 3% hydrogen peroxide is effective on cuts and bruises.
2. Test pineapple and other fruits, fresh and canned, to see if they affect the formation of gelatin.
3. Under your teacher's supervision, determine the approximate temperature at which enzymes are inactivated. Take fresh pineapple juice and heat portions of it to 30°C, 35°C, 40°C, 45°C, etc. Test the heated juice with hydrogen peroxide and determine the temperature above which no reaction occurs.

Analysis of Commercial Vitamin C

Small Scale Lab 80

APPLICATION

Text reference: **Chapter 27**

Introduction

Vitamin C occurs naturally in many fruits and vegetables, including oranges, kiwis, kumquats, papayas, potatoes, and hot green chilies. Chemically, vitamin C is known as ascorbic acid, $H_2C_6H_6O_6$. Its structure is shown in Figure 80–1.

Figure 80–1 *Ascorbic Acid (Vitamin C)*

Vitamin C is an important nutrient in your diet. It is essential in the formation of collagen, a protein found in the connective tissue of your ligaments and tendons. It is involved in the metabolism of several amino acids and in the absorption of iron. It aids in the healing of wounds. It also acts as an antioxidant because it prevents the oxidation of other vitamins, such as A and E.

The recommended daily allowance of vitamin C is 60 mg. Some people claim that much larger amounts—1000 to 3000 mg per day—may help prevent diseases such as the common cold, cancer, and heart attacks. Large doses, however, are toxic in 2 to 5 percent of the population. Therefore, anyone considering taking large doses of vitamin C should first consult a physician. If you eat three to five servings of fruit and two to four servings of vegetables each day, you should be getting adequate amounts of vitamin C.

In this investigation, you will employ analytical methods to determine the amount of vitamin C in a commercially produced vitamin tablet. You will conduct an acid-base neutralization reaction using sodium hydroxide to neutralize the ascorbic acid in the tablet. Phenolphthalein, an acid-base indicator, will change from colorless to pink when the neutralization is complete. By employing principles of stoichiometry, you then will be able to calculate the amount of vitamin C in the tablet and compare this amount with the amount claimed by the manufacturer.

Pre-Lab Discussion

Read the entire laboratory investigation and the relevant pages of your textbook. Then answer the questions that follow.

1. What is the molar mass of ascorbic acid?

   _____

2. Write a balanced equation for the reaction of sodium hydroxide with ascorbic acid. NOTE: Only one of the hydrogen atoms of the ascorbic acid is replaced in this reaction.

   _____

3. What hazards are involved in working with the sodium hydroxide solution and what safety precautions should you take? _____

   _____

   _____

4. What is phenolphthalein and what is its function in this experiment? _____

   _____

   _____

5. In what position should the pipet be held while delivering drops of sodium hydroxide? Why? _____

   _____

   _____

Problem

How can titration techniques be used to determine the amount of ascorbic acid in a commercial vitamin C tablet?

Materials

chemical splash goggles
laboratory apron
vitamin C tablet, 500-mg
laboratory balance
graduated cylinder, 50-mL
beaker, 100-mL
distilled water
stirring rod

phenolphthalein solution, 1%
standardized sodium hydroxide
   (NaOH) solution
beaker, 50-mL
2 micropipets
graduated cylinder, 10-mL
well plate
4 toothpicks

Safety

Wear your goggles and lab apron at all times during the investigation. Sodium hydroxide is caustic and can cause permanent eye damage, so avoid direct contact with it. If contact occurs, immediately wash the affected area with plenty of cold water and inform your teacher. Clean up all spills immediately. Note the caution alert symbols here and with certain steps of the Procedure. Refer to page *xi* for the specific precautions associated with each symbol.

Procedure

1. Put on your goggles and lab apron. Find the mass of the vitamin C tablet and record this value.

2. Place the tablet in the 100-mL beaker and add 50 mL of distilled water.

3. Dissolve the tablet in the distilled water. The binder that holds the tablet together will not completely dissolve, so use the stirring rod to break up the undissolved part of the tablet into very small pieces.

4. Add three drops of phenolphthalein indicator to the vitamin C solution. Set the solution aside for use later.

5. Obtain 15 mL of standardized sodium hydroxide solution in a clean, dry 50-mL beaker. Note and record the exact molarity of this solution. Fill a micropipet with some of this solution. **CAUTION:** *NaOH is caustic; take care not to come into direct contact with it. If you spill any, wash the area with plenty of cold water, and inform your teacher.*

6. Calibrate a micropipet for use with sodium hydroxide solution as follows: Fill a 10-mL graduated cylinder with sodium hydroxide to exactly 5.0 mL. Then count and record how many drops are needed to increase the volume to 6.0 mL, then 7.0 mL, then 8.0 mL. Calculate the average number of drops per mL from these values. Record the numbers in the Observations section. Hold the pipet vertically while counting the drops. If you tilt the pipet, the NaOH will adhere to the sides of the pipet and the drops will be too large. Do not allow the drops to touch the sides of the cylinder. Be sure to read the volume by sighting the bottom of the meniscus at eye level.

7. Return all the NaOH solution in the graduated cylinder to the beaker. Rinse the cylinder first with tap water and then with distilled water. Using the procedure in Step 6, calibrate the second pipet for use with vitamin C solution, and calculate the number of drops of vitamin C per mL. Double this number to determine the number of drops in 2 mL.

8. Using the number of drops you just calculated, add 2 mL of the vitamin C solution to each of four wells of a 12-well plate. Touch the tip of the pipet to the side of the well to remove the last drop of solution from the pipet.

Name_____

9. Titrate the vitamin C solution in the first well with the sodium hydroxide solution as follows: Use the micropipet to add sodium hydroxide one drop at a time, stirring with a toothpick after each drop, until the solution remains a faint pink color. Count and record the total number of drops needed to do this. Be sure to hold the pipet in a vertical position. Repeat this process for the remaining three wells containing vitamin C solution.

 10. Discard the waste chemicals in the sink, flushed with plenty of water. Wash all equipment, rinsing the well plates and the pipets with distilled water. Clean up your work area and wash your hands before leaving the laboratory.

Observations

Mass of vitamin C tablet	_____
Molarity of NaOH solution	_____
Number of drops of NaOH/mL (3 trials)	_____ _____ _____
Average number of drops of NaOH/mL	_____
Number of drops of vit. C/mL (3 trials)	_____ _____ _____
Average number of drops of vit. C/mL	_____

Number of drops of NaOH solution
used to turn the solution faint pink:

Trial 1	_____
Trial 2	_____
Trial 3	_____
Trial 4	_____

Calculations

1. From the data, determine the average volume of one drop of the sodium hydroxide solution delivered by the pipet.

2. Determine the average number of drops of sodium hydroxide solution necessary to react with the ascorbic acid in 2 mL of vitamin C solution. Convert the average number of drops to mL.

3. Determine the volume of sodium hydroxide that would have been necessary to react all the vitamin C in the entire 50 mL of vitamin C solution (VC).

4. Determine the number of moles of vitamin C in the 50 mL of solution.

5. Using the molar mass you determined in Pre-Lab Question 1, determine the number of milligrams of vitamin C in the 50 mL of solution. (This is the number of milligrams present in the entire tablet.)

Critical Thinking: Analysis and Conclusions

1. How does your experimental result compare to the manufacturer's claim of 500 mg of vitamin C in each tablet? Are you within experimental limits or not? Explain. *(Making comparisons)* _____

_____

_____

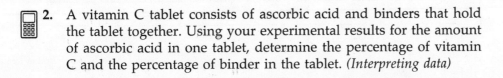

2. A vitamin C tablet consists of ascorbic acid and binders that hold the tablet together. Using your experimental results for the amount of ascorbic acid in one tablet, determine the percentage of vitamin C and the percentage of binder in the tablet. *(Interpreting data)*

3. Being as specific as possible, predict the effect of each of the following scenarios on the experimental result for the amount of vitamin C in the tablet. *(Making predictions)*

a. The binders reacted with the sodium hydroxide solution. _____

_____

_____

b. The pipet was not held vertically for each drop delivered.

_____

_____

c. One drop more of sodium hydroxide was added than was necessary. _____

_____

Critical Thinking: Applications

1. This experiment was based on the assumption that only one of the protons in ascorbic acid reacted with the sodium hydroxide. If both protons reacted with the NaOH, how would you change the calculations to obtain an accurate analysis of the amount of vitamin C in the tablet? *(Making predictions)*

Name_____

2. Cranberries contain quinic acid, $HC_7H_{11}O_6$. Suppose you titrated 20.00 g of cranberry juice with 0.1123 M sodium hydroxide solution until all the acid was neutralized. In the process, you used 39.9 mL of sodium hydroxide. What percentage of the cranberry juice was quinic acid? (*Applying concepts*)

3. Why will the method used in this investigation not work for the analysis of the amount of vitamin C in orange juice? Design an experiment that would allow you to measure the amount of vitamin

C in orange juice. (*Designing experiments*) _____

_____

_____

Going Further

1. The method used in this investigation can be applied to find the acid content of a variety of commercial products. Under the supervision of your teacher, try this method to determine the amount of acetic acid in vinegar.

2. With your teacher's help, obtain a computer interface that uses a pH probe or a standard pH meter. Use this instrumentation to analyze a vitamin C solution. You can determine the ionization constant, K_a, by first measuring the pH of the initial vitamin C solution and then titrating the 50 mL of vitamin C solution with standardized sodium hydroxide. Measure and record the pH after adding each 1.0 mL of sodium hydroxide. Make a graph of pH versus the number of mL NaOH used in order to determine the equivalence point. Then calculate the total moles of ascorbic acid and the ionization constant. This method will work with most fruit juices, with vinegar, and with other acid-containing products.

3. Health-food stores do not come under Food and Drug Administration guidelines and are allowed to sell "natural vitamins" without warnings or guarantees of actual content of vitamins. There is a move by some organizations to have these products fall under government regulations. Research this controversy. You may find Food and Drug Administration publications helpful.

APPENDICES

The Chemical Elements

THE CHEMICAL ELEMENTS WITH THEIR SYMBOLS, ATOMIC NUMBERS, AND ATOMIC MASSES

Element	Symbol	Atomic Number	Atomic Mass	Element	Symbol	Atomic Number	Atomic Mass
Actinium	Ac	89	227.0278	Neptunium	Np	93	237.048
Aluminum	Al	13	26.98154	Nickel	Ni	28	58.69
Americium	Am	95	(243)[a]	Niobium	Nb	41	92.9064
Antimony	Sb	51	121.157	Nitrogen	N	7	14.0067
Argon	Ar	18	39.948	Nobelium	No	102	(259)
Arsenic	As	33	74.9216	Osmium	Os	76	190.2
Astatine	At	85	(210)	Oxygen	O	8	15.9994
Barium	Ba	56	137.33	Palladium	Pd	46	106.42
Berkelium	Bk	97	(247)	Phosphorus	P	15	30.97376
Beryllium	Be	4	9.01218	Platinum	Pt	78	195.08
Bismuth	Bi	83	208.9804	Plutonium	Pu	94	(244)
Boron	B	5	10.81	Polonium	Po	84	(209)
Bromine	Br	35	79.904	Potassium	K	19	39.0983
Cadmium	Cd	48	112.41	Praseodymium	Pr	59	140.9077
Calcium	Ca	20	40.078	Promethium	Pm	61	(145)
Californium	Cf	98	(251)	Protactinium	Pa	91	231.0359
Carbon	C	6	12.011	Radium	Ra	88	226.0254
Cerium	Ce	58	140.12	Radon	Rn	86	(222)
Cesium	Cs	55	132.9054	Rhenium	Re	75	186.207
Chlorine	Cl	17	35.453	Rhodium	Rh	45	102.9055
Chromium	Cr	24	51.996	Rubidium	Rb	37	85.4678
Cobalt	Co	27	58.9332	Ruthenium	Ru	44	101.07
Copper	Cu	29	63.546	Samarium	Sm	62	150.36
Curium	Cm	96	(247)	Scandium	Sc	21	44.9559
Dysprosium	Dy	66	162.50	Seaborgium[b]	Sg	106	(263)
Einsteinium	Es	99	(252)	Selenium	Se	34	78.96
Erbium	Er	68	167.26	Silicon	Si	14	28.0855
Europium	Eu	63	151.96	Silver	Ag	47	107.8682
Fermium	Fm	100	(257)	Sodium	Na	11	22.98977
Fluorine	F	9	18.998403	Strontium	Sr	38	87.62
Francium	Fr	87	(223)	Sulfur	S	16	32.066
Gadolinium	Gd	64	157.25	Tantalum	Ta	73	180.9479
Gallium	Ga	31	69.72	Technetium	Tc	43	(98)
Germanium	Ge	32	72.61	Tellurium	Te	52	127.60
Gold	Au	79	196.9665	Terbium	Tb	65	158.9254
Hafnium	Hf	72	178.49	Thallium	Tl	81	204.383
Helium	He	2	4.00260	Thorium	Th	90	232.0381
Holmium	Ho	67	164.9304	Thulium	Tm	69	168.9342
Hydrogen	H	1	1.00794	Tin	Sn	50	118.710
Indium	In	49	114.82	Titanium	Ti	22	47.88
Iodine	I	53	126.9045	Tungsten	W	74	183.85
Iridium	Ir	77	192.22	Unnilennium	Une	109	(266)
Iron	Fe	26	55.847	Unniloctium	Uno	108	(265)
Krypton	Kr	36	83.80	Unnilpentium	Unp	105	(262)
Lanthanum	La	57	138.9055	Unnilquadium	Unq	104	(261)
Lawrencium	Lr	103	(260)	Unnilseptium	Uns	107	(262)
Lead	Pb	82	207.2	Uranium	U	92	238.0289
Lithium	Li	3	6.941	Vanadium	V	23	50.9415
Lutetium	Lu	71	174.967	Xenon	Xe	54	131.29
Magnesium	Mg	12	24.305	Ytterbium	Yb	70	173.04
Manganese	Mn	25	54.9380	Yttrium	Y	39	88.9059
Mendelevium	Md	101	(258)	Zinc	Zn	30	65.39
Mercury	Hg	80	200.59	Zirconium	Zr	40	91.224
Molybdenum	Mo	42	95.94				
Neodymium	Nd	60	144.24				
Neon	Ne	10	20.1797				

[a] Approximate values for radioactive elements are listed in parentheses.
[b] The name of Element 106 has not yet been certified.

Formulas of Common Ions

Positive Ions (Cations)

aluminum	Al^{3+}
ammonium	NH_4^+
barium	Ba^{2+}
calcium	Ca^{2+}
cobalt	Co^{2+}
copper(I)	Cu^+
copper(II)	Cu^{2+}
hydrogen, hydronium	H^+, H_3O^+
iron(II)	Fe^{2+}
iron(III)	Fe^{3+}
lead(II)	Pb^{2+}
lithium	Li^+
magnesium	Mg^{2+}
manganese(II)	Mn^{2+}
potassium	K^+
silver	Ag^+
sodium	Na^+
strontium	Sr^{2+}
zinc	Zn^{2+}

Negative Ions (Anions)

acetate	CH_3COO^- or $C_2H_3O_2^-$
bromide	Br^-
carbonate	CO_3^{2-}
hydrogen carbonate	HCO_3^-
chlorate	ClO_3^-
chloride	Cl^-
fluoride	F^-
hydroxide	OH^-
hypochlorite	ClO^-
iodate	IO_3^-
iodide	I^-
nitrate	NO_3^-
nitrite	NO_2^-
oxalate	$C_2O_4^{2-}$
oxide	O^{2-}
permanganate	MnO_4^-
phosphate	PO_4^{3-}
monohydrogen phosphate	HPO_4^{2-}
dihydrogen phosphate	$H_2PO_4^-$
sulfate	SO_4^{2-}
hydrogen sulfate	HSO_4^-
sulfide	S^{2-}
hydrogen sulfide	HS^-
sulfite	SO_3^{2-}
hydrogen sulfite	HSO_3^-

Important Formulas, Equations, and Constants

Density (d)

$$\text{density} = \frac{\text{mass}}{\text{volume}} \qquad d = \frac{m}{V}$$

Percent Error

$$\text{percent error} = \frac{\text{measured value} - \text{accepted value}}{\text{accepted value}} \times 100\%$$

Percent Yield

$$\text{percent yield} = \frac{\text{actual yield}}{\text{expected yield}} \times 100\%$$

Percentage Composition

$$\text{percentage composition by mass} = \frac{\text{mass of element}}{\text{mass of compound}} \times 100\%$$

Planck's Equation

$E = h\nu$

where h is Planck's constant, E is energy, and ν is frequency

Kinetic Energy (KE)

$$\text{kinetic energy} = \frac{\text{mass} \times \text{velocity}^2}{2}$$

$$KE = \frac{mv^2}{2}$$

Gravitational Potential Energy (GPE)

$$\text{gravitational potential energy} = \text{mass} \times \text{acceleration due to gravity} \times \text{height}$$

$GPE = mgh$

Amount of Gas (n) in a Sample

$$n = \frac{\text{mass}}{\text{molar mass}} = \frac{m \,(g)}{\mathcal{M} \,(g/mol)}$$

Boyle's Law

$P_1 V_1 = P_2 V_2$

Charles's Law

$V_1 T_2 = V_2 T_1$

Avogadro's Law

$V = k_3 n$

where k_3 is Avogadro's law constant and n is the number of moles

Dalton's Law of Partial Pressures

$P_T = p_a + p_b + p_c + \cdots$

Ideal Gas Law

$PV = nRT$

Molarity (M)

$$\text{molarity} = \frac{\text{moles of solute}}{\text{liters of solution}}$$

Molality (m)

$$\text{molality} = \frac{\text{moles of solute}}{\text{kilograms of solvent}}$$

Mole Fraction (χ)

$$\text{mole fraction} = \frac{\text{moles of solute or solvent}}{\text{total moles of solution}}$$

Boiling Point Elevation

$\Delta T_b = K_b m$

where K_b is the molal boiling point elevation constant

Freezing Point Depression

$\Delta T_f = K_f m$

where K_f is the molal freezing point depression constant

Rate of Reaction

$\text{rate} = k[A]^x[B]^y$

where $[A]$ and $[B]$ are molar concentrations of reactants and k is a rate constant

Entropy Change

$\Delta S = S_{\text{products}} - S_{\text{reactants}}$

Gibbs Free Energy

$\Delta G = \Delta H - T\Delta S$

Avogadro's number	6.02×10^{23}
Speed of light in a vacuum	3.00×10^8 m/s
Atomic mass unit (amu)	1.66054×10^{-27} kg
Charge of an electron	1.60×10^{-19} C
Mass of an electron	9.11×10^{-31} kg
	0.0006 amu
Mass of a proton	1.0073 amu
	1.6726×10^{-27} kg
Mass of a neutron	1.0087 amu
	1.6749×10^{-27} kg
Planck's constant (h)	6.6262×10^{-34} J-s
Gas constant (R)	0.08206 atm-L/mol-K
	8.314 Pa-m³/mol-K
	8.314 J/mol-K
Molar volume of a gas at STP	22.4 L

Standard Reduction Potentials

(Ionic Concentrations 1 M Water at 298 K and 101.3 kPa)

Half Reaction	E° (volts)
$F_2(g) + 2e^- \rightarrow 2\,F^-$	+2.87
$8\,H^+ + MnO_4^- + 5e^- \rightarrow Mn^{2+} + 4\,H_2O$	+1.51
$Au^{3+} + 3e^- \rightarrow Au\,(s)$	+1.50
$Cl_2(g) + 2e^- \rightarrow 2\,Cl^-$	+1.36
$14\,H^+ + Cr_2O_7^{2-} + 6e^- \rightarrow 2\,Cr^{3+} + 7\,H_2O$	+1.23
$4\,H^+ + O_2(g) + 4e^- \rightarrow 2\,H_2O$	+1.23
$4\,H^+ + MnO_2(s) + 2e^- \rightarrow Mn^{2+} + 2\,H_2O$	+1.22
$Br_2(l) + 2e^- \rightarrow 2\,Br^-$	+1.09
$Hg^{2+} + 2e^- \rightarrow Hg\,(l)$	+0.85
$Ag^+ + e^- \rightarrow Ag\,(s)$	+0.80
$Hg_2^{2+} + 2e^- \rightarrow 2\,Hg\,(l)$	+0.80
$Fe^{3+} + e^- \rightarrow Fe^{2+}$	+0.77
$I_2(s) + 2e^- \rightarrow 2\,I^-$	+0.54
$Cu^+ + e^- \rightarrow Cu\,(s)$	+0.52
$Cu^{2+} + 2e^- \rightarrow Cu\,(s)$	+0.34
$4\,H^+ + SO_4^{2-} + 2e^- \rightarrow SO_2\,(aq) + 2\,H_2O$	+0.17
$Sn^{4+} + 2e^- \rightarrow Sn^{2+}$	+0.15
$2\,H^+ + 2e^- \rightarrow H_2\,(g)$	0.00
$Pb^{2+} + 2e^- \rightarrow Pb\,(s)$	−0.13
$Sn^{2+} + 2e^- \rightarrow Sn\,(s)$	−0.14
$Ni^{2+} + 2e^- \rightarrow Ni\,(s)$	−0.26
$Co^{2+} + 2e^- \rightarrow Co\,(s)$	−0.28
$Fe^{2+} + 2e^- \rightarrow Fe\,(s)$	−0.45
$Cr^{3+} + 3e^- \rightarrow Cr\,(s)$	−0.74
$Zn^{2+} + 2e^- \rightarrow Zn\,(s)$	−0.76
$2\,H_2O + 2e^- \rightarrow 2\,OH^- + H_2\,(g)$	−0.83
$Mn^{2+} + 2e^- \rightarrow Mn\,(s)$	−1.19
$Al^{3+} + 3e^- \rightarrow Al\,(s)$	−1.66
$Mg^{2+} + 2e^- \rightarrow Mg\,(s)$	−2.37
$Na^+ + e^- \rightarrow Na\,(s)$	−2.71
$Ca^{2+} + 2e^- \rightarrow Ca\,(s)$	−2.87
$Sr^{2+} + 2e^- \rightarrow Sr\,(s)$	−2.89
$Ba^{2+} + 2e^- \rightarrow Ba\,(s)$	−2.91
$Cs^+ + e^- \rightarrow Cs\,(s)$	−2.92
$K^+ + e^- \rightarrow K\,(s)$	−2.93
$Rb^+ + e^- \rightarrow Rb\,(s)$	−2.98
$Li^+ + e^- \rightarrow Li\,(s)$	−3.04

Vapor Pressures of Water

Temperature (°C)	Pressure (mm Hg)	Temperature (°C)	Pressure (mm Hg)
0	4.6	33	37.7
2.5	5.5	34	39.9
5	6.5	35	42.2
7.5	7.8	36	44.6
10	9.2	37	47.1
11	9.8	38	49.7
12	10.5	39	52.4
13	11.2	40	55.3
14	12.0	41	58.3
15	12.8	42	61.5
16	13.6	43	64.8
17	14.5	44	68.3
18	15.5	45	71.9
19	16.5	46	75.6
20	17.5	47	79.6
21	18.7	48	83.7
22	19.8	49	88.0
23	21.1	50	92.5
24	22.4	60	149.4
25	23.8	65	187.5
26	25.2	70	233.7
27	26.7	75	289.1
28	28.3	80	355.1
29	30.0	85	433.6
30	31.8	90	525.8
31	33.7	95	633.9
32	35.7	100	760.0

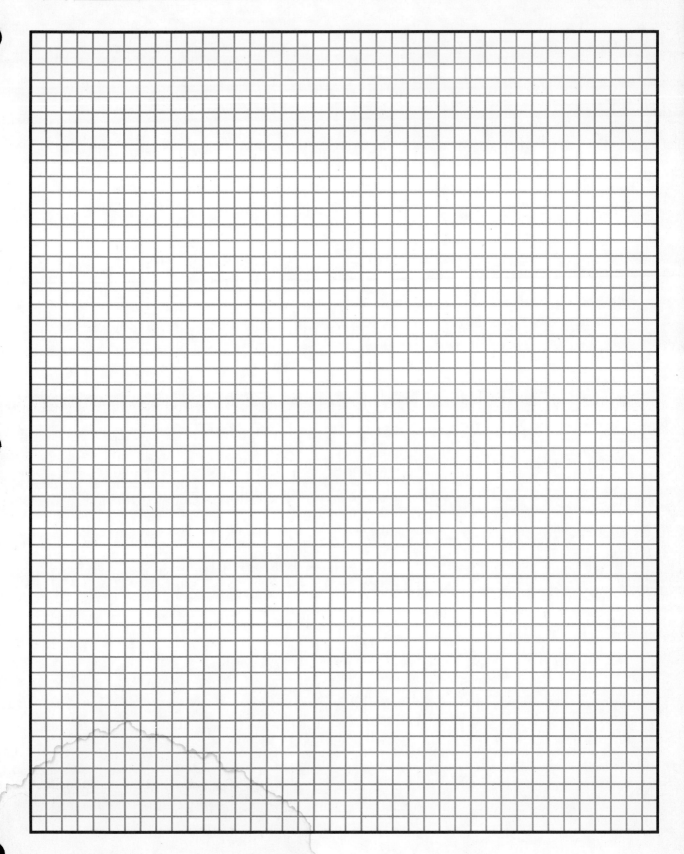

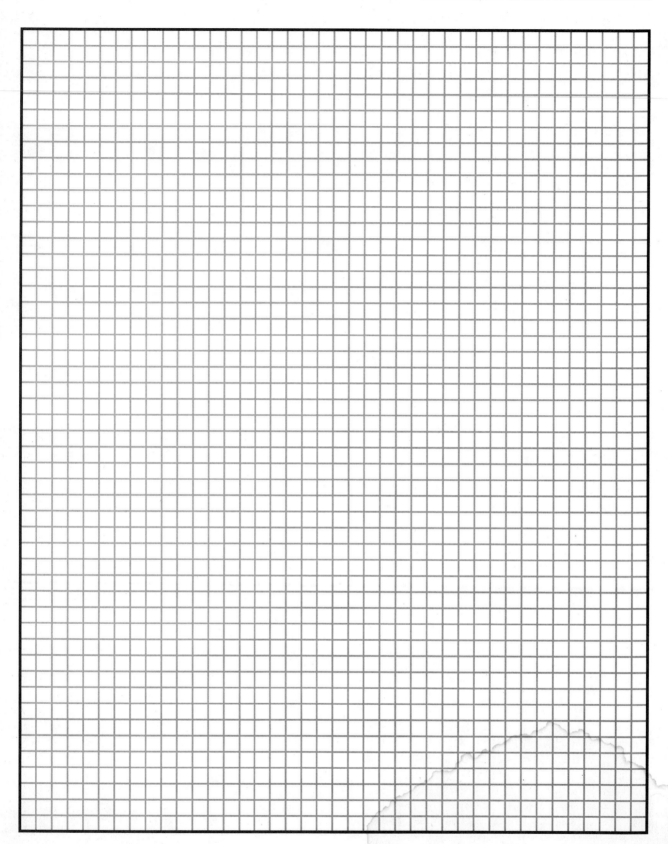

454

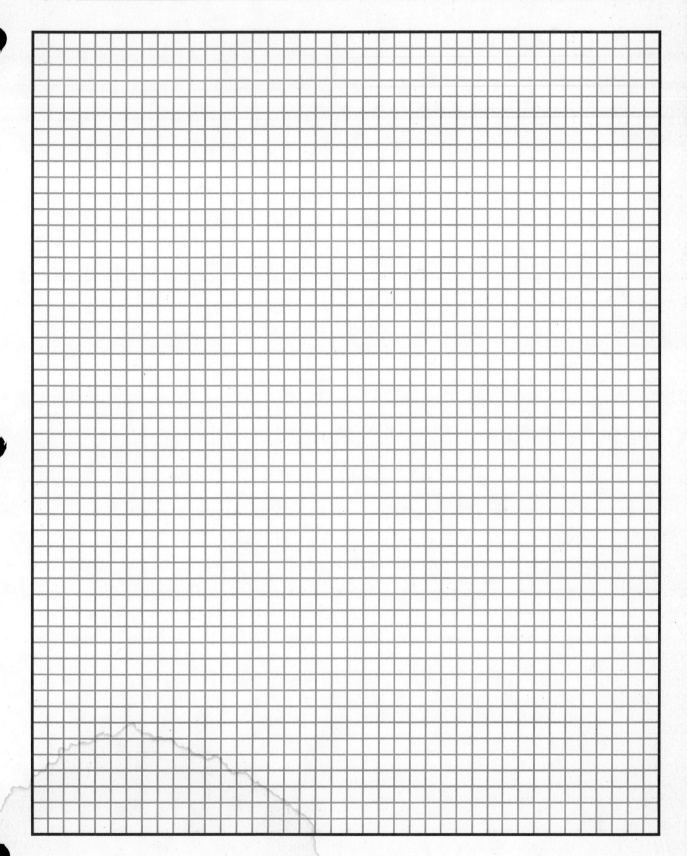

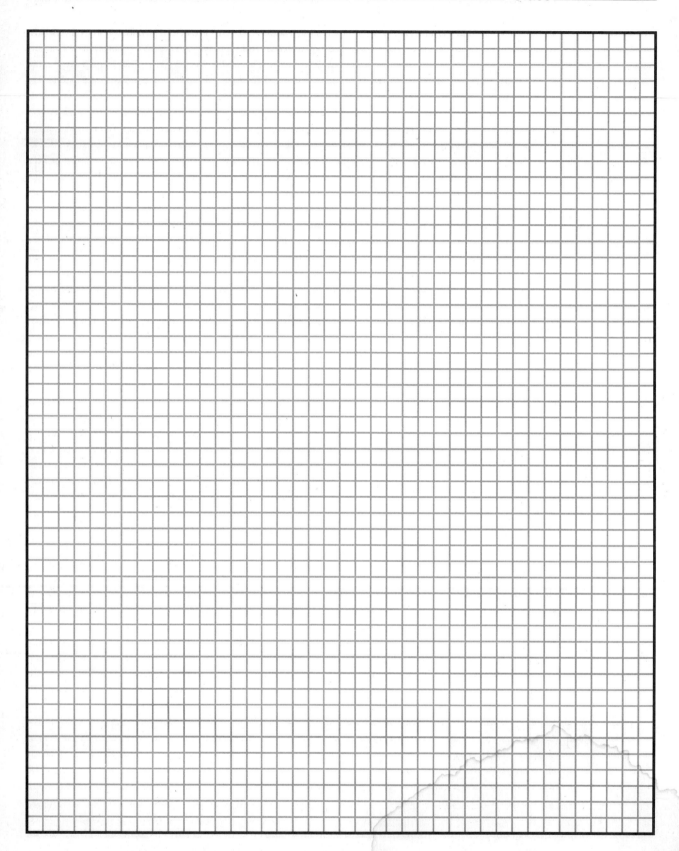

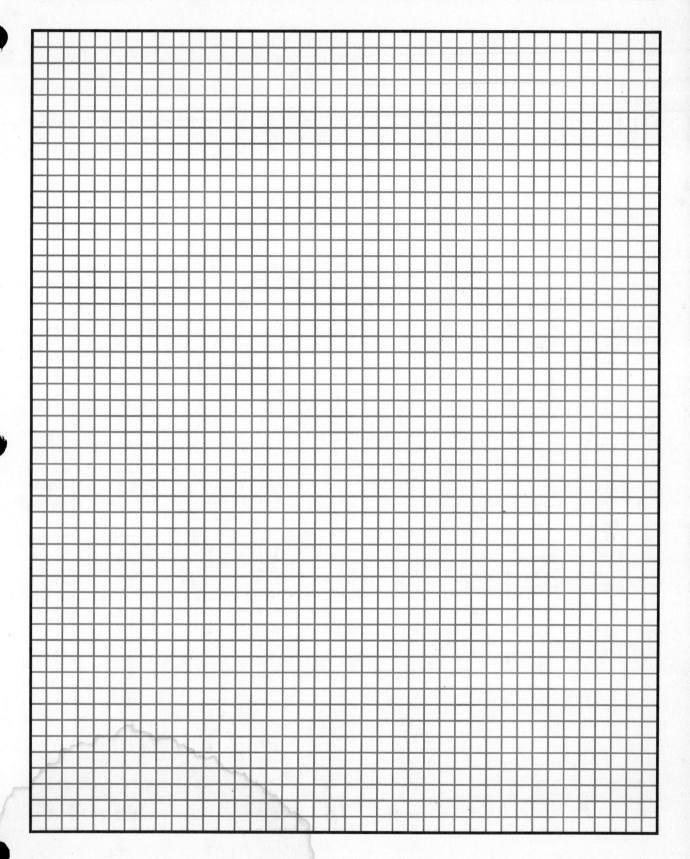

1
1A

1
H
Hydrogen
1.00794
$1s^1$

Key

6
C
Carbon
12.011
$[He]2s^2 2p^2$

Atomic number —— 6
Element symbol —— C
Element name —— Carbon
Atomic mass —— 12.011
Electron configuration —— $[He]2s^2 2p^2$

2
2A

3	4
Li	**Be**
Lithium	Beryllium
6.941	9.01218
$[He]2s^1$	$[He]2s^2$

11	12
Na	**Mg**
Sodium	Magnesium
22.98977	24.305
$[Ne]3s^1$	$[Ne]3s^2$

3 3B	4 4B	5 5B	6 6B	7 7B	8	9 8B
19 **K** Potassium 39.0983 $[Ar]4s^1$	20 **Ca** Calcium 40.078 $[Ar]4s^2$	21 **Sc** Scandium 44.9559 $[Ar]4s^2 3d^1$	22 **Ti** Titanium 47.88 $[Ar]4s^2 3d^2$	23 **V** Vanadium 50.9415 $[Ar]4s^2 3d^3$	24 **Cr** Chromium 51.996 $[Ar]4s^1 3d^5$	25 **Mn** Manganese 54.9380 $[Ar]4s^2 3d^5$
					26 **Fe** Iron 55.847 $[Ar]4s^2 3d^6$	27 **Co** Cobalt 58.9332 $[Ar]4s^2 3d^7$

(Row 4 continued)

19	20	21	22	23	24	25	26	27
K	**Ca**	**Sc**	**Ti**	**V**	**Cr**	**Mn**	**Fe**	**Co**
Potassium	Calcium	Scandium	Titanium	Vanadium	Chromium	Manganese	Iron	Cobalt
39.0983	40.078	44.9559	47.88	50.9415	51.996	54.9380	55.847	58.9332
$[Ar]4s^1$	$[Ar]4s^2$	$[Ar]4s^2 3d^1$	$[Ar]4s^2 3d^2$	$[Ar]4s^2 3d^3$	$[Ar]4s^1 3d^5$	$[Ar]4s^2 3d^5$	$[Ar]4s^2 3d^6$	$[Ar]4s^2 3d^7$

37	38	39	40	41	42	43	44	45
Rb	**Sr**	**Y**	**Zr**	**Nb**	**Mo**	**Tc**	**Ru**	**Rh**
Rubidium	Strontium	Yttrium	Zirconium	Niobium	Molybdenum	Technetium	Ruthenium	Rhodium
85.4678	87.62	88.9059	91.224	92.9064	95.94	(98)	101.07	102.9055
$[Kr]5s^1$	$[Kr]5s^2$	$[Kr]5s^2 4d^1$	$[Kr]5s^2 4d^2$	$[Kr]5s^1 4d^4$	$[Kr]5s^1 4d^5$	$[Kr]5s^2 4d^5$	$[Kr]5s^1 4d^7$	$[Kr]5s^1 4d^8$

55	56	71	72	73	74	75	76	77
Cs	**Ba**	**Lu**	**Hf**	**Ta**	**W**	**Re**	**Os**	**Ir**
Cesium	Barium	Lutetium	Hafnium	Tantalum	Tungsten	Rhenium	Osmium	Iridium
132.9054	137.33	174.967	178.49	180.9479	183.85	186.207	190.2	192.22
$[Xe]6s^1$	$[Xe]6s^2$	$[Xe]6s^2 4f^{14} 5d^1$	$[Xe]6s^2 4f^{14} 5d^2$	$[Xe]6s^2 4f^{14} 5d^3$	$[Xe]6s^2 4f^{14} 5d^4$	$[Xe]6s^2 4f^{14} 5d^5$	$[Xe]6s^2 4f^{14} 5d^6$	$[Xe]6s^2 4f^{14} 5d^7$

87	88	103	104	105	106	107	108	109
Fr	**Ra**	**Lr**	**Rf**	**Db**	**Sg**	**Bh**	**Hs**	**Mt**
Francium	Radium	Lawrencium	Rutherfordium	Dubnium	Seaborgium	Bohrium	Hassium	Meitnerium
(223)	226.0254	(260)	(261)	(262)	(263)	(262)	(265)	(266)
$[Rn]7s^1$	$[Rn]7s^2$	$[Rn]7s^2 5f^{14} 6d^2$	$[Rn]7s^2 5f^{14} 6d^2$	$[Rn]7s^2 5f^{14} 6d^3$	$[Rn]7s^2 5f^{14} 6d^4$	$[Rn]7s^2 5f^{14} 6d^5$	$[Rn]7s^2 5f^{14} 6d^6$	$[Rn]7s^2 5f^{14} 6d^7$

57	58	59	60	61	62
La	**Ce**	**Pr**	**Nd**	**Pm**	**Sm**
Lanthanum	Cerium	Praseodymium	Neodymium	Promethium	Samarium
138.9055	140.12	140.9077	144.24	(145)	150.36
$[Xe]6s^2 5d^1$	$[Xe]6s^2 4f^1 5d^1$	$[Xe]6s^2 4f^3$	$[Xe]6s^2 4f^4$	$[Xe]6s^2 4f^5$	$[Xe]6s^2 4f^6$

89	90	91	92	93	94
Ac	**Th**	**Pa**	**U**	**Np**	**Pu**
Actinium	Thorium	Protactinium	Uranium	Neptunium	Plutonium
227.0278	232.0381	231.0359	238.0289	237.048	(244)
$[Rn]7s^2 6d^1$	$[Rn]7s^2 6d^2$	$[Rn]7s^2 5f^2 6d^1$	$[Rn]7s^2 5f^3 6d^1$	$[Rn]7s^2 5f^4 6d^1$	$[Rn]7s^2 5f^6$